AN ITALIAN LORDSHIP
THE BISHOPRIC OF LUCCA IN THE LATE MIDDLE AGES

Published under the auspices of the

CENTER FOR MEDIEVAL AND RENAISSANCE STUDIES

University of California, Los Angeles

Publications of the
CENTER FOR MEDIEVAL AND RENAISSANCE STUDIES, UCLA

1. Jeffrey Burton Russell: Dissent and Reform in the Early Middle Ages
2. C. D. O'Malley: Leonardo's Legacy: An International Symposium
3. Richard H. Rouse: Guide to Serial Bibliographies in Medieval Studies
4. Speros Vryonis, Jr.: The Decline of Medieval Hellenism in Asia Minor and the Process of Islamization from the Eleventh through the Fifteenth Century
5. Stanley Chodorow: Christian Political Theory and Church Politics in the Mid-Twelfth Century
6. Joseph J. Duggan: The Song of Roland: Formulaic Style and Poetic Craft
7. Ernest A. Moody: Studies in Medieval Philosophy, Science, and Logic: Collected Papers, 1933–1969
8. Marc Bloch: Slavery and Serfdom in the Middle Ages
9. Michael J. B. Allen: Marsilio Ficino: The *Philebus* Commentary, A Critical Edition and Translation
10. Richard C. Dales: Marius: On the Elements, A Critical Edition and Translation
11. Duane J. Osheim: An Italian Lordship: The Bishopric of Lucca in the Late Middle Ages

DUANE J. OSHEIM

An Italian Lordship

The Bishopric of Lucca in the Late Middle Ages

UNIVERSITY OF CALIFORNIA PRESS
Berkeley, Los Angeles, London

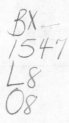

The emblem of the Center for Medieval and Renaissance Studies
reproduces the imperial eagle of the gold *augustalis* struck after 1231
by Emperor Frederick II; Elvira and Vladimir Clain-Stefanelli, *The
Beauty and Lore of Coins, Currency and Medals* (Croton-on-
Hudson, 1974), fig. 130 and p. 106.

University of California Press
Berkeley and Los Angeles, California

University of California Press, Ltd.
London, England

ISBN: 0-520-03005-2
Library of Congress Catalog Card Number: 75-7198
Copyright ©1977 by The Regents of the University of California

Printed in the United States of America

For Yvonne

Contents

Tables and Graphs

Preface

The period between the mid-eleventh and the mid-fourteenth centuries is commonly described as the "Italian Communal Age." Studies of this period correctly emphasize the growth of urban institutions and communal citizenship, and the slow breakdown of those institutions which could vie with individual communes for the allegiance of their citizens. The well-known conflict between the medieval empire and the papacy ended not in victory for either but in the virtual independence of the Italian towns. In their drive for autonomy, the cities came into conflict with a variety of groups that claimed immunity from communal control. Local religious groups were one of the first and most tenacious of the commune's opponents. The leader of the local clerics, the bishop, was the most visible and the most powerful churchman. Thus I have chosen to study him and his bishopric.

In the late eleventh and twelfth centuries the bishops were often virtual lords of their episcopal towns. By the mid-fourteenth century, bishops without exception had lost any semblance of civil power in their cities. What remained of their civil power was a limited dominion over certain areas of the countryside.

Paradoxically, no medieval Italian bishopric in that age of transition has been the subject of a modern major historical study. This accounts for some of both the challenges and the shortcomings of this book. I could not draw on comparative studies for investigative models or for data on developments in other parts of Italy, and thus many of the questions and approaches have had to be new.

The first and greatest problem facing the prospective historian of an Italian bishopric is the definition of the chronological limits and the various aspects of episcopal life to be studied. Scholars have concentrated primarily on the period before 1200, partially because external events, including monastic and papal reform and church-state controversies, made the bishoprics more

visible. After 1200, the rise and expansion of the communes overshadowed
the urban churches, which also had to compete with the new lay society of
merchants and bankers. Studies of this period have touched on only one or
two aspects of episcopal history and have dealt primarily with other questions. Episcopal lands have been investigated as a source for agrarian history, while the episcopal civil jurisdiction in the countryside has been examined only as a part of the general question of the relations between the
commune and its *contado,* that part of the surrounding countryside subject
to the commune. Scholars who do study the church have emphasized questions of theology or perhaps the actions of a few particularly active bishops.
I have chosen to include all the varied aspects of episcopal life in so far as
they relate to the temporal lordship of the bishopric of Lucca.

The words *bishopric* and *episcopate* (*episcopatus* or *vescovado*) may indicate the bishop's residence, his dignity, or his office. In the Middle Ages the
word was occasionally used, as it is today, as equivalent to *diocese.* In this
study, I use *bishopric* to designate the office of bishop to which all his rights,
duties, and properties belong.

Temporal and spiritual possessions and prerogatives pertain to the bishopric as much as to the bishop himself. The most common formula indicates
that officials represented the "bishop and bishopric" or that lands and rights
were the "bishop's and bishopric's." The relationship between the bishop
and bishopric is indicated especially by a document of 1201 in which lands
and jurisdiction were sold "to the venerable and most worthy lord Guido
Luccan bishop receiving [them] for the previously mentioned bishopric of
San Martino [of Lucca]. . . ."[1] Similarly, in 1281, when Bishop Paganello
exercised his spiritual right to select the *pievano* (or rector) of the *pieve* (baptismal church) of Padule, he acted "as patron for the bishopric," indicating
that the right of selection belonged to the bishopric which was under his protection.[2]

The *temporalities* of the bishopric refer to all the possessions of the bishopric that are not spiritual. Canon lawyers could and often did distinguish
between ecclesiastical lands, tithes, and offerings (the *res ecclesiasticae*) and
the lands and jurisdictions that, at least in theory, derived from a king or
emperor (the *regalia*). The distinctions between the church properties, tithes,
and the jurisdictions remained confused, and by the thirteenth century
theoretical differences were largely discarded. Robert Benson has observed
that the problem was related to the controversy over lay investiture and that

by redefining the episcopal office and its jurisdictional competence in purely ecclesiastical terms, by subjecting even the bishop's feudal obligations and prerogatives to
canonical criteria, and by ignoring the constitutive significance of regalian investiture,
the decretals and the canonists realized in practical fashion the old ideal of *libertas
ecclesiae.* Although many bishops continued to hold *regalia* thereafter, one can give a

clear—and not seriously misleading—account of the episcopal office during the thirteenth century without mention of the bishops' secular appurtenances.[3]

The canonical distinctions between *res ecclesiasticae* and *regalia* are not evident in administration. An inventory of episcopal possessions in Montecatini in 1201[4] included lands and tithes held *in feudum* as well as lands and jurisdictions held by lease for an annual payment. There was no attempt to distinguish between regalian and ecclesiastical possessions. An inventory of 1364, called a "Martyrology of income and rents of the Luccan Episcopate,"[5] contained the same mixture. Here rent payments and *pedaggio* payments (a road tax assessed on those who crossed the lands under episcopal jurisdiction) were arranged geographically with no attempt to classify payments as either secular or religious.

The only distinction made was that between purely spiritual matters and temporal affairs (including all finances). From the mid-thirteenth century onwards the bishops of Lucca appointed vicars who were specifically empowered to manage temporal affairs, including relations with rural communes under episcopal jurisdiction and the leasing of episcopal lands.[6]

From a practical viewpoint, canonical distinctions between church properties and regalia could never have been fully implemented. Administrative organization was geographical and it would have been impossible to incorporate into administrative practice these differences, about which even theorists disagreed. I do not attempt to draw distinctions that medieval administrators found unnecessary or impossible to use.

The reader might have wished for a more specific analysis of feudalism, but extant documents say very little about this enigmatic institution. Feudal terminology arrived late in Lucca, in the mid-eleventh century. Usually a feudal contract was little more than an alienation of properties to magnate families. Bishops did not use feudal institutions or prerogatives for administration or for military service. Thus feudalism does not appear to have been an important factor in the history of the bishop's temporal lordship.

I have also studiously avoided certain issues which would more correctly be seen as clerical prerogatives. I have not included questions concerning canon law and the prosecution of usury in the bishop's courts, or taxation and regulation of the clergy by communal officials. These questions occasionally affected the overall relations between commune and bishop, but they are canonical or religious questions and do not involve the bishop's temporal rights.

The Luccan bishopric is an exceptional subject for an investigation of episcopal lordship. The city was politically and economically one of the more important in central Italy. Its archiepiscopal archive, famous for its more than 1,500 documents from the period before 1000, also contains an exceptional number of administrative records from the thirteenth and early fourteenth centuries. The Fondo diplomatico of the Archivio arcivescovile preserves administrative documents, both originals and copies, for matters in the rural communes under the bishop's jurisdictional control and perhaps five hundred thirteenth- and fourteenth-century agricultural leases for episcopal lands as well as some partial inventories of episcopal possessions. For the period after 1250, we also have incomplete administrative records preserved in the so-called *Libri antichi*. While neither the parchments of the Fondo diplomatico nor the *Libri antichi* offer as complete a picture of the Luccan bishopric as we might like, episcopal records for the diocese of Lucca are perhaps the best preserved episcopal records in Tuscany.[7] This series, including thirteen extant volumes for the period between 1256 and 1350, preserves records of the bishop's civil and religious administration and leases and inquests concerning his landed possessions. The volumes range in size from only 54 pages to 374 pages. In theory, most of the volumes were divided into four or five sections reflecting all aspects of episcopal administration, but in fact a majority of the documents actually recorded dealt with the bishopric's temporal possessions.

This investigation begins in the eleventh century and continues through the first half of the fourteenth century. These chronological limits are broad enough to comprehend the development of episcopal administration as well as episcopal relations with the Luccan commune and the *jura* (the name used by the Lucchese to denote that area of the countryside under episcopal jurisdiction) and the exploitation of its economic resources.

This study derived from a dissertation on aspects of the temporalities of the Luccan bishopric presented to the University of California at Davis. I wish to thank Professor William M. Bowsky, who first suggested a study of the Luccan church and who offered assistance throughout this project. Sac. Giuseppe Ghilarducci, director of the Archivio arcivescovile, and Mons. Giuseppe Casali, director of the Archivio capitolare, both helped me explore the wealth of their archives. Don Lelio Mannari, parish priest of Santa Maria a Monte, shared with me his extensive knowledge of the history and geography of the many small towns in the lower Arno Valley. Professor Christine Meek gave me a great deal of help in the Archivio di Stato, including citations to important measures recorded in unindexed volumes of the city council deliberations. The necessary archival research was supported by grants from the Council on Research of the University of California at Davis and the American Philosophical Society.

I would especially like to thank my wife Yvonne, who has helped and encouraged me throughout the seemingly endless researching and writing of this book.

Abbreviations

ASI	*Archivio Storico Italiano*
ASL	Archivio di Stato di Lucca
Atti	*Atti della Accademia Lucchese di Scienze, Lettere ed Arti*
Bongi, *Inventario*	Salvatore Bongi, *Inventario del R. Archivio di Stato in Lucca,* 4 vols. (Lucca, 1872)
Endres, "Das Kirchengut"	Robert Endres, "Das Kirchengut im Bistum Lucca vom 8. bis 10. Jahrhundert," *Vierteljahrschrift für Sozial- und Wirtschaftsgeschichte,* 14 (1916), 240-92
Fiumi, *San Gimignano*	Enrico Fiumi, *Storia economica e sociale di San Gimignano* (Florence, 1961)
Guerra, Guidi, *Storia ecclesiastica lucchese*	Almerico Guerra and Pietro Guidi, *Compendio di storia ecclesiastica lucchese dalle origini a tutto il secolo XII* (Lucca, 1924)
Herlihy, "Agrarian Revolution"	David Herlihy, "The Agrarian Revolution in Southern France and Italy, 801-1150," *Speculum,* 33 (1958), 23-41.
Herlihy, *Pisa*	David Herlihy, *Pisa in the Early Renaissance* (New Haven, 1958)
Herlihy, *Pistoia*	David Herlihy, *Medieval and Renaissance Pistoia: The Social History of an Italian Town, 1200–1430* (New Haven and London, 1967)
Inventari	*Inventari del vescovato della cattedrale e di altre chiese di Lucca,* eds. Pietro Guidi and E. Pellegrinetti, Studi e Testi, 34 (Rome, 1921)

xiii

Jones, "An Italian Estate"   Philip Jones, "An Italian Estate, 900–1200," *Economic History Review*, 2nd ser., 7 (1955), 18–32

Kehr, *Italia Pontificia*   Paul F. Kehr, *Italia Pontificia*, III: *Etruria* (Berlin, 1908)

LA   *Libri antichi*

Martilogio   *Inventari*, No. XIV

Mem e doc   *Memorie e documenti per servire alla storia di Lucca*. III, i: Antonio N. Cianelli, *Dissertazioni sopra la storia lucchese* (Lucca, 1814). III, iii: *Statuto del Comune di Lucca dell' anno MCCCVIII*, eds. Salvatore Bongi and Leone Del Prete (Lucca, 1867). IV, i and ii: Domenico Bertini, *Dissertazioni sopra la storia ecclesiastica lucchese* (Lucca, 1818, 1836). V, i: Domenico Barsocchini, *Dissertazioni intorno alla storia ecclesiastica* (Lucca, 1844). V, ii: *Documenti relativi alla storia ecclesiastica lucchese*, ed. Domenico Barsocchini (Lucca, 1837). V, iii: *Raccolta di documenti per servire alla storia ecclesiastica lucchese*, ed. Domenico Barsocchini (Lucca, 1841). VII: Paolino Dinelli, *Dei sinodi della diocesi di Lucca, dissertazioni* (Lucca, 1834)

MGH   *Monumenta Germaniae Historica*

Migne, *PL*   J. P. Migne, *Patrologia Latina*

Nanni, *La Parrocchia*   Luigi Nanni, *La Parrocchia studiata nei documenti lucchesi dei secoli VIII–XIII*, Analecta Gregoriana, 47 (Rome, 1948)

Pacchi, *Garfagnana*   Domenico Pacchi, *Ricerche storiche sulla Provincia della Garfagnana* (Modena, 1785; reprinted Bologna, 1967)

Repetti, *Dizionario*   Emanuele Repetti, *Dizionario geografico fisico storico della Toscana*, 6 vols. (Florence, 1833–46)

RSI   *Rivista Storica Italiana*

Regesto del Capitolo, I–III   *Regesto del Capitolo di Lucca*, eds. Pietro Guidi and Oreste Parente, Regesta Chartarum Italiae, 6, 9, 18 (Rome, 1910–33)

Schwarzmaier, *Lucca*   Hansmartin Schwarzmaier, *Lucca und das Reich bis zum Ende des 11. Jahrhunderts*, Bibliothek des Deutschen Historischen Instituts in Rom, 41 (Tübingen, 1972)

Tolomeo, *Annales*

Die Annalen von Tholomeus von Lucca, ed. Bernhard Schmeidler, *MGH,* Scriptores rerum Germanicarum, n.s., 8 (Berlin, 1930; reprinted 1955)

Tommasi, *Storia di Lucca*

Girolamo Tommasi, *Sommario della Storia di Lucca* (Florence, 1847; reprinted with an introduction by Domenico Corsi, Lucca, 1969)

Tuscia

Rationes decimarum Italiae. Tuscia, I: *La Decima degli anni 1274–1280,* ed. Pietro Guidi. II: *Le Decime degli anni 1295–1304,* eds. Martino Giusti and Pietro Guidi. Studi e Testi, 58, 98 (Vatican City, 1932, 1942)

Violante, "I vescovi"

Cinzio Violante, "I vescovi dell' Italia centro-settentrionale e lo sviluppo dell' economia monetaria," in *Vescovi e diocesi in Italia nel medioevo (sec. IX–XIII),* Italia Sacra, 5 (Padua, 1964), pp. 193–217

Volpe, *Medio evo italiano*

Gioacchino Volpe, *Medio evo italiano* ([3rd ed.] Florence, 1961)

Volpe, *Pisa*

Gioacchino Volpe, *Studi sulle istituzioni comunali a Pisa* (Pisa, 1902; reprinted with an introduction by Cinzio Violante, Florence, 1970)

Volpe, *Toscana medievale*

Gioacchino Volpe, *Toscana medievale* (Florence, 1964)

Dating

Luccan documents before 1200 were dated according to the Incarnation in the Florentine style. The year began on March 25 instead of on the preceding January 1. After 1200, the Luccan year began on December 25, the Nativity. Some of the documents, for the most part those redacted in the Valdera, were dated from the Incarnation according to Pisan style, that is, the year began on the March 25 preceding January 1. Dates in the text and notes are in common style, unless otherwise indicated.

Measures

Luccan measures are similar to those used in most of Italy. Dry measures were based on the *moggio, staio* and *quarra*. A *moggio* contained 24 *stai,* "starium rectum lucanum venditorium nunc curens"; in the thirteenth century the number varied according to whether it was a *staio affictale, antico, terzino,* or *quartino.* The *quarra* was a fourth part of a *staio.* The *stioro* was the standard area measure used in thirteenth-century documents. One *cultra* equaled 22 *stiori* or 121 *scale.* (On weights and measures see Bongi, *Inventario,* II, "Elenco dei pesi e misure già usate in Lucca e nel territorio soggetto," 67–77.)

This was the Luccan system, though before the fourteenth century there were independent systems of measure in Moriano, Altopascio, Santa Maria a Monte, and Valdarno.

Money

The money of account in the Lucchese documents was a Lira (£) of 20 soldi or 240 denari. During the thirteenth century the Lucchese silver denario was roughly equivalent to the Pisan denario. Many documents allowed for payment in either coin. None of the surviving episcopal documents indicate the relationship between the Florentine florin and Lucchese coin, but the thirteenth-century florin must have been worth roughly 36 Lucchese soldi— a rate similar to the exchange rates in late thirteenth-century Pisa and Siena. See David Herlihy, *Pisa,* pp. 193–96; and William M. Bowsky, *The Finance of the Commune of Siena, 1287–1355* (Oxford, 1970), p. xx.

AN ITALIAN LORDSHIP

THE BISHOPRIC OF LUCCA IN THE LATE MIDDLE AGES

The Medieval Luccan Diocese

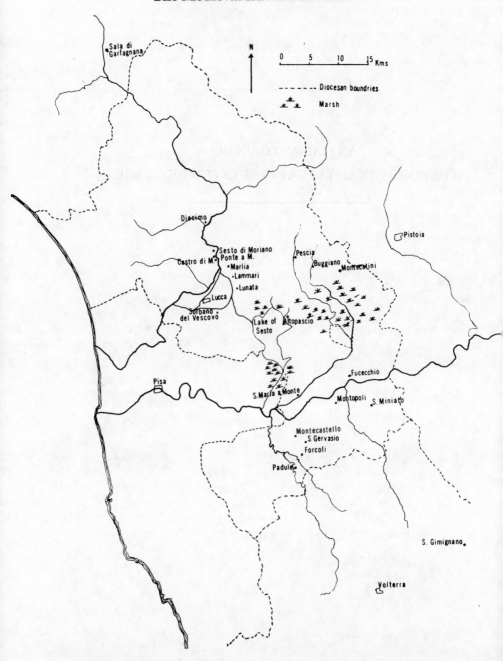

N

0   5   10   15 Kms

- - - - Diocesan boundries

⁂ Marsh

Sala di Garfagnana

Diecimo

Sesto di Moriano
Ponte a M.
Castro di M.
Marlia
Lammari
Lunata

Pescia
Buggiano
Montecatini

Pistoia

Lucca

Sorbano del Vescovo

Lake of Sesto

Altopascio

Pisa

Fucecchio

S. Maria a Monte

Montopoli   S. Miniato

Montecastello
S. Gervasio
Forcoli

Padule

S. Gimignano

Volterra

1

The Setting

Lucca is a child of rivers and roads. Lying about 70 kilometers west of Florence in northern Tuscany, it rises on a large plain between the Arno and Serchio (Ausar in the Roman age) rivers. Its position on the left bank of the Serchio allowed it to control the historically strategic road down the Serchio to the lower Valdarno. The first mention of "Luca" records the importance of this location when, in 218 B.C., Ti. Sempronius Longus retreated to Lucca after the Roman defeat by the Carthaginians at the Trebbia River near Piacenza. After such a crushing defeat he needed an easily defended point which would allow him to block any southward moves by the Carthaginians.[1]

Luccan territory was a borderland between Etruria and Liguria. Etruscan domination stopped at the left bank of the Arno, while the Ligurians settled primarily on the hills along the right bank of the Serchio and in the Valdinievole. Thus Ligurians and Etruscans intermingled on the plain of Lucca which stretches from the Serchio to the low hills along the Arno. Both Ligurian and Etruscan graves have been discovered at Bientina, a few miles south of the present city of Lucca. The Ligurians probably predominated, since the city's name derives from the Celto-Ligurian word *luc* meaning a marsh or swamp.

The actual founding of the present city of Lucca was left to the Romans, who established a *colonia* at Lucca in 180 B.C. and later, during the reforms of the first century B.C., made Lucca a *municipium*.[2] The Romans founded Lucca as a fortified center to control the road into the lower Arno Valley. Later, it served as an important post between Pistoia and Luna on the Via Cassia.

As the southernmost point in Liguria (rather than the northern outpost of Etruria), Lucca was Julius Caesar's choice to be the meeting place for the creation of the First Triumvirate. Only later, under Augustus, was Lucca added to Tuscany.

Roman Lucca quickly rose to challenge Pisa. Its Roman walls enclosed an area of 39 hectares while those of Pisa encompassed no more than 30. At the same time, the estimated population of Lucca was about 10,000, that of its neighbor to the southwest only about 8,000.[3] Despite the size of the city of Lucca and its strategic position north of the Arno, its Roman territory was surprisingly small. Lucca's municipium was bounded on the south by the Arno and probably did not reach the Tyrrhenian Sea. The largest part of the municipium was north of the city and included all of the Garfagnana.[4]

Lucca's role changed dramatically after the barbarian invasions and the end of Roman administration. The primary north-south road during the early Middle Ages was the Via Francigena (also called the Via Romea) rather than the Via Aurelia or Via Emilia. This road by-passed Florence by going through Siena to San Gimignano, crossing the Arno at Fucecchio, and joining the older Via Cassia at Lucca. The Lombards, recognizing Lucca's strategic value, located their capital of Tuscany there in order to command at once the Via Francigena and the important road up the Serchio Valley to Emilia.[5]

As an important Lombard center Lucca and its church found new prosperity. Taking advantage of gifts of lands, jurisdictions, and pievi from wealthy Lombards, the medieval diocese of Lucca extended to include all of the Roman municipium as well as parts of the municipia of Pisa, Volterra, Pistoia, and Luna.[6] As late as the ninth century, Pope Hadrian wrote to Italian bishops forbidding them to transfer churches forcibly from one diocese to another.[7] This injunction certainly applied to the bishops of Lucca. Their close relation to the Lombard nobility was a most important reason for the expansion of the Luccan diocese. The eighth-century bishop Walprando, for example, was the son of Duke Walprando and the brother of Count Pertifunso. These Lombards were munificent in their charity. During the eighth century, more than forty churches were founded and given to the bishops of Lucca.[8] Among the reasons for the foundation of these churches was the desire to provide for a son. According to Luigi Nanni, the church would be built and given to the bishop with the reservation that a son or relative of the donor should have possession of the church.

During the ninth century, the administrative center of Tuscany was moved back to Florence and the bishop's formerly close relationship with the Tuscan nobility was altered. Partly as a result of this, the bishop's influence diminished and gifts to the church declined sharply.[9] Despite these changes, the position of the Luccan bishops and the size of the diocese was by then assured. To the north and west the Luccan diocese included the whole of the Garfagnana, touching the dioceses of Luni, Reggio, and Modena. To the east and south it included the Valdinievole and lands south of the Arno touching the dioceses of Pistoia, Florence, Volterra, and Pisa. It also extended west to the Tyrrhenian Sea.[10]

The sixth to the eighth centuries therefore were critical for the construction of the medieval diocese. Unlike medieval Pistoia, where the basic political and economic orientation was a product of the Roman period,[11] Lucca's critical period of expansion was between the sixth and eighth centuries. Because of the changed political and economic relationships, and especially the new importance of the Via Francigena, Lucca dominated Tuscany during the Lombard period. At the same time, Lucca's diocese increased to almost twice the size of its Roman municipium.

Medieval Lucca, like the rest of Tuscany, saw an almost continuous demographic growth from at least the eleventh century to possibly as late as the fourteenth century. Fragmentation of the agricultural holdings in the Luccan countryside and an increase in trade and sale of these fragments seem to indicate growing population pressures, beginning in the very early tenth century and continuing into the very early twelfth century.[12] The increased urban population is indicated by the construction of new city walls begun about 1200 and finished about 1260.[13] These walls enclosed about 75 hectares, not quite double the 39 hectares enclosed by the Roman walls.

Lest we overemphasize the growth Lucca experienced, it should be remembered that the walls of other Tuscan cities often enclosed much larger areas. Pisa's walls, completed in the late thirteenth century, probably enclosed about 185 hectares,[14] while Florence's walls, completed about 1180, enclosed between 80 and 100 hectares.[15] Florence grew dramatically in the thirteenth century and, by 1335, enclosed over 500 hectares within its walls.[16] Even Pistoia, never one of Tuscany's most populous areas, contained an area of 117 hectares within its thirteenth-century walls.[17] These figures show that Lucca, though growing, was far from one of Tuscany's largest towns during the thirteenth century.

The surface areas of these cities give us no more than approximations of relative size. We cannot assume equivalent densities in all Tuscan cities.[18] More important, we must consider the people living just outside the walls. At Lucca, as at Pistoia, a large proportion of the population always lived outside the walls in suburbs protected by a series of canals. Until the late fourteenth century, one fork of the Serchio River encircled Lucca, providing an additional natural moat.[19]

The earliest indication of Luccan population is a notation from 1333 that 4,746 men took an oath to John of Bohemia. Karl Beloch,[20] using a conservative multiplier of 3.5 persons for each male who took the oath, estimated the population of Lucca to be about 15,000. At the same time, Luccan tax receipts indicated that Luccans consumed 168,300 barrels of wine, which according to David Herlihy would indicate a population of about 40,000.[21] Such a population figure is probably too high. A more reasonable figure would be about 21,000 to 23,000, based on 4,746 multiplied by 4.5-5.[22]

Lucca's demographic growth was not as pronounced as that of several of the larger Tuscan towns. Florence swelled from a moderate population of about 10,000 to 15,000 in the late twelfth and early thirteenth centuries to about 95,000 by 1300. Pisa, too, outdistanced Lucca. By 1315, Lucca's rival had an estimated population of 50,000.[23]

Lucca was of moderate size compared to Pisa and Florence and, like its larger neighbors, its economic and demographic expansion was based in part on its trade and manufacture. It was a distribution center for the smaller towns in the region. Luccan merchants, moreover, had agents in most of the major European cities, and they attended the most important trade fairs. They sold woolen and silk cloth besides acting as bankers.

The Luccan woolen industry did not expand as rapidly as the Florentine and Pisan wool trade. Manufacture at Lucca apparently retained a simple household organization throughout the thirteenth century. The earliest reference to a guild of weavers at Lucca is in 1320. In the thirteenth century, Luccan drapers were wholesalers for rural merchants and peddlers who traveled the Val di Serchio, the lower Valdarno, and the Valdinievole. These merchants and peddlers sold both locally manufactured and foreign made woolen cloth.[24]

The woolen industry was not large enough to explain either the distribution of Luccan merchants throughout Europe or their reputations as astute businessmen. The key to the Luccan economy was its control of the silk market. Raw silk originally was imported from the East and Sicily. Beginning sometime in the thirteenth century, silkworms were actually raised at Lucca. The cultivation of the worms doubtless corresponds to the introduction of mulberry trees into the Valdinievole by Francesco Buonvicini. The silk trade quickly expanded in the thirteenth century and was the chief product of the Luccan trading colonies that settled in commercial centers in Italy and the rest of Europe. Trade remained the primary occupation of the Luccan bankers who had settled in Bruges even in the mid-fourteenth century, long after the Luccans had lost their virtual monopoly on silk manufacture.[25] But like the woolen industry, silk production remained a modest household enterprise during the thirteenth century. A more rationalized, centralized manufacture only developed in the late fourteenth century after Lucca had lost its predominance in silk production.

The other crafts and industries at Lucca were of lesser importance, supplying, for the most part, local needs. Leather workers, stone cutters, and iron workers were present at Lucca just as in nearly every urban center. Except for the leather workers and butchers, who by statute were restricted to certain districts,[26] these craftsmen were distributed throughout the city and countryside.

Lucca's mineral wealth was minor. During the Middle Ages there was probably enough domestic iron ore to meet the needs of the city. Iron as well as silver was mined in Versilia, Garfagnana, and the Lunigiana, areas incorporated into the Luccan contado about the mid-thirteenth century. It was control of the silver mines in Versilia that provided a portion of the wealth of the powerful Castracani—the family of Castruccio Castracani degli Antelminelli, the early fourteenth-century lord of Lucca. When the iron mines could no longer fulfill Lucca's needs in the late fourteenth century, Paolo Guinigi chose to import iron from Elba rather than invest money in new explorations and excavations in the Luccan contado.[27] Because of its barely adequate mineral deposits, land remained valuable basically for its agricultural potential.[28]

Lucca had a viable economy in the Middle Ages, though by the late thirteenth and early fourteenth centuries it was not as strong as that of Florence or even Pisa. Lucca's major economic advantage was its silk trade. Other economic activities of the city pale in significance when compared with silk manufacture. It was in this environment that the government of Lucca developed.

The communal government of Lucca is visible from the late eleventh and early twelfth centuries, appearing early enough that Daniel Waley included Lucca in a list of "the more precocious cities."[29] Consuls are first mentioned at Lucca in 1107, though it is likely that they were present much earlier. The role played by the "people" in the struggle over church reform in the mid-eleventh century indicates a nascent autonomous commune.[30] Emperor Henry IV recognized the autonomy of the commune when, in 1081, he conceded to the people of Lucca jurisdiction in the city and the surrounding district up to a distance of six miles. The emperor promised that he would not build a palace within the city or castles in the surrounding district.[31]

Because of a series of sackings which destroyed many communal records, little is known about the government at Lucca before the early fourteenth century. The city seems to have experienced the difficulties common to other Italian towns. Early in the thirteenth century, reports the annalist Tolomeo of Lucca,[32] there was discord between the "people" and the "nobles." The people were victorious in this and other struggles which resulted in a greater participation of the middle class in government and administration. Popular participation in government at Lucca as in other Italian cities can at least partially be equated with the institution of the "Captain of the People" as a rival to the *podestà*, the chief administrative officer of the commune. Captains of the People appear regularly at Lucca after 1250.[33]

A primary function of the city government was to insure communal control of the contado. This involved matters of civil administration and economics as well as relations with other towns. Administratively, the commune strove to insure uniform criminal and civil statutes in the city and countryside.[34] The rural communes provided taxes and men for defense and many of the agricultural products necessary to sustain the urban population.

Control of potentially wealthy strategic border areas of the contado brought the commune of Lucca into almost inevitable conflict with neighboring communes. As early as 1005, the Luccans and Pisans fought for control of Versilia and Ripafratta, a vital ford on the Serchio. The wars with Pisa continued sporadically over the next three centuries. The two cities fought over the seacoast area of Versilia, the mountainous Garfagnana, and the left bank of the Arno, and especially over the Valdera.[35] Similar, and for Lucca more successful, struggles occurred with Pistoia along the eastern edge of the Luccan contado. The wars with the Pistoians did not last as long as the Pisan wars and they ended with Luccan and Florentine hegemony over Pistoia and its contado.[36]

The wars fought to control the contado help to explain the Guelf and Ghibelline sympathies of the cities. Lucca's neighbors, Pistoia and Pisa, were Ghibelline (usually supporters of the empire), and probably for that reason Lucca was Guelf (and theoretically a supporter of the papacy). Lucca's shift to Ghibellinism in the early fourteenth century was a reaction to the defeat of Pisa and the growing Florentine menace to Luccan jurisdiction in the Valdarno and the Valdinievole. At Lucca, the conversion to Ghibellinism may have been accompanied by an attack on local church immunities, but the Ghibelline policies also can be understood as a continuation of the attitudes of the "Guelf commune." The emperors who depended on Ghibelline lords such as Castruccio Castracani found these nobles to be more interested in securing their local power than in the lofty ideals of either the empire or papacy.[37]

Part of the inter-city strife in the countryside was for control of the roads, the means of contact with other parts of Italy and, indeed, with all of Europe. They were the very bands that held the contado together. Lucca was well served by its road network, better perhaps than any other major Tuscan city. Lucca was a main station on the Via Francigena, the most important medieval highway between France and Rome. This road connected Lucca not only to northern Europe, but also to its strongest economic and political ally, Genoa. The international traveler, almost without exception, had to cross the Luccan diocese and stay in one of the Luccan hospitals. There were 43 hospitals in the diocese of Lucca around 1300. The sheer number of the hospitals shows the importance of Lucca as a stopping place. There were almost twice as many hospitals in the diocese of Lucca (the greatest proportion along the major highways) as there were in any other Tuscan diocese.[38]

From Lucca the traveler bound for France on the Via Francigena crossed the Serchio, traveled up the Freddana Valley and crossed the Apuane mountains to Camaiore. West of Camaiore, the Francigena joined the Aurelian Way, the coastal road, and passed through the deserted Roman town of Luni on its way to Genoa. Control of this stretch of road was one of the issues in the almost continuous war with Pisa. From the mid-twelfth century, the Pisans maintained a coastal route, allowing travelers to leave the Via Francigena and by-pass Lucca on their way to Pisa.[39] The eight hospitals along the Via Francigena in the late fourteenth century, however, attest to the continued importance of this road.[40]

The Luccans not only fought Pisa over the Francigena but also exacted promises of safe passage for their merchants from the powerful bishop of Luni and the nobles of the Lunigiana. The pledges of passage without payment of the pedaggio soon led to Luccan hegemony in the area. By the early thirteenth century judges in the Lunigiana acted "for the venerable lord bishop of Luna and the commune of Lucca."[41]

The other route north traveled along the banks of the Serchio into the Garfagnana. There were roads on either side of the river, though the preferred one, judging by the placement of hospitals, was on the right bank passing through Moriano and Diecimo, lands within the bishop's jura. The traveler could continue up the Serchio and cross into the Lunigiana, and thus join the Via Francigena, or turn right near Castelnuovo in Garfagnana and cross into the diocese of Modena near San Pellegrino delle Alpi. Judging again from the placement of hospitals, the road that followed the Serchio into the Lunigiana was more important, though the Luccan commune valued the road to Modena. In 1222 and again in 1281, the Luccans and the communes of Reggio and Modena agreed to maintain that road.[42]

The traveler to Florence followed the Via Cassia, which owed its importance to the expansion of Florentine economic and political power. Although it was a minor road in the early Middle Ages, the rise in the number of hospitals along it attests to the increased use of the Cassian Way by travelers bound for Florence. There were, for example, five hospitals at Borgo a Buggiano by 1307, two of which had been built in the late thirteenth century.[43]

Like the Via Francigena, the Via Cassia followed the low hills rather than the marshy plains. The traveler would leave Lucca by the eastern gate, Porta San Gervasio, and pass through Lunata and by the hospital of Rughi. From there he would cross the low hills north of Montecarlo and travel through the towns of Pescia, Borgo a Buggiano, and Montecatini. In 1260, there were eleven hospitals along the roughly 25 kilometers between the walls of Lucca and Montecatini. By the mid-fourteenth century, the number had increased to fifteen.[44] The Via Cassia was important primarily because it connected Florence with the Via Francigena. By the end of the thirteenth century, Florentine travelers could also follow a newer road down the left bank of the Arno and join the Via Francigena at Fucecchio,[45] but the Via Cassia probably remained shorter and faster for those who wished to travel north.

To the south, the most important road was the Via Francigena. The traveler went to Altopascio, home of the wealthy and famous hospital of San Jacopo, and followed the high ground between the marshes of Bientina and Fucecchio. There were bridges and ferries across the Arno at the town of Fucecchio. From there he would travel to San Miniato—long the imperial stronghold in northern Tuscany. Then the traveler would climb the Elsa Valley to San Gimignano, Siena, and Rome.

For the traveler to Pisa three roads left Lucca.[46] The most direct was that over Monte Pisano. From the placement of hospitals in that area, we see that it was the earliest and remained the most popular throughout the Middle Ages. The other roads were north of Monte Pisano. The earlier and longer of the two ran west from Lucca to Lake Massaciuccoli and then followed the Via Aurelia to Pisa. This highway was probably more important as an entrance into the contested area of Versilia than as a way to Pisa. The third road followed the base of Monte Pisano and crossed the Serchio at Ripafratta. Rebuilt during the thirteenth century, it was probably the fastest way to move merchandise between Pisa and Lucca.

Unlike the modern province of Lucca, the medieval diocese clearly lay on a north-south axis. From this brief description of the major road systems and a careful notation of the hospitals located along them, it is apparent that very little traffic moved straight west of Lucca to the coast or to Pisa. It was Lucca's location on the Via Francigena and perhaps its connection with Florence that provided most of the traffic to Lucca.

This road system also explains some of Lucca's successes and failures in the arduous conflict for control of its contado. The Via Francigena and the road to Massaciuccoli allowed the Luccans easy and alternate routes into Versilia. Lucca, by the mid-thirteenth century, had driven the Pisans from Versilia and subsequently expanded its political influence throughout Versilia and Lunigiana. Lucca was not so fortunate to the south. Constrained by the mountains and the marshes of Bientina and Fucecchio, the Luccans could use but one road, the Via Francigena. To travel to the Valdera was a long and difficult trip, more easily made from Pisa. It is not surprising, therefore, that the Pisans controlled most, if not all, of the Valdera after the twelfth century.[47] In the south, the only part of the diocese incorporated into the Luccan contado was west of Santa Maria a Monte—and even this area fell to the burgeoning Florentine state in the early fourteenth century.

The lands controlled by the episcopate were concentrated in several areas within the diocese of Lucca. First and most important were the lands of the jura,[48] located in the upper Garfagnana, middle Serchio, on the Luccan plain, and in the Arno and Valdera regions of the diocese. In addition to the jura, the bishop also held extensive agricultural lands on the plain of Lucca, in the suburbs, and in the lower Valdarno. The episcopal lands were, for the most part, on the plains and lower hills—the wealthiest agricultural areas.[49]

Among the fairly diverse economic activities at Lucca, the episcopate's lands and wealth were almost exclusively agricultural. This specialization was provoked by changes that occurred in medieval society beginning during the reform movements of the eleventh century.

2

Formation of the
Medieval Luccan Bishopric

The nature of the Luccan bishopric's temporal possessions changed dramatically during the famous religious reform movements of the eleventh century. In this chapter we shall examine the episcopal temporalities prior to the reforms, the reforms at Lucca, and the changes and reactions to the new religious and social conditions after the reforms.

Traditional lists of Luccan bishops show a long line reaching back to San Paolino, allegedly a disciple of St. Peter and first bishop in Tuscany. The growth of the bishopric, however, should be dated from the time of San Frediano, the sixth-century Irish monk who, as bishop of Lucca, is credited with a miracle that changed the course of the Serchio River. In a less miraculous manner, he began a building program within the diocese, constructing not only the cathedral of San Martino and the basilica of San Vincenzo (later renamed San Frediano) in and near the city, but also 28 pievi within the diocese. This period of construction is the first indication that Lucca was recovering from the disorders of the early Middle Ages.[1]

THE BISHOPRIC BEFORE THE ELEVENTH-CENTURY REFORMS

The crucial period of expansion began in the eighth century when the bishops of Lucca began to benefit from extensive lay donations. Many of these to be sure were pious gifts, but others were for more practical reasons. In some cases lands were donated to churches in order to provide for a son or to bring the donor under the protection of the church. In many cases the Lombard nobility constructed proprietary churches, monasteries, and even hospitals,

10

providing them with lands in and around Lucca. These foundations typically remained in the hands of the founding families, who chose the rectors or abbots through the first three generations, but eventually they passed under the control of the bishops. The church of San Pietro Somaldi (later an important possession of the medieval bishopric) was originally a Lombard monastery just outside the Roman walls. It passed under episcopal control in the ninth century.[2]

A late ninth-century inventory of episcopal lands shows that most were small pieces lying near the city. Others were scattered in Versilia and Garfagnana. Most of the land, then, lay in the region between the middle Serchio and Monte Pisano. Though certain areas were designated as demesne lands and some manors (*corti* or *curtes*) were distinguished, the administration of the land was handled, in the main, by central authorities in Lucca.[3] We must not overemphasize the completeness of this inventory since a glance at the extant parchments indicates various holdings throughout the diocese. These territories may not have been included in the inventory because by the time the inventory was composed the bishopric may already have lost effective control of the lands.

In the eighth century, lands were let, for the most part, to small landholders by means of perpetual leases called *livelli*—theoretically, peasant leases given to individuals who worked the land directly and paid either an annual rent or a recognition payment (*censo*), usually in money. This was the theory, but increasingly in the ninth and tenth centuries livelli were given to rural magnates who did not work the land themselves. These livelli represented virtual alienation of property. By the end of the tenth century, many of the episcopal possessions had been let to aristocratic families and lost to episcopal control.[4]

The formula of the livello changed markedly in the same period. The normal peasant livello was a long-term lease (normally for thirty years or more), requiring that the lessee work and reside on the land. The livello further required that the lessee appear at his lord's court for justice. The livelli granted to magnates, on the other hand, did not contain all these requirements. While the duration of the contract remained the same, the requirements of residence and justice were dropped. The magnate was directed either to work the land himself, or to see that the land was worked by someone else. Where the peasant lease was for a single house and its lands, the magnate leases were for several houses and lands, or even for whole manors.[5]

Episcopal administration of the pievi and their tithes functioned in much the same way. The formula of the livello was used to appoint parish priests. During the eighth and ninth centuries the livello was the preferred notarial

formula for any delegation of possession or jurisdiction.[6] The practice probably began because of the lack of exempla which could be used to construct
documents delegating religious jurisdiction. The medieval notarial formu-
laries appeared only in the mid-eleventh century and later. The first extant
manual of notarial style is the mid-eleventh century *Breviarium de dictamine*
of Alberic of Monte Cassino.[7] The use of livelli to appoint parish priests
simplified the transfer of churches to laymen. Instead of the usual order
that the priest should say divine offices, the notarial form was changed (much
as in the magnate agricultural leases) so that the lessee needed only to "cause
divine offices to be said." In this way, control of local churches, their lands,
dues, and tithes passed into the hands of laymen. During the second half of
the tenth century, bishops even let fractions of pievi rather than leave a
church under the jurisdiction of a single pievano[8]—a further attempt to
maximize the possible income from the control of local churches.

The revenues paid to the bishopric were based primarily on the leases of
episcopal lands and churches to lay magnates, but the bishopric could also
take advantage of blurred lines of jurisdiction and gain additional income
by letting lands belonging to local churches, just as if the lands pertained
directly to the bishopric. In the ninth decade of the ninth century, for
example, Bishop Gherardo let lands in Moriano which belonged to the
basilica of San Frediano for an annual rent of six denari payable to himself.[9] In such cases the bishop was not letting religious control of the church,
but only control of certain of the temporal goods belonging to it. The policy
was adopted not only for the lands of the large and wealthy urban churches
and pievi, but also for certain of the smaller subaltern churches (churches
lacking baptismal and burial rights) throughout the diocese.[10]

In the tenth century signs of economic and spiritual decline are evident
in all areas. Lands and churches were alienated. Purchases of land by the
bishopric dropped to zero in the second half of the ninth and in the tenth
centuries (Table 1). Pious donations also declined dramatically. The period
of expansion had lasted about a century and a half (ca. 700–850) and was
followed almost immediately by a period of contraction. Between 850 and
1000, the bishopric lost control of much of its land and many of its pievi.
Philip Jones summarized agriculture on Luccan episcopal lands about 1000
simply by noting that "the bishop's economic position was not strong: his
properties were dissipated in the hands of the lay aristocracy and his rental
was modest and fixed"[11]—a dramatic change for bishops who in the late
eighth century were wealthy and influential.

There are several possible causes for this decline in vitality. The simplest
explanation would be that it was caused by the renewed barbarian invasions.
Early in the tenth century, the Hungarians passed through Lucca as they
plundered Italy. They probably moved down the Val di Serchio, since we

TABLE 1

Land Transactions of the Bishopric, 800–1000

	Number of Extant Documents	Donations		Purchases		Exchanges	
		(no.)	*(%)*	*(no.)*	*(%)*	*(no.)*	*(%)*
700–800	281	136	67.3	46	22.8	20	9.9
800–850	391	72	50.0	38	26.4	34	23.6
850–900	374	18	22.5	13	16.3	49	61.2
900–1000	1,710	4	3.8	--	--	100	96.2

SOURCE: Endres, "Das Kirchengut," p. 245 n. 12.

have reports that San Pietro a Vico was burned and that later a castle was built there to protect the road. Many of the contracts letting churches to laymen indicate that the churches had been destroyed, probably because of the unrest. Contracts often called for the reconstruction of the ruined churches and buildings.

Luigi Nanni judged the livelli more harshly, arguing that they "served the private interests of certain wealthy speculators. . . ." The leasing of destroyed churches, according to Nanni, was just another example of the deplorable moral condition into which the Luccan church had fallen.[12] Nanni's conclusions seem valid for the second half of the tenth century. These leases, however, probably did originate as improvement leases since a significant number of the ninth- and early tenth-century leases called for the construction and repair of buildings.[13] The shock of these invasions could have dislocated the economy. The destruction doubtless included trees and vines on episcopal lands which would have caused economic hardships for both the church and its tenants.

The transformation, however, occurred earlier. The decline in donations to the church and the end of land purchases by the bishopric began early in the ninth century. The increased proportion of magnate leases also recommenced a half-century before the invasions. Figures given by Robert Endres (Table 2) indicate that after the mid-ninth century, leases to magnates increased continually. The percentage of extant leases given to magnates nearly doubled in the second half of the ninth century. In the second half of the tenth century over 93 percent of the extant leases were given to magnates.

The declining episcopal vigor was probably related to the appearance of this new group challenging the episcopate's control of church lands. Powerful magnate families, variously called rural counts, *cattani, valvassori,* or

TABLE 2

Leases Given for Episcopal Lands, 800–1000

	Peasant Leases (no.)	(%)	Magnate Leases (no.)	(%)	Freehold Leases (no.)	(%)
800–850	17	36.17	16	34.0	14	29.83
850–900	26	11.58	79	64.51	33	23.91
900–950	36	23.37	106	68.91	12	7.72
950–1000	12	6.81	164	93.19	--	--

SOURCE: Endres, "Das Kirchengut," p. 277 n. 118.

lombardi, became prominent by the second half of the ninth century, after the decline of Carolingian administration in Italy. These families acquired powerful centers in the countryside. Later imperial concessions of jurisdiction to these families were simply acceptance of established fact.[14]

The Aldobrandeschi were one such powerful family. Though of Lombard origin, the Aldobrandeschi had cooperated with the Franks, and by 840 Eriprando, father of the eponymous count Ildebrando and of the Luccan bishop Geremia, was referred to as a "vassus domini imperatoris."[15] The family began to build a solid base in southern Tuscany when, in 803, Bishop Jacopo of Lucca let them the properties of the church of San Giorgio, located near Grosseto. The same bishop let land near Sovana (also near Grosseto) to the Aldobrandeschi six years later. The family continued to receive lands in the Luccan diocese throughout the ninth and tenth centuries, though their real center of power lay in southern Tuscany. These lords played an independent role in the struggles between the papacy and the empire. The Aldobrandeschi, Siena's primary opponents in the commune's conquest of coastal lands to the west, remained independent well into the fourteenth century.

In similar fashion, the bishopric leased houses and land during the second half of the tenth century to the "Lombardi" of San Miniato,[16] to the lords of Corvaia in Versilia,[17] and to the Porcaresi on the plain of Lucca,[18] as well as to other noble houses.[19]

The cession of lands and churches to these families probably occurred for two reasons. First, some of the bishops were related to these magnate families. Bishop Geremia (852–67) was an Aldobrandeschi; Bishop Corrado (935–64) was a Roladinghi; Bishop Guido I (979–83) belonged to the Donuccio family, the first lords of Porcari; Bishop Teudigrimo (983–87) was related to a noble family with extensive holdings in the Valdera and in the

Maremma; and Gherardo II (981–1003) was probably a Soffredinga of the lords of Anchiano.[20] Given the unrest of the period, caused first by the disappearance of Carolingian administration in Italy and later by the invasions, the bishops needed strong allies and probably—not unnaturally—followed dynastic policies similar to those of the Roman pontiffs. Often, too, the bishops let large tracts of land to families who could help the episcopate build fortresses in the countryside—an absolute necessity for any attempt to bring order to rural Italy.[21]

Secondly, the state of episcopal wealth and finance about 1000 was mixed at best. Pious donations either to the bishop or to local churches had ceased, and the bishopric only attempted to maintain what it already possessed. Though demesne lands still existed, they, like the local churches and tithes, had been leased to laymen for money rents to the episcopate. Rather than administer the lands, the bishops preferred or were constrained (we don't know which) to lease servile lands to wealthy laymen. The episcopal administration was passive, reacting to the changes and conditions created by others.

The situation changed radically in the eleventh century. Economic and social life was altered by renewed local and regional trade and an emerging urban class. At the same time a new spirituality appeared in the church, with a more positive attitude toward the secular world and toward the mission of the church.[22] It was this changed economic and spiritual environment that breathed life into the series of religious reforms that Gregory VII finally welded into a far-reaching concept of the "Liberty of the Church."[23]

THE ELEVENTH-CENTURY REFORMS AT LUCCA

At Lucca the issue of reform quickly centered on the state of the cathedral chapter. In question were attitudes toward the institution of common life and an end of clerical marriage.[24]

The cathedral canons of San Martino were present at Lucca from the eighth century. They were clerics attached to the bishop, and by pride of place, they were very probably the most important clerics in the diocese. In the earliest references (between the eighth and tenth centuries), they were referred to as "Sacerdotes nostri," "Filii Ecclesiae," or even "Nobiles Sacerdotarum." Originally, they were without any corporate structure or holdings outside those of the bishops and his episcopate. The growth of the chapter as a well-defined structure separate from the episcopate began in the tenth century, about the same time they began to be referred to as *canonici.*[25]

The gifts of lands and jurisdictions enabled the chapter to build its own jura in the area of Versilia, with centers at Massagrossa, Massarosa, Gualdo, Montignano, and Fibbialla. The canons received pious donations from laymen as well as from the nobility. In 932 and 941 King Ugo gave lands in Versilia and later Bishop Corrado contributed the tithe of the pieve of San Lorenzo of Segromigno. The canons' popularity and predominance in the tenth century reflect the growing influence of the judges and notaries—"a class of respected and rich families who," according to Hansmartin Schwarzmaier, "were in the position to supply their (legitimate and illegitimate) sons to the Cathedral Chapter."[26]

The jurisdiction was held in common, but the agricultural rents seem to have been divided into prebends by the early eleventh century. Erich Kittel has already shown that in the mid-eleventh century canons received rents from peasants for lands: "qui [the canon] habebat eam a S. Martino pro ordine suo."[27] This formula and its variants indicate that before the reform movement, and possibly from the beginning, the chapter's revenues were divided among the canons. The possibilities for abuse were many. The lands could be pawned, sold, or simply alienated by a canon who if he were married would naturally wish to pass his possessions on to his children. In 1048, Bishop Giovanni II instituted common life and ordered that prebends should be held only by those who followed common life. In the 1050s, Pope Leo confirmed Giovanni's declaration.[28]

The various events of chapter reform are difficult to follow because we have few documents that deal with the problem, but it appears that after Leo's declaration the problem of reform was slowly solving itself. During the pontificate of Anselmo I (1057–73), little was heard about the reformation of the chapter. One might suppose that Anselmo followed a moderate course, just as he did later as Pope Alexander II.[29] He did, however, show an interest in the reorganization of the chapter. In an undated bull, Alexander directed that the chapter should be made up of twelve priests, seven deacons, seven sub-deacons, and four clerics who would serve in the choir. This stabilization of the chapter's size is Alexander's only known contribution to the reform of the chapter. We might assume that he preferred to follow the moderate path of Giovanni and Leo and therefore felt that only time was necessary to complete the reforms.[30]

The problem of chapter reform burst out again with the accession of Anselmo II, the nephew of Anselmo I and later compiler of the *Collectio canonum*.[31] Anselmo II had been trained by his uncle and tapped as his successor in the see of Lucca before Alexander's death in 1073. Anselmo's position in the struggle over lay investiture was made clear when, after the Lateran Council of 1075, he resigned his office because he had received imperial investiture. He returned to the see of San Martino only at the urging of Gregory VII.

Anselmo's reaction to chapter reform was as uncompromising. By late 1076, he apparently had begun to agitate for continued capitular reform. The *Vita Anselmi* of Bardone notes Gregory VII's presence in Lucca during December 1076, and it is probably because of his visit that he wrote to the Luccan chapter forbidding entrance into the Luccan church until they had reformed themselves. The issue, however, was no longer simply regular life, but the continued existence of simoniacs among the chapter canons.[32] In a second letter, of 28 November 1078,[33] Gregory again referred to following common life and forbade recalcitrant canons to enter churches until they had brought themselves into line with their bishop and the reformed canons of the cathedral.

That the reformers still could not succeed is indicated by a letter from Gregory on 1 October 1079.[34] Again he appealed for reform, but in this case he wrote to the clergy and people of Lucca warning them that they risked excommunication by supporting the unreformed canons. Gregory's call for support failed, however, because the issue of local reform had become enmeshed in the larger struggle between empire and papacy. Part of the problem was doubtless familial loyalty. The chapter membership was chosen from the leading families of Lucca, while their opponents, the reforming bishops Giovanni II, Anselmo I, and Anselmo II, were all non-Tuscan.[35] But the "populus" of Lucca also cared more about their struggle for independence against the pro-reform countess Matilda than they did about the spiritual health of the chapter. In 1080 Anselmo, menaced by popular support for the rebellious canons, had to flee the city. He traveled first to his castles in the countryside and later to Countess Matilda's army. In 1081, Henry IV repaid the Luccans by granting a concession to "Lucanis civibus pro bene conservata fidelitate eorum," including jurisdiction within the walls and over the area within six miles of the city.[36] At this point, the reform of the chapter was effectively lost in the larger struggle until 1092, when a new bishop, Gottifredo, was selected by Urban II to administer the diocese. The first sign of reconciliation between chapter, town, and bishop is a donation made in Lucca to the canons "q[ui] . . . commune vitam duxerint."[37]

Though the local issue of common life for the cathedral chapter had been submerged in the larger issue of church, empire, and commune, by the 1090s collegial organization was usual in the pievi and large urban churches as well as in the cathedral chapter. Common life and the semi-monastic organization of churches was probably brought on partly by the prestige of the monasteries as centers of piety.[38] Collegial organization, bringing together all the clerics of a single church under a single head, strengthened ecclesiastical discipline: common life could aid in the spiritual renewal of the clergy and guard against concubinage and other evils. But perhaps most important, the institution of common life and common possession of the wealth of churches could rectify the situation created when the various parts of churches and their properties were let to individual clerics or laymen.[39]

This reorganization of the churches began in the eleventh century. Giovanni II and Anselmo I and Anselmo II extended the right of collegial organization to some churches within Lucca and to several pievi. The churches within the city received the right to canonical organization earlier than did the pievi, but by the end of the eleventh century at least eight pievi followed collegial organization. The reform brought a new tough administration to the churches of the city and the countryside.[40] The individual cleric no longer found himself free to live as he pleased or to use his church's possessions as his own. The properties of the local churches were now in the possession of strong corporate entities which could protect the church's wealth from bishops as well as laymen.

The collegiate churches and especially the cathedral chapter grew quickly in the eleventh and twelfth centuries, receiving possession of lands, tithes, and private churches. In the case of the cathedral chapter, many gifts came from pious laymen, but also some of the bishopric's rights were transferred to the chapter. In 1192, the canons appeared before the consuls of Treguana (a communal court which from the last quarter of the twelfth century was convened to hear cases involving the temporalities of the churches) claiming a part of the tithe of Santa Maria a Monte. One of the witnesses swore that "I have heard always that at the time of Bishop Gregorio [1146–64] the bishop gave one moggio of wheat to the canons for the tithe . . . ," and he added that the payments had continued to the present time.[41] The gift may have occurred earlier than Gregorio's pontificate. As early as 1107 Pope Paschal II confirmed the chapter's possession of part of the oblations at the altars of the cathedral, as well as "tithe receipts within the Luccan city and suburbs that you possess by episcopal provision."[42]

The chapter's economic power and its privilege to act as advisor of the bishop gave it considerable strength within the bishopric. Throughout the twelfth century when bishops ordained the rectors of pievi they did so "with the consent" of the chapter. Further, according to the twelfth-century privileges given to the chapter, it had the right to select bishops—a power it continued to exercise successfully throughout the thirteenth century.[43]

Episcopal administration, however, underwent other equally significant changes. In the eleventh century, many of the most important churches, monasteries, and hospitals were placed under the protection of the Holy See.

Before the twelfth century five churches are mentioned as being under apostolic protection.[44] According to the late twelfth-century *Liber censuum,* the number of dependent churches had grown to sixteen.[45] And according to the Tithe of 1276–77,[46] there were 42 churches, monasteries, and hospitals listed as exempt, that is, under papal protection. In a related move, the cathedral chapter and other churches acquired the patronage of pievi and subaltern churches and thereby reduced episcopal control over some churches of the diocese.

The concession of papal protection given to the basilica of San Frediano reveals the importance of these reforms. Alexander II first offered papal protection to San Frediano. He specifically named the possessions of that church in the Maremma and elsewhere and declared the canons and their lands exempt from lay interference. Paschal II expanded the powers of the canons of San Frediano to include the collection of all tithes from their parish and the right "to dispense [the tithes] in the use of the chapter."[47] Paschal also guaranteed the canons the right to select the rector of San Frediano, except for that part of the selection which pertained to the cathedral chapter. Papal protection offered to the churches and monasteries did not excuse them from episcopal spiritual discipline, but it did protect their temporal possessions from interference. After such grants of protection, the bishopric could no longer let the lands of pievi, monasteries, and hospitals for its own profit.

THE POST-REFORM BISHOPRIC

The reform movement, which affected canonical organization so drastically, did not have the same effect on the tithe. The *quartesium,* the quarter of the tithe that was given to the parish church, indeed was protected by the Luccan bishops, but the reformers do not seem to have attempted to regain control of the other three quarters of the tithe. Bishops Giovanni II and Anselmo I, in fact, continued the policy of leasing certain local tithes. Giovanni let parts of the tithe within the pieve of Controne in 1042, and in 1068 Anselmo let the tithe of Usilliano.[48]

The episcopal leasing of tithes continued during the twelfth century. In 1159 Bishop Gregorio gave the tithe of Pinocchio, a small village south of the Arno, to the consuls of Pinocchio. He further promised that the tithe would not be transferred to anyone else in the future.[49] Twenty-one years later Bishop Guglielmo, with the consent of his archdeacon, gave the tithes of five pievi to the hospital of San Jacopo of Altopascio.[50] The bishopric did not seem to care (or was unable) to retain the tithes. The bishop may have found that it would cost more to collect the tithes than they were worth.

The leasing of the episcopal portion of the tithes may thus have been similar
to the farming of taxes in medieval communes: it could be more efficient for
the commune to lease the right to collect the tax and have an assured sum
than to face the difficulties and uncertainties of collecting the taxes themselves.[51]

The bishopric may have attempted a form of tax farming, but the sums
more resemble recognition payments than significant revenues. The hospital
of Altopascio paid a mere three pounds of wax for the tithes of five pievi and
their subaltern churches. For unspecified tithes within the city of Lucca, a
notary, Turcho, and his associates paid ten soldi annually. At the same time
the church of Pedogna paid five soldi "for the privilege of the tithe."[52]

The sums collected in the fourteenth century suggest that the bishopric
never exploited the tithes to their fullest. Even when the bishopric did try to
reclaim the tithe it was not always successful. In 1197, Bishop Guido tried
to recover lands, tithes, and the patronage of the pieve of Piano (in the
Valdera) which were in the hands of a group of men from that area.[53] The
case was heard by Orlando Mascia and Buonacurso Boccio of Vico, men of
the area selected as judges by the litigants. The case was heard on 1 April
and the judges presented their decision on 13 June. The judges ordered
that the men should have the lands that they held by "jure tenimenti seu
libelli" for their customary rent payment. The judges added:

Likewise we direct, concerning the tithes and their income, that so long as their children, like the children of the first indeed, who held it from the bishopric by livello,
live they shall have [the tithes and their income]. Likewise we say and define by judgment that the aforesaid pieve certainly shall be free and absolved from the patronage [*a jure patronatus*] that the abovementioned men said that they have in the aforementioned church and pieve. . . .

The indication is that although the tithe was lost, at least the liberty of the
church and episcopal control of its pieve were protected. But the judges continued:

that three out of all these, namely Ranuccione and his descendants and similarly two
others, must be examined by the bishop or by his nunzio, and they shall be with him
when selecting the pievano, and when they have consented the bishop shall select . . . .

Clearly the bishopric de facto lost the right to the tithe and the patronage.

For the 150 years before the reform movement, the episcopate had been
unable to control the leases given to lay magnates. The lands leased had
been, for the most part, lost. Similarly, church discipline was difficult, if
not impossible, to maintain while the bishops were leasing the tithes and
patronage of the various local churches to the lay nobility. These old meth-
ods of administration doubtless were bankrupt by the time of the reform.

But additionally, the bishopric faced new problems during the eleventh century. Along with a renewed urban life, new groups, which can be associated with new wealth, appeared to challenge the position of the bishop within the church. The rise of the canons of San Martino and other collegially organized churches with defined rights and privileges, for example, meant that new religious corporations could compete with the bishopric for the patronage of pievi and subaltern churches. The resumption of tithes, where it did occur, often left the tithes in the hands of monasteries, chapters, and collegiate churches. Monasteries especially gained from pious donations to the church.[54]

The diffusion of wealth also is reflected in the renewed gifts or *benificenze*, donations made for the care of the poor and infirm and for the foundation of hospitals. These donations were given to the chapter, pievi, monasteries, and hospitals throughout the diocese. There were only four gifts recorded between 824 and 1008, while there were 22 during the remainder of the eleventh century.[55]

Citing the foundation of the hospitals of San Martino (1076), Santa Reparata (1097), San Frediano (1099), San Donato (1102), San Michele in Foro (1111), Santa Maria Forisportam (1111), and San Pietro Maggiore (1140), Hansmartin Schwarzmaier observed that there was "a new intensification of spiritual life" in the late eleventh and early twelfth centuries. This new spirituality was felt in the countryside as well as in the city. In addition to the famous hospital of San Jacopo of Altopascio, hospitals were founded at Quiesa (1084), Camaiore (1086), and Fucecchio (1108).[56] The growth of hospitals, like the rise of the cathedral chapter, was not an unmixed blessing for the episcopate. Many of the most important hospitals were taken under direct papal protection, leaving their secular wealth exempt from episcopal control. The hospital of San Jacopo of Altopascio held not only the tithes of five pievi and large amounts of land within the diocese, but also subject houses throughout Europe.

This diffusion of religious life is also evident in the construction of new churches and the rebuilding of older ones. The reconstruction of the cathedral of San Martino was completed in 1069, according to Tolomeo of Lucca. During the course of the eleventh and twelfth centuries countless other churches within the city also were rebuilt: San Michele in Foro and San Alessandro were reconstructed in the eleventh century; the churches of San Giovanni and Santa Maria Corteorlandini were rebuilt in the twelfth century.[57] The same reconstruction occurred in the countryside. The pievi built before 1000 were of wood and have vanished without a trace. The first stone pievi, many still visible in the countryside, seem to have been built, for the most part, in the eleventh and twelfth centuries. Calixtus II in 1122 ordered that no more churches should be built without the approval of the bishop—possibly a sign that too many churches had been built.[58]

The new centers did not simply provide secular and ecclesiastical administration; they were also new *foci* of piety. The pious donations of the eleventh and twelfth centuries often benefited the collegially organized pievi as well as the monasteries and hospitals.[59]

Donations additionally were made to the autonomous Opera di Santa Croce, which had charge of the physical plant of the cathedral and managed the sale of candles and the money collected on certain feast days.[60] The rise of these autonomous bodies, all competing with the bishopric for pious donations and for money to carry on the church's activities, made it imperative that the bishop seek out new areas of power and new forms of revenue.[61]

The ideas of the reformers were stated in traditional terms, but the results were hardly traditional. In striving to regain lost lands and to purchase new ones, the reform bishops traded much of their "treasure" for lands and jurisdictions. The use of treasure as "substitute money" has been documented in northern and central Italy; not surprisingly, its use was most common about 1070 and thereafter began a steady decline.[62] Church reformers urged that treasures not be kept locked away but used to expand the land holdings of the church. The emphasis was first of all on the purchases and improvement of small properties, the *res massaricia* or servile peasant holding. Bishops pawned lands to moneylenders in order to buy or improve lands and thereby to strengthen their economic position. Bishop Anselmo I of Lucca had to pawn lands in 1057 to gain funds for his almost empty treasury. Within eleven years he could claim that he had cleared lands in Vallebuia and leased them to small farmers.[63]

At the same time that Anselmo was clearing and improving the episcopate's lands, he was also receiving donations and purchasing lands. Both the donations and the purchases began about the same time in the early eleventh century. In certain respects they cannot be easily separated.

The bishopric of Lucca, like so many other religious bodies, profited from a renewal of pious donations during and after the reform period. The most famous patron was, of course, the countess Matilda of Tuscany, who, in addition to her support of the reform popes, aided local religious groups in Tuscany and Emilia. Though her most famous castle, Canossa, lay in Emilia, the countess always specially favored the Luccans—possibly because of her close relationship with Bishop Anselmo II. Upon his succession, Gregory VII counseled Matilda to beware of the unreformed Lombard bishops and commended to her instead the reform bishop Anselmo II, who previously had been her chaplain.[64] Matilda's donations to the Luccan bishopric, in fact, did occur before the death of Bishop Anselmo in 1086.

Though Matilda's donations were the most famous and dramatic, the new wave of pious donations had begun almost a half century earlier, when, in 1026, one Count Ugo bought one half of three portions of the "monte, poio, castello et curte" of Potiosturli from Viscount Gherardo and gave it to Bishop Giovanni I.[65] Most of the pious donations that follow occurred during the episcopates of Giovanni II, Anselmo I, and Anselmo II—the most famous of the Luccan reform bishops. The donations continued into the twelfth century, though they were less frequent.

There are striking differences between these donations and those of the eighth and ninth centuries. In the earlier period, donations were, for the most part, of two types. There were donations of churches constructed on private lands, usually including lands and revenues to support a priest. These donations often included the prescription that the monastery, church, or convent would be held by a son or daughter of the donor.[66] The other donations were lands, given for the most part by small landholders rather than by magnates. These gifts were of moderate size, and often the lands were returned to the donor by livello.[67]

The donations made in the eleventh and twelfth centuries, on the other hand, were gifts of extensive holdings, often including a "castello et curte." In some cases, the donations were made because a family had died out. The last Cadolinghi count of Fucecchio, for example, willed his extensive holdings to the bishops of Pistoia, Lucca, Florence, and Volterra.[68] At other times there was a wish to strengthen the secular power of the bishop. Countess Matilda's gifts, for example, included portions of the castles of Diecimo, San Gervasio, and Montecatini, all strategically placed in the diocese.

Many other transfers of land are almost impossible to analyze because the meaning of the document is not clear. A sale to the bishopric usually was completed in more than one document. In the first, the lands were transferred to the bishop, and in the second, the donor, having received a "meritum" (some valuable used as substitute money and often of a defined value), promised not to molest episcopal possession of the lands. In the first document, the owner usually proclaimed that he was giving the property "for the care of the soul," which seems to indicate a pious donation, but in the second document the meritum seems to indicate a sale. It is possible, however, that the meritum (especially when the document does not indicate its value) had only a symbolic value to make the donation legal according to Lombard law.[69]

The vagueness of these documents as to the difference between sales and donations makes it difficult to know the significance of many donations. Some doubtless sprang from piety, though the sheer size of the pieces of land being offered makes one suspicious about their nature. The safest way to analyze these transactions is to consider them in relation to what clearly were sales of land to the bishopric, since the rise in donations paralleled a rise in purchases by the bishopric.

The purchases of land in the twelfth century, unlike the earlier buying of the eighth and ninth centuries, were not primarily purchases of small holdings. Although the early reform bishops, Giovanni and the two Anselmi, continued to buy individual pieces and unimproved lands, the extant documents from 1109 to 1153 record almost exclusively sales of demesne lands and fortified centers in the countryside. Only 21 of the 76 transactions by which the episcopate acquired or resumed control of lands were clearly concerned with small holdings. Some of the other transactions may represent small individual holdings, but they appear to be transfers of demesne lands and multiple peasant holdings. On 10 July 1120, the bishopric resumed control of lands in Sorbano del Vescovo which were described as "omnes terras, casas et cassinas, prata et pascua, paludes et piscationes, buscaria et omnia super predictis terris vel in illis habentia. . . ."[70] This policy was followed most assiduously during the first half of the twelfth century, although there were occasional purchases as late as the early years of the thirteenth century.

One of the earliest of these sales was that in 1076 by which the bishopric bought the castle and corte of San Gervasio in the Valdera from the sons of the late count Malaparte for £55 "pro paterno debito solvendo."[71] In this case the reason for the sale was made clear in the document, but it is unclear how the bishopric was able to get into a position where the sale would be made to it.

In many of the other sales, the original entry of the bishopric into partial possession of a castle was related to a pawn. In the mid-twelfth century, the Gherardesca counts sold and pawned lands and jurisdictions to the Luccan bishopric. Count Guido called "Malaparte" del fu Guido sold his portion of the castle and corte of Forcoli (in the Valdera) to the episcopate in 1131 for 140 soldi. One year later, Guido's brother Ugo pawned his portion of the same castle to the Luccan bishopric for a meritum of 240 soldi. Later, in 1153, Guido del fu Ugo sold one third (presumably including the one-sixth part pawned by his father) of the castle and district of Forcoli "for the repayment of my father's debt." Earlier in the twelfth century, Bishop Rangerio already had received one third of the castle and corte of Capannoli (also in the Valdera) from Guido Malaparte's brothers, Ugo and Raniero. And in 1145 another Gherardesca, Count Raniero, promised to Bishop Ottone that he would free the castle of Colcarelli.[72] The Luccan bishops seem to have obligated the nobles in any way possible and then bought out their lands when they were impoverished.

The process was accomplished because of the politically untenable position in which the Gherardesca found themselves. While they were bending under the pressures from the Luccan bishopric, they also were pawning lands to the archbishop of Pisa. In 1120, Raniero sold his portion of the castle of Ricavo to the archbishop of Pisa, and in 1126 Guido Malaparte sold his portion of the castle of Forcoli. The Gherardesca were caught in a struggle with the communes of Pisa, Lucca, and Volterra, as well as the rural communes in the Valdarno and Valdera. Count Guido del fu Ugo was constrained to swear before the archbishop of Pisa in 1141 that he would aid the citizens of Pisa and that he would not obligate lands within the contado of Pisa (which at least according to the Pisans included the Valdera in the diocese of Lucca) to anyone except the cathedral of Santa Maria of Pisa. He further promised to pay his father's debts and to free the castle of Forcoli from the bishopric of Lucca.[73] The conflict over control of the area continued into the thirteenth century. Though the possession of the castle of Forcoli had been divided between the two churches, it remained under the control of the Pisan commune.

The purchasing of lands and jurisdictions by the bishopric was concentrated in three areas: below the Arno, in the middle Val di Serchio, and in the eastern part of the diocese near Montecatini. The episcopate may have been cooperating with the Luccan commune in an attempt to secure these contested border areas. Certainly the Valdera remained a contested area into the thirteenth century. Montecatini and the area near the swamp of Fucecchio was similarly on the border of the Pistoian contado. In 1129, for 480 soldi, the bishopric bought all the lands between the Nievole River and the city of Lucca belonging to the monastery of San Tommaso of Pistoia.[74] This purchase, along with episcopal possession of the castle of Montecatini and the castle of Monsummano, effectively prevented any Pistoian claims to any parts of the Luccan diocese, except for the swamp of Fucecchio which remained part of the Pistoian diocese.[75]

This policy was only a partial success at best in the Valdarno and Valdera. The southwestern part of the diocese was under Pisan control. During the twelfth and thirteenth centuries Pisan measures predominated there. The documents redacted in that area were almost always dated "Pisan style," that is, from the Incarnation, while at Lucca documents were dated from the Nativity after about 1200. Pisa's control of the area was contested through much of the twelfth century, but with little success. Bishop Rodolfo of Lucca even tried to get the Lateran Council to intervene in 1116, but the churchmen chose to disregard the matter.[76]

The episcopal purchases in the eastern part of the diocese were more important and of more lasting consequence to both the bishopric and the commune of Lucca. While the bishopric failed to protect its lands southwest of Santa Maria a Monte from the Pisans, it did succeed in ending most Pistoian influence in the eastern part of the diocese. The marsh of Fucecchio remained part of the Pistoian diocese, but it was surrounded by lands owned and controlled by the bishopric and commune of Lucca.[77]

Acting in concert with the commune of Lucca, the bishop was actively engaged in securing the area of the two Pescia valleys and the Valdinievole. In 1159, the bishop received assurances from Transmundino of Pescia that he would be a fidelis of the bishopric and that, if necessary, he would aid the bishop in the recovery of lands against all except the emperor or Duke Guelfo of Tuscany. Tolomeo of Lucca records that in 1182 the men of Montecatini swore fidelity to the commune of Lucca.[78]

Although the Pisans controlled vast portions of the Luccan diocese, there were certain similarities between the eastern and southwestern parts of the diocese. In both areas, the bishopric lost the jurisdictional control implied by the possession of castles. Thus the investment in effort and money ended with the bishopric left only with control of large rental properties, mostly agricultural, in the countryside.[79] The result of episcopal activity was a greater dependence on agricultural lands and revenues.[80]

EPISCOPAL PENETRATION OF THE COUNTRYSIDE

We have investigated the changes in the structure of the episcopal temporalities in the eleventh and early twelfth centuries, but we have yet to establish how and why this change in structure was possible. The sudden economic activity is difficult to explain, because it did not follow the pattern of activity established in the eighth and ninth centuries. Instead of purchasing individual pieces of agricultural land, during the eleventh and twelfth centuries, the bishopric was interested in demesne lands. This meant the purchase not only of lands but also of jurisdictions. The reasons that the rural lords would divest themselves of jurisdictions are far from clear.[81]

If the crisis was but another aspect of the conquest of the contado by the nascent urban forces, the purchases of jurisdictions would seem to indicate an attempt by the commune and the bishop (acting for the commune) to unify politically the whole area of the diocese. The purchases then would be only an aspect of a total policy which included military actions such as the destruction of the castle of Vaccoli in 1088 by the Luccan commune.[82] The period after the mid-eleventh century was thus a period of competition among the various communes attempting to extend their control into the countryside. Gioacchino Volpe has noted that the wars between Pisa and Lucca began in the early eleventh century—a sign, he said, of the developing commune.[83]

It cannot be denied that competition between communes played a part in this crisis. The record of attempts by the Luccan bishopric to control the castle, corte, and district of Forcoli was matched, almost document for document, by the archbishop of Pisa. The lords of Forcoli pawned and sold portions of their jurisdictions to both. There is also no denying that religious leaders occasionally acted for their communes, especially in the earliest period of communal development. The Pisans required that nobles swearing aid to the citizens of Pisa eschew pacts with the commune or the bishopric of Lucca.[84] There are also indications that the same cooperation existed in the Valdinievole, where in 1107 both the consuls and the Luccan bishopric involved themselves in the construction of a castle at Colle San Martino.[85]

At the same time, there is no indication that the bishop participated directly in the wars of the commune to subdue the independent nobles of Versilia or the Garfagnana. The commune participated in the defense of areas where the episcopate had interests, but the commune felt no need to have the bishopric act for it in other areas in which the episcopate had no interests.[86]

The Luccan reform bishops of the eleventh and twelfth centuries may have bought rural lands not to aid communal expansion but as a balance against growing communal feeling in Lucca. The cathedral canons were, as noted earlier, sons of the leading judges and notaries, the men who formed the nucleus of the primitive commune. The bishops who over nearly a century struggled to reform these canons were without exception foreigners: Giovanni II, Anselmo I, Anselmo II, and Rangerio all were non-Tuscans. These bishops could claim little popular support within the commune; indeed, communal feeling forced Anselmo II into exile. Facing a commune whose interests did not necessarily coincide with episcopal policies, the reformers originally may have desired rural fortresses simply as a base from which they could resist communal pressures.[87]

Communal expansion and episcopal policy do not explain fully, however, why some lords could not resist the pressures of the communes while others (especially in the northern and western parts of the diocese) managed to retain their autonomy, at least temporarily. The Gherardesca lost control of Forcoli in the twelfth century, but the feudal lords in Versilia and Garfagnana were not subdued finally until well into the thirteenth century.

The sales of castles, corti, and districts probably are part of that juridic change in the structure of the Italian countryside which has been described as "territoriality."[88] In Italy, unlike north of the Alps, juridic relationships in the twelfth century were not based on personal ties, but came to be defined territorially. Jurisdiction resulted from possession of geographical areas. The key to this territorial order was the corte and its district. The system began to develop as early as the ninth century and probably is related to the popularity of the corte as a local marketing center.[89] During the unrest caused by the tenth-century invasions, these local market centers were natural defensive points for the population. Because of the disorders, the right to construct castles was conceded with little hesitation to those capable of protecting the local areas. Along with the right to construct the castles these rural lords received immunity from interference by imperial officials.[90]

The decisive change in this territorial development was, according to Pietro Vaccari, the emergence of these corti as independent juridic personalities—as *curiae*. This occurred when the rights to jurisdiction over the castle or corte were divided among two or more individuals or groups. This divided jurisdiction was evident as early as the eleventh century when most sales made to the episcopate were for only a part of the castle or corte—"meam portionem ex integro."

The formation of this new juridic personality, the curia, still does not explain why castles and corti were sold and pawned in the eleventh and twelfth centuries. To understand this we must look again at the function that the corti and the castles had fulfilled. The primary importance of local trade and market centers throughout western Europe in the period before 1050 has been noted. After the ground-breaking works of Pirenne and Dopsch, historians have re-examined the origins of trade and commerce and have placed new emphasis on the growth of local market centers.[91]

Both castles and corti seem to have been designed to provide for essentially local needs. By the mid-eleventh century, however, the corti seem to have been of less importance. Though the bishops and communes bought the rights to local centers, they organized them on a regional rather than a local basis.

The use of the word *curia*, for example, is not common in the documents of the bishopric, and where it does occur, it does not describe what Vaccari called the "mixed lordship" of a corte. Many of the land leases in the Valdarno and south of the Arno describe the lands being let as within the "curia of Santa Maria a Monte," though these lands in reality lay closer to other corti or castles. The rents usually were carried to the granary at Santa Maria a Monte rather than to other centers which were closer.[92]

What developed was a new system of regional centers within the diocese. There were other castles and corti in the area of Moriano, but the episcopate's leases in that area required that the rents be delivered to Castro di Moriano, at the episcopal granary.[93] The curia of Santa Maria a Monte was a gathering point not only for rents collected in the immediate area but also for those collected on lands south of the Arno. An inventory for that curia composed in the 1180s included labor services of carting wine from Colcarelli in the Valdera to Santa Maria a Monte.[94] Others surely carted wheat and other grains to the same episcopal center. Similar centers were located at Sala di Garfagnana, Montecatini, and Montopoli. The reform bishops reorganized their possessions along new lines related to new centers within the countryside.

This explains why, in certain areas, the local rural nobles could no longer compete: their local markets were not economically necessary. Cinzio Violante argued that the development of markets did not work to the advantage of the small landholders or of the tenants, but rather to the advantage of those who supervised the urban markets.[95] Similarly, I would contend, those whose markets were simply local could not compete with those who held regional markets. The reform bishops, by buying jurisdictions and extending their possession of lands, showed an understanding of the importance of direct control. They were building vast centralized estates created for the purpose of supplying the expanding urban markets.[96]

There is indirect evidence that Lucca's population was expanding. Lucca had begun construction of its medieval walls by 1200. Leases of two-storied houses without surrounding lands were not uncommon even in the twelfth century in the area around the church of San Pietro Somaldi (on the northeastern edge of the city just outside the Roman walls). The construction of church buildings beginning in the eleventh century is inconceivable without a ready labor supply. New population and a new movement of people is also reflected by the rise of the subaltern churches in the twelfth century and by jurisdictional disputes between pievi. Luigi Nanni rightly notes that the jurisdictional disputes occur, for the most part, in urban areas. As early as 1135, the basilica of San Frediano (in the northern suburb of the city) objected that the monks of San Donato (on the western edge of the city) had usurped rights of burial which belonged to San Frediano. Several years later, the canons of San Frediano again appealed to the bishop, this time because the canons of San Michele in Foro (in the center of the city on the site of the old Roman Forum) had illegally claimed burial rights.[97] Such questions arose simply because of the larger population: the ill-defined boundaries between the various urban churches were no longer satisfactory.

The post-reform bishopric differed sharply from the earlier episcopate. Where formerly lands were spread throughout the diocese and let to nobles, after the reform episcopal lands were concentrated in enclaves in the southern part of the diocese, on the plain of Lucca, and in the middle Serchio Valley. Where before the reform the bishopric had managed to share a portion of the revenues of its pievi and subaltern churches, it now was faced by collegially organized and papally protected religious bodies which controlled their own revenues. Although the bishopric tried to regain spiritual control of pievi and subaltern churches, it left tithes in the hands of the chapter, monasteries, hospitals, and rural communes. One reason for many of these changes was urban growth, but the paradoxical result was to leave the temporalities of the bishopric with a decidedly rural character.

3

Administration of Episcopal Temporalities

The changes in episcopal structure and organization just described established areas of economic interest that remained important to the Luccan bishopric throughout the later Middle Ages. But how effective were these changes? By studying episcopal temporal administration in the post-reform period, we can determine how far the bishop and his officials attempted to distinguish between their temporal and spiritual rights and duties. Analysis of the episcopate's administrative machinery also will identify those groups and officers that played an active role in shaping episcopal policies and therefore had some responsibility for the changes in the economic and political influence of the episcopate in later medieval Italy.

Church administration, even in areas with exceptional episcopal registers like those found in parts of England, remains an ill-defined subject. Given the nature of the available sources, no completely satisfactory picture is likely to be drawn. An investigation of a single episcopate, however—that of Lucca—will clarify and refine our present knowledge of Italian episcopal administration and provide suggestions for studies of other episcopates.

Traces of the bishop's administration appear as early as the ninth and tenth centuries, but it is only in the twelfth and thirteenth centuries that documentation is sufficient in either number or variety to allow reasonably secure conclusions about episcopal government. Before the twelfth century, the bishop tended to handle his affairs himself, and only rarely did he delegate any authority. Even when others acted for the bishop, the form of the documents indicates that the official's role was severely limited. One Albone, called "Carbone," del fu Lamberto promised Bishop Giovanni II on 16 October 1043 that he would not contest the episcopate's possession of certain lands at Santa Maria a Monte. For this promise to the bishop, who was not

30

present, Carbone received a meritum from Moretto del fu Gherardo.[1] Moretto had no title nor any mandate from the bishop, except to give the meritum to Carbone. The two Anselmi also used laymen in occasional transactions. In 1059, Falniero del fu Guido promised Bishop Anselmo I (who was not present) that since he had received a meritum worth 20 soldi from Villano del fu Rolando "pro persona Anselmi Episcopi," he would not molest episcopal possession of a house near the pieve of San Genario.[2] Anselmo II bought the corte of Suverto in 1081 in a similar action where the venders received a meritum from an imperial judge "pro persona Anselmi Episcopi."[3] In the twelfth century, Bishop Benedetto used an untitled official when the widow Itta sold to the bishop and bishopric her portion of the castle of Valivo di Sopra.[4] The bishops handled most other trades and sales themselves.

The untitled officers do not follow any simple pattern, except that typically they are recorded paying the money the bishopric owed for its purchases. The only other examples of an official acting for the bishop would be members of the cathedral chapter who occasionally acted in the bishop's name. In 1072, for example, the archdeacon, archpriest, and *primicerio* (the chapter's prior or administrative head) of San Martino received a promise that a chapel near Diecimo would remain under the bishop's jurisdiction.[5] The others who acted for the bishops came from no single group. They were judges, notaries, castaldi, and clerics, who seem to have been chosen simply because they were in the area where the transaction was to take place. They were ad hoc officials who do not appear to have had permanent administrative functions within the bishopric.

LAY OFFICIALS

The earliest and most visible of the episcopal titled officers were the advocates and the *visdominus*.[6] The advocate, a lay judicial officer of the episcopate, acted for churchmen in judicial matters since clerics were forbidden to take oaths. This officer can be found in the fourth and fifth centuries, but first appeared in Italy during the ninth and tenth centuries. The episcopal advocate appeared in court requesting and receiving lands, and litigating over temporal rights. The earliest examples I have found of advocates at Lucca are from the tenth century. In 901, Bishop Pietro was represented by Eliazar called "Elbonizo" del fu Eriteo, his advocate in an appeal to Emperor Lodovico.[7] Fourteen years later, Bishop Pietro appeared before the court of Odelrico, an official of King Berengario. In this case he came to court "una cum item Petrus scavino huius comitato et advocatus suis," who may be the same "Petrus notarius et scabinus" who appeared as a witness to many of Pietro's acts. The only other document in which the notary Pietro appeared as an active participant records an exchange of land between Bishop Pietro and one "Pietro notario et scabino."[8]

Since the notary Pietro was in almost constant attendance at the episcopal court one might be tempted to assume that the office of advocate belonged to the leading layman at the episcopal court. Unfortunately, the only two other references to the office of advocate seem to indicate an entirely different situation. In 941, Bishop Corrado appeared before the court of the marchese Uberto on March 14 and again on March 25. In the first case Teuperto del fu Rodolfo served as advocate. In the second a judge named Giovanni was the advocate. Like the earlier advocate Pietro, Teuperto and Giovanni occasionally appeared as witnesses to episcopal documents.[9] The most likely conclusion to be drawn is that in the tenth century, the advocate was appointed ad hoc and did not serve a term of any defined length.

Anselmo I, after he was selected as Pope Alexander II, appointed the first advocate of whom we have record to serve a term with a general mandate. In 1068, Anselmo "elected Berengario, son of Donuccio of good memory, who will be the advocate of the aforesaid church of the episcopate of San Martino, [and] who henceforth shall have the power to enter into court, make appeals, give security, and give and receive oaths for the goods of the aforesaid episcopate. . . ."[10] Considering the extent of his powers, one would expect Berengario to have been very busy. In actuality, there is no record that he was. The only document in which we find him mentioned records an appearance before the court of Countess Beatrice, mother of Countess Matilda.[11]

In the period following the reforms, the advocates continued to represent the bishopric in most judicial matters. Actually, clerics, and at times the bishop himself, would represent the bishopric in matters not heard in a court, that is when the affair was heard by arbiters selected by the litigants. In 1135, Bishop Uberto represented the bishopric before arbiters at Marlia. In 1205 and 1218, Bishop Roberto represented the bishopric.[12] In cases heard by the communal courts of Lucca, however, the bishopric was invariably represented by an advocate.

Most of the litigations occurred before the "Consuls of the Court of the Treguana," a communal court formed by the mid-twelfth century to hear cases involving the temporal possessions of clerics. During most of the thirteenth century, the court was composed of one judge and two other consuls without legal training. By 1292 (possibly by 1288) one of the consuls was normally a cleric appointed by the bishop. Although it was a communal court, there is no indication that the bishop or other clerics objected to its jurisdiction. The bishopric probably accepted the court because it was not obligatory. To the early thirteenth-century statute defining the competence of the consuls, the commune added the phrase that the consuls were to hear cases involving religious corporations "if they wish to litigate before them [the consuls]." Thus, when it was easier or more advantageous to use arbiters, the bishopric was free to use them.[13] Of the 14 twelfth-century cases of which we have record, 13 were heard by the consuls of the Treguana.[14]

Occasionally, cases were also brought before the "New Court of Justice." This court, which seems to have first appeared in the 1220s, was a court of appeals to which a claimant could go if the sentence of a previous court had not been observed.[15] Out of a total of 69 litigations over temporal matters recorded between 1135 and 1311, nine (or approximately 13 percent) were heard by this court.

In the rural communes some distance from Lucca, advocates were seldom used. A special proctor or a castaldo[16] normally represented the bishopric, in these areas. The episcopal castaldo at Santa Maria a Monte (about 40 kilometers by road south of Lucca), Guido del fu Tediccione, represented the bishopric in a controversy decided by Federigo Tonni, the podestà of Montecalvoli, on 11 June 1203.[17] In the nine other acts in which Guido appeared as a principal, he made leases and bought lands for the episcopate. Giunta del fu Accurso of Segromigno was appointed castaldo of Santa Maria a Monte in 1269 "ad . . . petendum et proseguendum et defendendum. . . ."[18]

As the advocate's role in the thirteenth century was often confused, and occasionally joined to the office of *visdominus,* it may be best to consider the two offices together. In the early tenth century, the visdominus was a cleric who, theoretically, had charge of the bishopric's temporal administration.[19] If, however, we examine those cases in which he was present, it becomes evident that he had little or no control over the temporalities. Typically, the visdominus appeared as witness only when a priest was ordained or when other religious matters were handled. From the lists it also appears that the visdominus was one of the lesser members of the cathedral chapter.[20]

In the last quarter of the tenth century, a layman appeared as visdominus. In 980, one Austrifuso or Ostrifuso "judex et visdominus" is mentioned as a witness. Between 980 and 989, Ostrifuso witnessed at least twelve documents, received a lease of five pieces of land at Sorbano from the episcopate, and exchanged lands at Sorbano, Pieve San Paolo, and Scragio with the bishop.[21] Ostrifuso's assumption of the title of visdominus was not unusual. In the late tenth century, Italian visdomini were most commonly laymen who, according to Gioacchino Volpe,[22] became the bishop's "viscount" and judge of his court.

The office of visdominus often became the hereditary possession of powerful families. This was the case at Massa Marittima, Siena, and Florence.[23] At Lucca, the Avvocati family (so called because they were the imperial advocates in Tuscany) held the office. This family probably did not gain hereditary possession of the visdominate before the mid-eleventh century, though one Flaiperto, "vassus domini imperatoris," recorded at the episcopal court in 873, is commonly thought to be a member of the Avvocati family. The family received concessions from Emperors Frederick I, Henry VI, and Frederick II. Frederick II recognized them as "counts palatine" and "*missi* of the Emperor." Frederick II's concession added: "Moreover, we confirm the advocacy they possess from the marquis of the whole March [of Tuscany] and the visdominate that they have from the Luccan episcopate. . . ."[24] The family's possessions included the castle of Col di Pozzo (near Matraia on the northern edge of the Luccan plain), the patronage of the pieve of Marlia, and "possessions and benefices" in the Pisan and Luccan contadi.

The Avvocati apparently retained their independent private jurisdiction while at the same time they held Luccan citizenship and played an active role in communal politics. As early as 1192, Normanno del fu Sesmondino degli Avvocati was described as a Luccan citizen.[25] Members of the family served in the consulate in 1184 and 1234.[26] This participation did not cost them their immunities. As late as 1360 they still possessed independent civil and criminal jurisdiction at Col di Pozzo and elsewhere.[27]

The Avvocati possessed the office of visdominus throughout the twelfth century, but there is little evidence of their activity in temporal administration. Duodo degli Avvocati, identified as "advocate of the Luccan episcopate," did let lands near Lucca in 1195, but there is no other record of his serving the bishopric. Normanno del fu Sesmondino appeared with Bishop Guglielmo in 1181, when the bishop gave a perpetual lease to the rector of the pieve of Santa Maria a Monte. Two years later, Normanno was at Montecatini conducting an inquest into what lands the bishopric possessed at that castle.[28] The few agricultural leases in the twelfth century were let by the bishops themselves.[29] Lay representatives of the bishopric were not used regularly before the last two decades of the twelfth century. Where laymen did act for the bishopric, they are usually found at the local level. In the late twelfth century, two castaldi, Riccardo del fu Ubertello at Moriano and Guido del fu Tediccione at Santa Maria a Monte, acted for the bishopric making leases, receiving confessions of rents owed, and representing the bishopric in litigations in local courts.[30] The only other active episcopal officials were the advocates.[31]

That the Avvocati family did not often exercise their office of the visdominate during the twelfth century may have been due to the reforming zeal of the bishops. The eleventh- and twelfth-century reformers tried to exclude laymen from the control of ecclesiastical offices, and as we noted earlier the visdominate was originally a clerical office. In fact when in 1120 Sigismondo degli Avvocati acted as visdominus, he may have held that office only because he was a cathedral canon. In the mid-twelfth century, Tancredo, the Younger, did not claim to be visdominus. In 1165 he appeared simply as "comes sacri palatii." Earlier, in 1159, he claimed an episcopal title, but not that of visdominus—"imperatoria dignitate lucensis episcopi advocatus."[32] It is doubtless significant that when we do find Avvocati acting for the bishopric they are most often called "advocates" rather than "visdomini."

The Avvocati enjoyed renewed influence between 1220 and 1240. Like the visdomini at Massa Marittima,[33] they attempted to combine the traditional role of visdominus with the advocate's role. Members of the family acted in the traditional role of visdominus (though they did not call themselves visdomini in the documents), making leases and buying lands. The extent of the family's influence can be inferred from an appeal in 1240 made by the episcopal advocate, Manso, that Rainerio degli Avvocati not molest the bishop concerning leases of houses and lands, incomes of the castaldi, or any other payments owed to the bishopric. The advocate also asked that Rainerio not be allowed to receive any food or sustenance at the episcopal palace in Lucca.[34] The family's most active period was between 1231 and 1236, when the Avvocati assisted in the administration of a vacant see.[35] Between 1232 and 1243 members of the family also appeared in court acting as advocates. They did not dominate episcopal administration, however, since they remained under the control of the primicerio and the archdeacon of the cathedral chapter. In 1236 Buono del fu Buonacurso degli Avvocati acted "per parabolam et mandatum domini Ubaldi Primicerii." They also had to compete with other laymen: at the same time that the Avvocati represented the bishopric, one Orlanduccione del fu Tedesco Bonzomori was actively engaged as an advocate for the bishopric.[36]

It is likely that the Avvocati family wished to control the advocate's office as well as the visdominate. The Avvocati probably considered the advocate's office, like the visdominate, to be their hereditary possession—extending the rights granted them by imperial sanction. But in 1241 their hopes were stymied and Rainerio del fu Tancredo degli Avvocati found himself in a controversy heard by the court of the podestà of Lucca.[37] Rainerio claimed that his right to act as episcopal advocate had been usurped. Answering him, Manso, son of Saraceno del fu Buonaconte, "advocate of the Luccan bishopric," argued that Rainerio's right to act as advocate had been revoked. It is not surprising that no decision is recorded since both men, and their families, could rightly claim to have served as advocates for the bishopric.[38]

This controversy and the almost complete disappearance of the Avvocati from episcopal administration after 1241 indicate the extent of the change in the Avvocati's position. Various laymen exercised the role of advocate on an ad hoc basis and no single family dominated the office thereafter.

Nor did the Avvocati maintain uninterrupted control of the visdominate. The bishops of Lucca seemed to use the title indiscriminately, interchanging it with that of viscount. Originally the viscount was a secular official. At

Lucca, however, the viscount as well as the visdominus served as an administrator of the episcopal patrimony, and by the late twelfth century the two offices had merged. In the thirteenth century the title of viscount was preferred.

Frate Ricovero was the most active of the viscounts. During the 1240s and 1250s he gave leases, negotiated contracts, and held inquests into the rents owed to the bishopric throughout the diocese. If Ricovero were a representative example, we could conclude that the office had again become a clerical office and that the viscount was one of the primary administrative officers. In truth, however, the official was usually a layman of lesser importance in the administration. In 1215, we find one Giova del fu Carnelevare, the castaldo at Santa Maria a Monte, also called a viscount. Later in the 1220s, Riccomanno degli Avvocati was called a viscount in one of the four documents in which he was named as a principal. In the 1250s Arrigo, son of Morello, and ser Ricco del fu Jacopo, both from Coreglia, served in the office. In 1261, Riccomanno, rector of the hospital of San Ansano at Ponte di Moriano, was viscount. In 1274, another of the Avvocati family, Orlando del fu Cipriano, was the viscount. There is no indication that the viscount, whether lay or religious, regularly played a dominant role in administration.[39]

All laymen who were part of the episcopal administration were described as members of the bishop's family. These *familiares* received food, clothing, and housing in return for their services. When Bishop Roberto appointed Orlanduccione del fu Tedesco Bonzomori to his family in 1222, he promised food and shelter in return for Orlanduccione's services.[40] In 1241, Manso del fu Saraceno had a house from the bishopric in return for his services as advocate.[41] And in the 1320s ser Betto of Coreglia received an annual rent of 11 stai of wheat and a house within the cloister of San Martino for services as a syndic, notary, and occasionally as an advocate.[42] But even the term *familiaris* is not completely satisfactory. Enrico Fiumi, observing the bishop's family at San Gimignano, noted that "these people come from the category of '*boni homines,*' who transform themselves from councilors, judges of the bishop, arbiters, and public appraisers into the consuls of the commune."[43]

The twelfth-century Luccan familiares (like the Avvocati) may well have become thirteenth-century consuls; the thirteenth-century familiares, however, are not necessarily the same. They were an extremely mixed group including notaries and lay members of several noble families. Thus, even the notation that episcopal officials were all members of the bishop's family tells us little about the groups that could affect episcopal administrative policy. To discover the lines of influence we must examine the background and associations of the officers of the bishop.

Among episcopal lay officers, the first group to appear is the lay nobility. We have already noted the prominence of the Avvocati family in the 1230s and their changed role in the mid-thirteenth century. Other identifiable magnate families acted during the mid-thirteenth century as special judges and as podestàs in the rural communes under episcopal jurisdiction. Gualterio di Calcinaia wrote to Enrico degli Avvocati in 1257 that they were to travel to Santa Maria a Monte and act as arbiters in a question between Bishop Guercio and the "noble men of the *domo Berlingorum*."[44] The same year Buono degli Antelminelli, a member of a noble family with extensive holdings in the area of the middle Serchio, was sent to Montopoli to serve as a special judge in a dispute over the disposition of a dowry.[45] Members of other Luccan families served as podestàs of the communes located in the bishopric's jura, usually for one-year terms. Members of the Mansi, Montemagnese, and Malaprese families all served occasionally in that office.[46]

Another lay group, the notaries, increasingly took part in administration during the thirteenth century. Notaries were necessary for the validation of all legal documents. Their very ubiquity has made them seem to disappear from sight. Their influence upon episcopal matters began at the most practical level. It was they who wrote the leases, documents making proctors, court decisions, and compromises. In matters of record keeping, they affected the formation of registers, inventories, and even the popular conception of papal documents.[47]

To record administrative acts is one thing, to participate in decision-making is quite another. As early as 1194, the notary Guglielmo acted as advocate for the bishop before the consuls of the Treguana.[48] The few notaries who acted for the bishopric between about 1190 and 1257 functioned primarily as advocates and arbiters in court cases. In 1231, the notary Jacopo di Lucchese Almosnieri, the episcopal advocate, served as arbiter in a controversy between the bishop and one Romeo of Marlia. In the same year the notary Guido was present and identified as a consul of the bishopric when the archpriest Opizone heard a confession that lands would be returned to the bishopric.[49] The first notary I have found giving a lease for the bishopric was one Giovanni identified in 1254 as a syndic of the bishopric.[50]

The notaries' active participation in episcopal government began in earnest during the episcopate of Enrico dei Rodalinghi (1257-69). Immediately upon his election, Enrico began to use lay notaries, as well as clerics, as syndics and proctors. The first and most active of Bishop Enrico's notaries was Ricco del fu Jacopo of Coreglia, who between 1257 and 1261 acted as proctor and leased lands south of the Arno at San Gervasio.[51] Between 1259 and 1263, Alberto del fu Magistro Ferrante, the notary who redacted some of Ricco's documents, appeared as a syndic and proctor of the bishopric, giving four leases at Santa Maria a Monte and San Gervasio.[52] Lest we overemphasize the role of notaries as episcopal proctors, we should remember that the episcopate of Enrico was a very active period for the bishopric: in the late 1250s episcopal officials seem to have reentered the area south of the Arno which had been in Pisan hands. Also, the notaries represented the bishopric in only a small proportion of the nearly 170 agricultural leases made between 1257 and 1269.

The use of notaries as proctors continued throughout the thirteenth and fourteenth centuries. Like Ricco and Alberto, they seem to have been assigned to a particular area where they were alternatively proctor and recording notary.

Notaries occasionally acted as castaldi, though this was the exception rather than the rule. In 1280, Gualando del fu Guidone Gualandi of Pisa served as the castaldo and syndic of the bishop at Santa Maria di Villa, south of the Arno near the pieve of Corazzano.[53] The significance of this is difficult to determine. Santa Maria di Villa was a center of secondary economic and political importance to the bishopric. If we dare generalize from this one example, it would seem that notaries functioned as castaldi only in the minor centers of the bishopric. On the other hand, Santa Maria di Villa lay in an area continually contested by the Luccans, Pisans, and, eventually, the Florentines. It is likely that Gualando, a Pisan citizen, was chosen because at that time the area was under Pisan control. Notaries may have served as castaldi of other minor centers, but since the castaldi of these centers almost never appear in the extant documents, there is no way to discover them.

The notaries, as representatives of the bishopric, never attained a position comparable to that of the clerics or the noble Avvocati family. They were most evident acting as special proctors in areas at some distance from Lucca—especially in the Valdarno and to the south.[54] Their relatively sudden appearance as principals in episcopal administration is probably linked to the declining visibility of the noble Avvocati noted in the early 1240s.

Despite the lack of direct evidence, these two changes in episcopal administration may be related to a political change well documented throughout central and northern Italy—the emergence of the "popolo."[55] The popolo represented the wealthier craftsmen and professions against the magnates who had controlled the consulates. After 1250 the Luccan government was firmly in the hands of the popolo, with certain of the magnate families excluded from high government office. Among the excluded families, at least according to the list contained in the constitution of 1308, we find "Omnes et singuli de domo Advocatorum."[56] The virtual banishment from episcopal government was a price the Avvocati paid for their power during the period of the consulate.

The notaries and the Avvocati (after the 1240s) served the bishopric as ad hoc officials, usually designated proctors or syndics, in roles paralleling those of various titled officials. The vicar, advocate, or viscount, in fact, often might be described simply as a syndic or proctor. Bishop Roberto designated Martino, abbot of Serena, proctor for one half of the bishopric's possessions in the contado of Pisa in 1209, "because of the present inquietude," that is, the almost constant state of war between Lucca and Pisa.[57] Presbyter Guglielmo acted as "proctor, syndic, and factor" in 1228, receiving lands from the commune of Pisa.[58]

The use of syndics and proctors increased in the mid-thirteenth century until certain of them seem to have been named as semi-permanent officers. In the 1260s and 1270s, Ugolino del fu Jacopino was "castaldo and proctor of the Luccan episcopate" at Santa Maria a Monte, while one Guinivalle del fu Personaldo held a similar position at San Gervasio. Rainerio di Seggio was called "proctor and castaldo" at Moriano for nearly twenty years (ca. 1261–79). The title of syndic was added to other titles in order to give the officer necessary authority and to make his actions binding in court.

On the local level, the office most often combined with the title of syndic or proctor was that of the castaldo. *Castaldo,* or *villicus,* was a vague title that could designate men who acted simply as agents collecting rents, as well as those who were in charge of the bishop's most important fortified centers and who possessed authority to act for the episcopate in court. These castaldi probably grew out of the manorial office of villicus, since they are primarily concerned with managing episcopal lands and rents. They may have existed in the episcopal centers between the ninth and twelfth centuries, but I have found no record of them before the 1140s. We find "Rodolfino et Martinello de Moriano missi et castaldi octoni [i.e., Ottone] lucani episcopi" acting for the bishopric in litigation of 1146 over a piece of land near the monastery of San Quirico. In 1181, Riccardo del fu Ubertello appeared as "villicarius domini Guilielmi" in Moriano, and in 1187 Guido del fu Tediccione acted as castaldo of Santa Maria a Monte.[59]

We have indications of salaries for only two of the episcopal castaldi. In 1193, Ranuccino del fu Bernardo of Cascina promised Bishop Guglielmo's proctor that he would collect all rents, pensions, and entry fines (*servitia*) owed to the bishopric within the district of Migliano (south of the Arno). For his services he was allowed to retain one sixth of all the revenues.[60] In an inquest over rents owed to the bishopric at Alica (south of the Arno) in 1236, the notary recorded that the castaldo (unnamed) held three pieces of land "pro ufficio suo."[61] We can only guess at the worth of such salaries, but it probably was not great. Castaldi such as Ranuccino only collected rents. He could not conduct inquests, make leases, or litigate for the bishopric.

When extraordinary business was conducted, a special syndic or proctor was sent. This circumscription of the castaldo's powers was most evident during the flurry of activity when the bishopric reoccupied its lands south of the Arno in 1258. Ugucione del fu Guidotto d'Albiano, "sindicus domini Episcopi Henrigi ultra Arnum," conceded 21 leases in the area of Monte-castello and San Gervasio.[62] The castaldi of the two areas did not take part in the granting of the leases.[63]

Only the castaldi of the large and more important episcopal centers, primarily Santa Maria a Monte and Moriano, played an active role in administration. Men such as Giunta del fu Accurso of Segromigno, the castaldo of Santa Maria a Monte in 1269, had the power to make and dissolve leases, collect rents, and appear in court for the bishopric.[64] The geographical extent of these castaldi's jurisdictions is difficult to assess. The district of Santa Maria a Monte, for example, seems to have extended from Lavaiano, south of the Arno, northeast along the canal of Usciana almost to the marshes of Fucecchio. The castaldo of Moriano at one time may have had jurisdiction over the episcopal possessions throughout the Garfagnana. In 1261, Rainerio di Seggio was described as castaldo of Bishop Enrico I alternately in Moriano and in Garfagnana.[65] Leases and inquests indicate that the bishopric had other castaldi in Garfagnana, at Diecimo and at Sala for example, but it is possible that only Rainerio had authority to make leases throughout Garfagnana.

The castaldo's authority may have been circumscribed, but he could still occasionally profit greatly from his office. As we noted earlier, the castaldo, Ranuccino, retained one sixth of the payments at Migliano. Over a century later, in 1297, Bishop Paganello named the notary Solomino del fu Martino of Montopoli "viscount, castaldo, syndic, and proctor . . . in the lands across the Arno." Solomino was empowered to collect rents for the next three years, paying to the bishopric 16 soldi of Pisan money for each Pisan staio of wheat and 6 soldi for each staio of millet, barley, or beans. In the preceding dec-ade one staio of wheat had sold in the Pisan market for as much as 45 soldi! Normal prices seem to have fluctuated between 20 and 29 soldi. Only once in the 1290s did the price drop below 20 soldi, to 15 2/3 soldi in 1299. Even given the high cost of overland transportation, a significant profit remained for the castaldo.[66]

These men seem to have been members of contado families. The most important Luccan families, such as the Avvocati, Mansi, and Porcaresi, do not seem to have been interested in such positions. Notaries appeared as castaldi only irregularly.[67] Among the castaldi of whom we have notice, we do not find clear indications of a hereditary claim to office. Since our castaldi are identified only by patronyms, it is difficult if not impossible to know the extent to which certain families did control the office.

In the southern part of the diocese, at Santa Maria a Monte, there are indications of some family continuity. In the 1230s, two brothers, Nenita and Ventura di Rustico, served as castaldi, and it is possible that the Rustico who in 1204 was castaldo of San Gervasio (south of Santa Maria a Monte and across the Arno) was their father.[68] There was another possible father-son combination recorded at Santa Maria a Monte. One Giova del fu Carnelevare served as castaldo and occasionally as syndic, proctor, or advocate between 1214 and 1224. Later, between 1259 and 1262, one Gualfreduccio del fu Giova served as "syndic, castaldo, and proctor of Lord Enrico."[69]

At the same time that these men acted for the bishopric, they and their relatives were actively involved in the economic and political life of Santa Maria a Monte and its district. While Giova del fu Carnelevare was castaldo, he and his brothers Rubaconte and Gilione participated in various financial transactions in and around Santa Maria a Monte. In 1211, the brothers sold a piece of land in the district of Santa Maria a Monte for 20s. 9d. of Pisan money. They later appear buying, selling, and leasing lands from the bishopric. When the bishop made an agreement over the governance of Santa Maria a Monte with the men of that commune in 1233, one of the members of the minor council of Santa Maria a Monte was Giova's brother Rubaconte. Finally, in 1238, Giova (no longer called castaldo) and his sons purchased the right to collect the pedaggio (a road tax) for the next twenty years, for an annual payment of £32 and 22 stai of salt delivered to the castaldo of Santa Maria a Monte.[70] A later castaldo, Giunta del fu Accurso of Segromigno, gives further evidence of the castaldi's wealth. In 1274, Giunta, who had been a castaldo under Bishop Enrico and continued to serve under Bishop Pietro, received possession of the episcopal mill at Piediripa in the district of Santa Maria a Monte, as well as the right to collect the pedaggio for an unspecified term and at an unspecified rent.[71] We do not know that he was related to any other castaldo, but his being chosen to collect the pedaggio shows that he possessed a certain wealth and administrative ability. Further, while serving as castaldo, Giunta leased five pieces of land in the district of Santa Maria a Monte on a thirty-year lease.[72]

These cases suggest that although no single family dominated the office of castaldo at Santa Maria a Monte, the castaldi were probably chosen from several of the leading families in the town and its district. Lacking the noble pretensions of some urban families, they nevertheless carried a great deal of influence in episcopal administration because they had at least moderate wealth and they resided in the important centers of the contado. They also held the most profitable of the episcopate's rights and properties in these rural districts—control of the pedaggio and of the mills. Only occasionally did their influence extend to Lucca itself, but the very fact that they served as proctors and syndics in the important episcopal centers reveals the bishop's dependence upon their abilities.

CLERICS IN EPISCOPAL ADMINISTRATION

A common trait of the laymen we have discussed was the narrow nature of
their competence. Except for the noble Avvocati family, lay officials usually
were restricted to certain centers of the diocese. To find officials who customarily acted throughout the diocese we must look to the clerics in the
bishop's administration.

One of the earliest offices to appear with relatively well-defined functions
was that of the treasurer, or *camerarius* or *camarlingo*. There is little evidence that the bishopric had a treasurer in the twelfth century, though the
office did exist in the cathedral chapter and in the monastery of San Pietro
of Pozzeveri. The chapter's treasurer certainly functioned in his office by
1140 and possibly as early as 1112. The monastery's treasurer acted as a
major official, making leases from as early as 1145.[73] In the earliest references, the treasurers acted as general administrators in all the affairs of
chapter and monastery, rather than simply as supervisors of accounts.

The chapter's treasurer may have handled the episcopal accounts in the
twelfth century. A document of 1183 lists the episcopate's credits and debits
for each month of that year as well as giving totals for the year, but it does
not include the name of the treasurer who had charge of the accounts.[74]
Written without notarial sign or protocol naming the responsible official,
the document gives the total income which the treasurer had received and
then lists the individual expenses. "In the month of January we had £129,
out of which the bishopric had £86, and the canons £43." Following the
total receipts, the redactor included the various expenses of the bishopric,
but not those of the chapter. This would seem to indicate that the document
had been prepared by a common treasurer: since we know that the chapter
had a treasurer, apparently the bishopric simply used him to prepare its
accounts.[75]

The episcopal treasurer appeared in the early thirteenth century, and the
office expanded quickly between 1230 and 1280. During this half century,
the treasurer can be found conducting inquests, making leases, accepting
rents, and, in short, playing a major role in administering the episcopal
temporalities. In 1236 and 1237, for example, we find the treasurer Bon-
insegna preparing an inventory for the bishop-elect Guercio dei Tebalducci.
Five years later, the treasurer Baleante made agrarian leases for the bishopric at Marlia, on the Luccan plain, and at Santa Maria a Monte, along the
Arno River.[76]

The treasurer's functions and the term of his office are not clear. In the
extant portions of the constitutions of Bishop Enrico, completed about 1300,
there is no rubric which treats the functions of the office. The treasurer seems
to have served an undefined term at the pleasure of the bishop. This officer
was most visible in the mid-thirteenth century, during the episcopates of

Bishop Guercio and Enrico I, between 1236 and 1269. Presbyter Baleante, a cathedral canon, acted as treasurer between 1238 and 1245, and later as vicar or "vicar for the temporalities." There are 25 documents in which Baleante participated actively and was called treasurer, and 15 others in which he was designated a vicar.[77] After the nearly ten-year period that Baleante served as treasurer, the office was filled for relatively short terms by a variety of men, almost always ecclesiastics.[78] Presbyter Jacopo, a canon of Santa Maria Forisportam, filled the office in 1256; a year later, one Agolante di Guidone of Rocca Mozzano was treasurer. In 1258 and 1259, the officer was Presbyter Guido di Gragno of the cathedral chapter. Presbyter Jacopo was again treasurer in 1265.[79] Though the office continued to exist, the treasurers were less active in the last quarter of the thirteenth century. In 1323, the treasurer appeared presenting his accounts to the cathedral chapter, but he was clearly subordinate to Francesco di Casale, the rector of the pieve of Segromigno and vicar general of the late bishop Enrico II.[80]

The vicar, like the treasurer, was busiest in the middle of the thirteenth century. Although Presbyter Baleante was called "vicarius" it is likely that in his case at least, the vicar's role consisted only in administering the temporalities, since in two of the documents he was called "vicarius in temporalibus." The problem of defining this office is much like that of defining the treasurer's office. No document specifically defines the office and its competence. We do know that when a see was vacant the cathedral chapter selected vicars, and in some cases the chapter would choose a vicar to serve after a bishop's selection.[81]

Before the vicars served the bishopric regularly, special syndics and proctors handled affairs. The change was more than verbal. Proctors and syndics possessed only ad hoc powers; the vicar's term of office was longer, his mandate more general. The office first appeared regularly in the 1230s when Pope Gregory IX appointed the primicerio and the archdeacon of the cathedral chapter as vicars for the temporalities of the bishopric while the diocese was under suspension. The dissolution of the diocese was a result of the competition between Gregory IX and the Luccan commune for control of the Matildine lands in Garfagnana. Gregory placed the commune under interdict, handing over spiritual administration of the diocese to the bishop of Florence and temporal affairs to the two vicars.[82] The next vicar, Baleante, was likely little more than a treasurer. In this period, the real administrative powers lay with the viscount, Frate Ricovero. Ricovero acted for the bishopric at least 37 times, making leases and conducting inquests between 1242 and 1258.[83]

The vicars developed a more general competence during the second half of the thirteenth century. By 1315, we find Uberto di Uzza, rector of the pieve of Triano, described as "vicarius in spiritualibus et temporalibus generalis."[84] The vicar general's office probably originated earlier in the thirteenth century. As early as 1262, we find vicars designated for specific geographical areas, indicating that by the episcopate of Enrico I the diocese of Lucca had been divided into vicariates similar to those found in the twentieth-century church. The competence of the office does not seem to follow any definable rule. Soffredo, vicar in the Valdinievole in 1262, had certain temporal duties, since we find him letting a house in Montecatini. Gerardo, vicar in the lands south of the Arno in 1267, however, possessed a specifically spiritual mandate. According to his title he was "vicarius . . . in spiritualibus super ecclesiis ultra Arnum et populis earumdem."[85]

Ten years before Gerardo's term as vicar, Bishop Enrico had a vicar for temporal matters, "Galganus vicarius domini lucani Episcopi in terris qui sunt ultra Arnum. . . ." Galgano served primarily as a judge in the bishop's courts. He appointed guardians and heard disputes over lands, defaulted loans, and contested dowries.[86] Unlike other vicars, Galgano did not administer lands, make contracts, or supervise spiritual matters. The castaldi in the area continued to manage the lands, and the bishop himself supervised the selection of rectors and other spiritual matters.[87]

The use of vicars for specific geographical areas may have begun at the same time that the commune of Lucca divided its contado into vicariates. It is even possible that the bishopric acted under communal influence. The first indication I have found of any division into vicariates by the Luccan commune comes nearly forty years before the records of Galgano, the first known episcopal vicar of a geographical area. In 1218, Diodato del fu Buonagiunta, the judge of the Luccan podestà for the Valdinievole and the corte of Pescia, returned a piece of land to the episcopal advocate, Buono del fu Buonacurso. Diodato, like Galgano, apparently functioned only as a judge in court.

The geographical similarities between the communal and ecclesiastical vicariates are striking. The commune divided its contado into twelve vicariates. Two of these, at least, carried the same names as the bishopric's vicariates—Valdinievole and Valdarno. The two vicariates of the Valdarno were not coterminous, however, since part of the episcopal vicariate lay in the Pisan contado. The functions of the vicars were also similar. The commune's vicars were primarily judges, handling civil and criminal cases in their vicariates.[88]

THE CHAPTER'S INFLUENCE

In our investigation of the clerics we have noted a variety of offices. It remains to determine just who these clerics were. While we lack any information about their families, we can see which ecclesiastical corporations they represented.

The earliest and most important group was the cathedral chapter. Its power was based on its possession of lands, and even of complete temporal jurisdiction over several corti and castles in Versilia. The chapter's independent possession of these temporalities was protected from episcopal interference by papal concession. The bishopric, on the other hand, was not similarly protected from the chapter. After the eleventh-century reforms, Pope Calixtus II in 1122 conceded to the cathedral chapter the right to select the bishop.[89] This right by itself did not imply administrative control, but combined with the power to appoint vicars for the temporalities while a see was vacant, it gave the chapter a powerful position in episcopal administration.

The chapter's most notable activity came between 1231 and 1236 when Lucca was under interdict and the chapter had complete control of the episcopal temporalities. The two vicars were the primicerio Ubaldo and the archdeacon Opizone, two of the leading officers of the cathedral chapter. Ubaldo and Opizone visited all parts of the diocese, conducting inquests, leasing lands, and litigating for the return of lands and back-rent payments. In the seven years between 1229 and 1236, Opizone appeared as a principal in eight documents, Ubaldo in 24.[90]

The reasons for this new activity are unclear. Possibly the loss of the spiritualities made the chapter more concerned about the episcopate's temporal rights. Perhaps too, the profits from the temporalities were even more necessary during the costly negotiations over lifting the interdict. Whatever the reason, the episcopal administration was much more active under its capitular vicars than it had been previously.

Pope Gregory raised the interdict and appointed a new bishop in 1236, but the chapter retained control of the administration. The papal choice as bishop of Lucca, Guercio dei Tebalducci of Siena, a familiaris of the pope, was unable to leave Rome immediately and left control of the administration in the hands of the chapter. The chapter continued to dominate episcopal administration even after Guercio arrived. Of the eleven clerics recorded serving Guercio as vicars, syndics, or proctors between 1236 and 1256, six are identified as being chapter members; only four are definitely not cathedral canons.[91] The most active of Guercio's officers were canons. Presbyter Baleante, who is recorded in forty documents and called alternately camerarius, syndicus, vicarius, or familiaris, was by far the most active official, moving throughout the diocese and conducting inquests, negotiating exchanges, and receiving goods.[92]

The episcopate of Guercio, possibly the high point of the medieval Luccan church, certainly was the period in which the chapter was most conspicuously active. Gregory's former familiaris visited the institutions of his diocese, held a synod, and made important arrangements with the commune for the defense of Santa Maria a Monte.[93] The chapter, at that time, established its right not only to administer the temporalities during a vacant see, but also to nominate vicars, treasurers, and other syndics of the bishop-elect.[94] After the chapter selected Enrico I as bishop in 1256, it chose two cathedral canons to act as vicars for the bishop-elect "until the Luccan church will have been reorganized by the pastor."[95]

Such power naturally gave the chapter an enormous influence, although theoretically the bishop's entire family advised him. In 1261, Bishop Enrico gave an agricultural lease "with the consent of the archpriest Alemagno and the primicerio Ildebrandino." The holdings were extensive, including all the episcopal lands "at Arsicia, Pratolungo, and Campo a Pietro," near Fucecchio and Montefalcone. In the early thirteenth century, this type of extensive lease usually was made with the consent of the bishop's family; in this case, only the two cathedral canons took part.[96]

Only in certain purely spiritual matters could the chapter's influence regularly outweigh that of the whole family. According to an agreement between the chapter and Bishop Paganello in 1286, concerning selection of some of the priors, pievani, and other religious officials within the diocese, "the venerable father, the lord Luccan bishop, by law and by custom, must call and consult the Luccan chapter and must have their consent in confirmation of that which shall be done concerning priors, abbots, and pievani and other prelates and rectors of churches of the Luccan city and diocese."[97] This continued to be the chapter's role in spiritual matters throughout the thirteenth century.

The chapter's temporal role in administration seems to have been indirect after the episcopate of Enrico I, a former cathedral canon. During his regime more and more of the direct administration passed into the hands of proctors who were not members of the chapter. Presbyter Jacopo, a canon of Santa Maria Forisportam, acted as treasurer six times between 1256 and 1266.[98] He was not the only official who was not a cathedral canon: Riccomanno, rector of the hospital of San Ansano at Ponte a Moriano, is recorded as "viscount of Lord Enrico, Luccan bishop."[99] The new activity of clerics who were not members of the cathedral chapter was evident on the local level as well as among officers serving under a more general mandate. The most active of Bishop Enrico's syndics was Presbyter Orione, rector of the church of Sirico, in the pieve of Fosciana in northern Garfagnana. Between 1260 and 1268, he gave leases for lands south of the Arno near San Gervasio and Palaia.[100]

At Enrico's death in 1274, the chapter again selected the new bishop, the Luccan Dominican Pietro III, as well as the vicars, who were chapter members. But the two vicars did not follow the earlier precedent and administer the temporalities personally. They selected two "custodians," Angelo and Francesco, monks of San Michele of Guamo, located a few kilometers south of Lucca, and gave them complete power to administer the diocese "in spiritual and temporal business and dealings."[101] This pattern was followed in the fourteenth century. We find a notary, ser Betto del fu Bonano of Coreglia, acting for the cathedral canons in 1324 and 1327 while the see was vacant.[102]

Various reasons for this change in the chapter's role are possible. Perhaps the late thirteenth-century bishops tried to de-emphasize the chapter's part in administration. Before the 1230s, the bishopric had been represented by ad hoc officials acting irregularly. In Guercio's episcopate, officers with definite mandates were more common and they were, for the most part, cathedral canons. Because he was Sienese and not a chapter member, Guercio may have been willing to allow the chapter to play an increasingly dominant role in temporal administration. Before Guercio every bishop since Anselmo II had been a chapter member and most, where we have information, came from Lucca.[103] Again, although no single family had been able to control the episcopal see at Lucca as the Pannocchieschi did in early thirteenth-century Volterra, the Luccan bishops probably did try to use family members as supports just as many medieval popes depended upon their aristocratic Roman relatives. The native-born Enrico I dei Rodalinghi, a former chapter member, chose to use a large number of ecclesiastics who were not members of the chapter and may have been related to him. We are better informed in the case of Bishop Paganello of the noble Porcaresi family. In 1291, he selected a relative, Lord Parente del fu Gerardo di Porcari, as his viscount over the episcopal lands south of the Arno. In the 1280s, the same Parente had served as the bishop's podestà in Montopoli and San Gervasio.[104] Guglielmo II also used relatives. In his instrument making Pietro di Montalbano, rector of the pieve of San Gervasio, his vicar general, Guglielmo called him "discreto viro Petro . . . plebano . . . et diletto nepoti nostro. . . ."[105] We lack further examples of nepotism, but there is no reason to believe that these are unique. In any event, the use of non-chapter members and relatives would certainly have weakened the chapter's role in administration.

Though such an explanation suggests an attempt to shift the balance between the bishop and chapter, it does not account for the success of the change. The cathedral chapter, after all, had protected its spiritual rights from a similar attack by Bishop Paganello in the late thirteenth century and it did have the right to select vicars general for the bishopric. It seems unlikely that the canons should voluntarily have acquiesced in this new relationship in temporal matters.

The shift in the chapter's fortunes was, perhaps, part of an economic and spiritual "crisis" in the later thirteenth century.[106] That the level of economic vigor might reflect spiritual or administrative vigor is possible, especially when one recalls the close relationship between spiritual, economic, and administrative changes during the eleventh-century reforms. The declining prestige of the chapter may be related to a transfer of the centers of piety away from the cathedral to local churches and monasteries.

Such a change has already been noted at Pistoia by David Herlihy. Using tithe payments recorded in the *Tuscia* volumes of *Rationes decimarum Italiae* for the late thirteenth century and the *catasto* declarations of 1428, Herlihy concludes that "the years between 1276–77 and 1428 thus witnessed a remarkable growth in the relative wealth of hospitals and of the Opera di San Iacopo. . . ."[107] This phenomenon and a related change in piety was, according to Herlihy, essentially a fourteenth-century phenomenon because the tithe receipts in 1296–97 showed only a slight change in the wealth of the various religious corporations.

It is tempting to try to follow the changes in relative wealth of the various churches and monasteries by using these recorded tithe payments. The records, unfortunately, do not lend themselves easily to such an analysis. Some of the most important institutions did not pay the tithe, because their rectors were chosen as collectors. The entry for the Canonica of San Alessandro in the Luccan tithe receipts of 1276–77, for example, records "nichil solvit, quia prior est collector decimarum."[108] More important, all the tithe payments between 1274 and 1304 seem to have been made according to the same initial levy. The bishopric of Lucca, for example, paid £157 10s. in 1276–77, and the document records that the payment includes both of the semi-annual payments—"pro I et II solvit." The payment in 1302 is simply recorded as £78 15s. or exactly half of its earlier payment. The chapter's payments in 1302–03 were also exactly half of its earlier payment. Since the tithe payments at Pistoia show the same ratio, it seems likely that all the payments recorded in the tithe volumes were made according to a single estimation of wealth. Herlihy's conclusion that "the order of relative wealth, in so far as we can judge it with some omissions in the later tithe, changed only slightly," is inconclusive.

The tithe payments should be compared to another source, one dependent on another estimation of ecclesiastical wealth. Fortunately, there was a second thirteenth-century inquest at Lucca. This *"Estimo* of the Diocese of Lucca of 1260" probably was levied by the papacy to pay the expenses of the bishop of Monopoli (near Bari) and other papal legates in affairs (unexplained) between the Holy See and Lucca. This *estimo* lists the total income of all churches in the diocese, both "exempt" and "non-exempt" from local episcopal jurisdiction. Since the tithe payments of the *Rationes decimarum* record only the actual payments, and not the total wealth, the two sources cannot be compared directly. We can, however, perceive changes in the wealth of one religious body in relation to the wealth of another (Table 3).

Using such a system of comparison, we find that the relative wealth of the chapter declined between 1260 and 1276–77. An examination of the changing ratio of wealth between the monastery of San Michele of Guamo and the

TABLE 3

Changes in Relative Ecclesiastical Wealth

	1260 Estimo *of Total Income*		*Tithe Payments, 1276–77*	
	(sum)	*(%)*	*(sum)*	*(%)*
Bishopric	£ 3,500	27.8	£157 10s.	35.9
Chapter	4,200	33.3	125 --	28.5
S. Maria Forisportam (canonica et hospitale)	3,100	24.6	73 18s.	16.8
San Michele of Guamo	1,800	14.3	82 8s.	18.8
TOTAL	£12,600	100.0	£438 16s.	100.0

SOURCE: The *Estimo* of 1260 is edited in the Appendix of *Tuscia,* I, 243–73. The sums are found in *Tuscia,* I, Nos. 4191, 4208, 4235, 4239, 4240, 4707, 4708, 4712, 4713, and 4835.

chapter leads to the same conclusion. In 1260, it was 1:2.3; by 1276–77 it had slipped to 1:1.5. While these figures do not prove a changed relationship between the bishopric, the chapter, and other churches and monasteries, they do show the declining relative economic vigor of the chapter.

The chapter's exercise of its right to select the bishop also changed. In 1269 the chapter chose as bishop the Dominican Pietro degli Angiorelli of Lucca. Pietro was the first Luccan bishop elected by the chapter since the Benedictine Anselmo II (1073–86) who was not a member of the cathedral chapter. In the fourteenth century the chapter did not select the bishops. In 1300, the chapter tried to choose one of its members, Rainerio of Montemagno, as the new bishop. Pope Boniface set aside the election and provided the diocese with the Franciscan Enrico II di Carretto, from Liguria. In 1330, after Enrico's death, the papacy again provided a bishop—the Sienese Dominican Guglielmo II Dolcini of Montalbano. The chapter had lost one of the most important supports for its power within episcopal administration.

If new centers of piety made this change possible, it is not unreasonable to believe that the impetus for it came from new entities and ultimately from the laity who supported them. This raises the question of the bishop's role in the administration of his bishopric. Rural communes, other churches, monasteries, and hospitals all played a role in the selection of rectors for pievi and subaltern churches. Even when the bishop refused to recognize the right of laymen to select rectors for their local churches, he often did, in fact, follow their wishes. Bishop Opizone quashed the selection of a rector for the pieve of Padule made by the residents of the district, but he still nominated the candidate they had selected to be the pievano.[109] The bishop maintained the fiction of independent selection, but at Lucca, as later in Renaissance Florence, the laity retained a lively interest in local spiritual matters.[110]

The record in secular affairs is less clear. One is reduced to noting indirect signs of episcopal activities. Lacking clear descriptions of administrative structure, one is forced to investigate the individual acts of administrative officers.

The bishops themselves do not seem to have been active in temporal matters. In more than twenty years as bishop of Lucca, Bishop Roberto acted directly in only thirteen documents. Only nine documents record Bishop Guercio acting directly—an incredibly low number when we recall the activities of his officers. The bishops of Lucca, although they headed a large administration, do not seem to have been critical for the operation of their bishopric. The very continuity of actions during vacant sees suggests that the bishops themselves took very little part in the bishopric's temporal activities during the thirteenth and fourteenth centuries.

The figure of the bishop in administration is, then, less prominent during the thirteenth and fourteenth centuries than it had been in the eleventh and twelfth centuries. The bureaucratic administration, stimulated initially by the renewed prestige of the bishop and cathedral chapter, grew; the position of the cathedral declined. The administration of the bishopric clearly reflected changes that occurred in both secular and religious society in the thirteenth and fourteenth centuries.

4

The Episcopal Jura

The potentially most controversial aspect of the bishopric's temporal possessions was its secular jurisdiction over certain areas of the countryside. These areas were under episcopal law: legal actions of all kinds were heard in episcopal courts; police powers belonged to the bishopric; the bishop held all rights to taxation. The totality of the areas under the bishop's temporal jurisdiction was called the *jura*. The history of the Luccan jura during the later Middle Ages includes not merely the varying fortunes of the bishopric, but also the rise of the rural communes. Studying the jura and the rural communes within it means, in turn, investigating the various social classes in the countryside.

At Lucca, the lands of the episcopal jura were not treated as a unity. They were scattered over almost all parts of the diocese, including the mountains of upper Garfagnana (near and including Piazza al Serchio and actually in the diocese of Luni), Sorbano del Vescovo, Santa Maria a Monte, Moriano, Diecimo, Montopoli, Montecastello, and San Gervasio. The bishop of Lucca continued to exercise temporal jurisdiction over at least some of these areas until 1726.[1]

A limiting factor in any study, of course, is the nature of the available sources. There is no extant constitution for the whole jura, or for any of its individual communes, before the mid-fourteenth century. The statutes of Santa Maria a Monte for which the vicar general, Francesco di Casale, approved emendations in 1330 and similar constitutions for other areas have been lost.[2] The only document which approximates communal statutes is an exemplum of the oath sworn by the consuls or podestà of Santa Maria a Monte, dating from the late twelfth or early thirteenth century.[3]

For the period before 1260, we must be satisfied with occasional parchments. The most common documents concerning the episcopal jura are procurations before the officials of the bishopric for the appointment of podestàs and rectors of local churches. Other parchments record litigations between the rural communes of the jura and the bishopric, and leases (usually for the collection of tithes or possession of mills or waterways). The twelfth-century parchments seldom even mention the existence of rural communes. This does not prove, however, that they did not exist. As Gioacchino Volpe observed, a lease of the local tithe collections to a group of men from that locality may actually indicate primitive communal organization.[4]

For the period after 1260, we possess additional parchments and the volumes of the *Libri antichi*.[5] These volumes, however, do not contain all the acts of the bishopric. Only irregularly do they record the appointments of podestàs. They do not always record the payments made by rural communes to the bishopric or the names of all the *pedaggiores,* men appointed to collect road taxes in the jura. These books include only one list of men taking an oath to the Luccan bishopric—the kind of document so valuable for demographic, social, and economic history.[6] In sum, the archiepiscopal archive does provide sources for a study of the jura, but it does not offer enough documentation for quantitative analysis or for a detailed investigation.

The state archives of Lucca serve the prospective historian of the jura no better. The communal register, often cited by Tolomeo of Lucca as his source for matters in the twelfth and thirteenth centuries, no longer exists. We also lack tax records, deliberations of the city council, records of the *Anziani* (the small council), and the records of the communal courts before about 1330.[7]

The lacunae of the Archivio di Stato, and possibly some of those in the church archive, result from Lucca's tumultuous politics in the early fourteenth century. In the first third of that century, Lucca suffered three sacks. On 14 June 1314, Uguccione della Faggiuola, the Ghibelline lord of Pisa, captured Lucca and put its archives to a systematic sacking. Uguccione's interest in the episcopal archives was doubtless related to the conflicting claims of the Luccan bishopric and the Pisan commune south of the Arno. In 1329, Louis the Bavarian captured Lucca and again the archives were sacked. The extent of the damage is recorded in an act of 1334 which states that tax contracts made between 1320 and 1329 shall remain valid. The act was necessary, "since because of the fire sent upon the city on March 29, 1329, many books, indeed almost all of the books and writings of the Luccan camera, and the Luccan commune and gabelles, were burned and ruined."[8]

The final destruction was done in 1333 by the sons of Castruccio Castracani degli Antelminelli who destroyed the records of sentences passed against them. What remained in the Archivio di Stato include occasional notices of the jura, mostly concerning the period after 1333. While neither of the Luccan archives is completely satisfactory, together they do allow us to investigate in broad outline the history of the bishopric's medieval jura.

ORIGINS OF THE JURA

The first recognition of the areas within the jura is a bull of Alexander II (1061–73) in which he prohibited the lease or alienation of episcopal lands, castles, and possessions "unless to peasants or laborers." Named in the bull we find most of the lands which in the thirteenth century were under episcopal civil jurisdiction.[9]

Episcopal possession of immunities and jurisdictions may in some cases have been based on alienations of royal and imperial lands during the ninth and tenth centuries. In other cases claims of civil jurisdiction originated when the bishops gained de facto control of the districts.[10] Jurisdiction over some castles had been claimed as early as 1063. In fact, we can trace episcopal possession of castles back to the first quarter of the tenth century.[11] The castle of Anchiano (near Diecimo in the Serchio Valley) was first mentioned in 925 when Bishop Pietro let half of it to the lords of Anchiano. Similarly, the bishopric possessed castles in Moriano and south of the Arno long before they were mentioned in papal or imperial privileges. The earliest papal and imperial instruments simply acknowledge civil jurisdictions already exercised by the bishopric. Thus, the growth of episcopal civil administration paralleled the assumption of political power by the so-called rural counts of the tenth century who held fortresses in the countryside.[12]

As early as the ninth century the bishopric possessed lands in most of the areas which would become integral parts of its jura. Some of these came into its possession through pious donations made by old Lombard and Carolingian families. The eighth-century bishop Walprando, son of Walprando, duke of Tuscany, donated half of his personal possessions to the cathedral of San Martino. The bishop doubtless had significant holdings throughout the diocese of Lucca and elsewhere in Tuscany.[13] In 803, the presbyter Ildiperto del fu Auderamo similarly donated all of his possessions at Villa to the bishopric.[14]

In other cases the bishopric gained lands through its control of the patronage over local churches. At Santa Maria a Monte, the lands being let in the tenth century belonged "to your [the bishop's] church of Santa Maria that is called 'a monte,' which is under the power of your episcopate of San Martino."[15] The case of the church of San Terenzio of Marlia exemplifies how the bishopric gained control of these churches. In 728, one Transvaldo gave to the bishopric half of the church of San Terenzio, which he had built, as well as half of all the lands belonging to it. Sometime during the eighth century, the church was destroyed and so, in 802 and later in 850, the bishopric let the church and its lands in order that the church might be rebuilt. It is significant that these ninth-century leases let not the one half that had been given to the bishopric, but *all* of the lands of the church.[16] The bishopric may have gained full possession of the church when Transvaldo's family died out, or perhaps the family lost interest in the church when it needed costly repairs, or the bishopric may have purchased the remaining portion and subsequently lost the bill of sale. In any case, by the early ninth century, the bishopric had uncontested control of the church of San Terenzio and its lands.

It seems clear that during the eighth and ninth centuries, the bishopric gained lands in the areas which would become the jura. There is, however, no mention of castles, but only of churches, corti, and houses. At Sala in Garfagnana, for example, the bishopric may have had property as early as the middle of the ninth century. Emanuele Repetti reported that "this villa belonged, from the eighth century, to Walprando, bishop of Lucca, who willed his villa at Sala to the Luccan episcopal *mensa.*" The testament to which Repetti refers, but does not cite, only notes that the cathedral of San Martino should receive one half of his possessions. Repetti probably deduced that Sala di Garfagnana belonged to Walprando from a document in which Walprando's brother traded to him "parte mea de sala . . . [editor's ellipsis] sundriale quem avere visum sum in loco, qui dicitur Tocciano. . . ." Domenico Barsocchini placed Tocciano in the district of Sovana (near Massa Marittima); actually, Tocciano is probably the "Tucciano" described in a document of 753 as being near Luciano in the pieve of Triano, south of the Arno in the Luccan diocese.[17] In 883, Bishop Gherardo let a house and lands "ubi jam antea fuit case et curte domnicata," as well as the dependent lands held by serfs (*cum casis et rebus massariciis*) at Sala di Garfagnana. The lease was given to one Cunimundo who, according to Domenico Pacchi,[18] is believed to be the first of the de' Nobili family. By 1110, and possibly as early as 983, the de' Nobili family held a castle at Sala in the corte they had received from the bishop. We depend on almost chance mentions to learn of the existence of castles. In most cases, the castle is mentioned in an act only if the document was redacted there. Given the silence of the documents, we often can but guess when the castle was built.

The situation was similar at Moriano. The earliest reference to Moriano may be a document of 725 mentioning the foundation of the church of San Casciano.[19] The pieve of Moriano, Santa Maria a Sesto, is first mentioned in a document of 762. The earliest references to the pieve of Moriano suggest that the rector of the pieve was independent of episcopal patronage. The first indication of episcopal control over the rector comes in 772,[20] when the rector traded lands with the consent of Bishop Peredeo. It seems likely that the episcopal sanction was necessary only to insure that the transaction did not alienate any of the pieve's wealth, and that the bishop's consent did not represent exercise of rights of patronage. In the following years the rector,

Rachiprando, continued to receive donations and to buy and sell lands without reference to the bishopric. The holdings of the pieve of Sesto were impressive, including lands and houses at Brancoli and Quaranzana, in Versilia, and in the city of Lucca. Its rectors exercised control over the pieve and its wealth, independent of the episcopate's control, until 844 when the bishop took possession of the lands of the pieve. How this change occurred is not known, but in 844 and thereafter Bishop Ambrogio let lands belonging to the pieve and required rent payments to the bishopric.[21]

At that point the bishopric controlled the pieve and its lands, but there was no mention of a castle in the region. A castle at Moriano was first mentioned in 915 when Bishop Pietro leased to Urso del fu Luperto a piece of land "infra castello in loco et finibus Moriano" for an extremely low *censo* of two denari of silver each year. In the lease Urso promised that "we shall have to close with a wall that portion of the castle which is fourteen and a half feet [according to the measure of King Liutprand]; and on the above-written piece of land we shall have to raise, close, and cover a house."[22] This document probably records the completion of a new castle rather than the repair of an old one. Had there been a house or a wall on a piece of property being leased, the ruin ordinarily was mentioned. More significantly, the earliest reports of castles in the countryside all date from the early tenth century, the period of unrest throughout Europe caused by the Vikings, Saracens, and Hungarians. In 925, the bishop built a castle at San Pietro a Vico.[23] It is possible that many other fortresses throughout the diocese were constructed during the rest of the tenth century, but the argument remains theoretical since the first mention of most of the castles dates from the eleventh century, some even from the twelfth century.[24] In any case, we do not know when the castles were constructed.

The rent contract requiring the enclosure of the castle at Moriano may actually reveal how these castles were built. In a similar lease in 925, Bishop Pietro let half of the castle of Anchiano to Giovanni del fu Leofredo, Pietro di Adalperghe, Ghisalperto del fu Ghisi, and Ghisalperto del fu Ghisalprando, and Domniperto del fu Domniprando, the lords of Anchiano. These men promised to build a wall twenty feet long for the castle.[25] Unfortunately these are the only examples we have of how the castles of the jura may have been built.

During the tenth century, castles were a necessity to preserve a tenuous order in the countryside. At the same time the bishopric found itself in a period of financial crisis. Donations to it were few and the bishopric was itself leasing large parts of its landed wealth to powerful rural lords.[26] If the bishopric did not have the resources necessary to fortify the countryside, we could expect it to turn to the one means of improving its possessions that did not

require outlay of liquid capital—that is, improvement leases. During the
tenth century, the bishopric quite regularly let lands with the understanding
that within a year a house would be built on the property. Similarly, destroyed churches and the lands belonging to the churches were let in order
that the churches might be rebuilt.[27]

Such a system of financing the construction or completion of castles
has several advantages. The bishopric would not have to tie up its limited
capital in the construction of castles. Those who built the wall would presumably be responsible for its defense. And, if those people lived in the castle,
they would obviously have an interest in the maintenance of the castle as a
whole.

The weakness of this system of financing construction was simply that
those who built the wall would own it and a portion of the jurisdiction of the
castle. At Anchiano, where the bishopric had let a part of the castle for a
promise to complete a portion of the wall, a second lease was given in 1005
to Fulchardo del fu Ildiberto, again for a recognition payment of six denari
per year. Similarly, Bishop Anselmo let that castle in 1062 to Ildebrando,
Arigo, and Sigefrido del fu Sigefrido. At this point even theoretical control
of the castle passed from the bishopric. Pope Alexander II (Bishop Anselmo
I) did not include Anchiano among the castles listed in his bull of 1063–73.[28]

In the high Garfagnana, at Sala, the bishopric must have made a similar
agreement for the construction of a castle sometime during the late twelfth
century. At Sala, there was no mention of episcopal jurisdiction until 1179
when the castle at Sala was divided according to a pact between Bishop
Guglielmo of Lucca and the de' Nobili family of Sala and the counts of Lavagna.[29] The bishopric was to hold two thirds of Castelvecchio di Garfagnana
and its tower, while the nobles received the other third. For their third
portion, Ugo, Cunemundo, and Superbo swore fealty to the bishop. They, as
well as all the other inhabitants of the castle, were to swear to make peace
or war in the district of Sala and the district of Castelvecchio according to
the wishes of the bishop or his representative in the district. This contract
was considerably more than just a simple feudal contract, for the de' Nobili
and the counts of Lavagna could take possession of any unused part of the
episcopal portion. Similarly, though the bishop's jurisdiction was to be protected, the pact specified that his military power could not be greater than
that of the lay lords:

And if the mentioned lord Guglielmo, bishop of Lucca, or his successors, does not
have men living [ad habitandum ad logatos] without fraud in his two parts of the
aforesaid castle, from that time [when this contract begins] to the constituted term of
twelve years, the aforesaid Ugo, Cunemundo, and Superbo and their heirs shall have
as a fief from the Luccan bishop that residue which remains of the two portions that
is not inhabited such that [the lords' total portion] with their third portion and with

that residue it shall not exceed or go beyond one half of those two parts and of the parts of the area within the fortifications. . . . And if it pleases the said Luccan bishop, or his successors, to build a tower on his portion of the area within the fortifications, that he may do, and similarly, Count Ugo may build a tower . . . so that however high either one is, they shall be of equal height. . . . Indeed, the men of the bishop and the men of the abovewritten counts shall swear to the abovewritten [agreement]. . . .

A later document exhibits the extent to which laymen had taken control of Sala. In 1278, the de' Nobili and the counts of Lavagna each held one half of the castle, with no mention of the episcopal portion.[30] Although the earlier document gave the nobles partial possession of the castle, some of the episcopal agricultural lands in the district were exempted from the partition by the restriction "that the bishop's meadow and all land that shall be vineyard shall remain free to the Luccan bishop. . . ." By 1302, however, the nobleman Dino del fu Filippo de' Nobili, a member of the ruling *consorteria,* also held the bishop's two mills and a fulling mill at Sala beside the Serchio. At Dino's death his lands passed to his son, including the mills, ten pieces of land held from the bishop (rent free), and one fourth of Castelvecchio for which he was to pay a recognition rent of five soldi each year.[31]

The actions of the reformed bishopric were partially a reaction to the problem of lay possession of castles.[32] In some cases the bishopric was more successful than it was at Sala. In the later eleventh century, Bishop Anselmo II litigated with one Itta for the jurisdiction of the corte and castle of Mammoli in Moriano.[33] Three men of the district of Mammoli were selected to testify as to the possession of the area, and they agreed that the men of the area "were accustomed to make law and justice in the presence of the bishop of Lucca and his representative. . . ." Itta's claim to the castle and jurisdiction is not explained, but it may have originated in a lease for the construction of defenses at Mammoli—like the lease the bishop gave for the fortification of nearby Castro di Moriano.

The bishopric also repossessed the castle of Diecimo during the eleventh century. The corte of Diecimo probably belonged to the bishopric when Bishop Corrado appealed to the marquis Ugo of Lucca in the mid-tenth century, saying that one Immilga and her son Rofredo illegally held the corte and land belonging to the pieve of Diecimo which was under the patronage of the bishopric.[34] The first indication of a castle at Diecimo is found in Alexander II's bull (1063–73). The episcopal possession was not yet complete, however, since in 1078 Countess Matilda donated her part of the castle to the bishopric.[35] After 1078, the bishopric held Diecimo continuously until the eighteenth century.

The bishopric repossessed the castle of Porcari in 1044, but with less satisfactory results.[36] At that time one Teutio, called "Barcarello," gave the bishopric his lands at Porcari and one fourth of the castle, which seems to indicate that the bishopric wanted clear title to the castle. Two years later such hopes were dashed when an imperial judge, Bishop Odalrico of Trent, decided that Bishop Giovanni of Lucca had unjustly reclaimed half of the castle from one Stirico del fu Donnuccio and that Stirico should be allowed to retain from the bishop his portion of the castle and its lands. The decision did not explain the reason for the judgment or what Stirico's rights and duties should be.[37]

Episcopal penetration of the countryside did not proceed simply by repossession of alienated church lands. In 1026, Count Ugo donated to the bishopric one half of three portions of the castle and corte of "Potiosturli" to which the bishopric apparently had no prior claim.[38] Similarly, the bishopric received parts of castles at Fondagno (near Diecimo), at Montecatini (in the Valdinievole), at Capannoli and Forcoli (in the Valdera), and at Castiglione Berardesta (in the diocese of Volterra).[39]

The policy of gaining control of castles continued into the twelfth century. The bishopric bought lands and received donations and pawns of castles, expecially south of the Arno and along the eastern edge of the diocese near Montecatini—areas where the rural magnates found themselves hard pressed militarily and economically by the bishop and the rural communes. The frequency of purchases and resumptions began to decline about 1160, and after 1202 the bishopric no longer bought or received castles.

Many of the castles and corti quickly passed from episcopal control. The castle of Vaccoli was destroyed by the commune of Lucca in 1088. By the mid-thirteenth century, Monsummano and Montecatini belonged to the Luccan commune. Similarly, between 1180 and 1240, many of the episcopal lands in the Valdera were incorporated into the Pisan contado.[40] But the lands that remained were the medieval jura, formed from possessions which the bishopric had held since the ninth and tenth centuries as well as some territories newly obtained during the eleventh and twelfth centuries.

RURAL COMMUNES

The bishopric expended a great deal of money and energy securing its possessions against the rural counts, yet at the same time it found itself sharing its jurisdictions with a new and more formidable power: the rural communes. These communes probably appeared as early as the larger communes, that is during the second half of the eleventh century. A sale document of 28 April 1076 mentions four rural communes in the Valdera and indicates that they had already received concessions from their rural lords.[41] Rolandino and Sigismondo del fu Count Malaparte sold to the bishopric part of the "castle and corte of San Gervasio" as well as the lands subject to the corte; the same day, "all the men of San Gervasio" met "ad consilium" in the canonica of San Gervasio, where they "confirmed and ratified" the sale and promised the bishop of Lucca that they would defend episcopal possession of San Gervasio.

Oaths similar to that sworn by the men of San Gervasio probably were the first recognition of early communal organization. The men of Moriano took such an oath in 1121. One year later the men of Valivo di Sopra in Garfagnana swore a similar oath. In 1159 and 1169, the men of Castro di Moriano and Colcarelli swore oaths to the bishop.[42] These oaths, like feudal oaths, are primarily negative. The men of Moriano swore, for example, that they would not take arms "against the honor of San Martino and the Luccan bishop," nor would they contend against episcopal possession of the castles and corte of Moriano; nor would they contend against those who would come to Moriano when the bishop was there nor against those episcopal officials who would come in the bishop's place.

The interests of these rural communes are difficult to perceive in such oaths. The nature of the oaths, primarily promises not to molest episcopal rights in the area and to protect episcopal possessions against others, does not differ from the oaths taken by rural nobles.

Like the rural nobles, these communes were interested in the tithes and patronage belonging to their local churches. The extent to which the local communes were able to control the tithes during the twelfth century is unknown. As mentioned above,[43] the commune of Pinocchio received the right to the tithes collected in that territory and a guarantee that the bishopric would not give the rights to these tithes to anyone else at a later date. We do not have other twelfth-century examples of leases of tithes to rural communes; a flurry of tithe leases did occur in the second half of the thirteenth and the early fourteenth centuries.[44]

Catherine Boyd noted that especially during the thirteenth century, the tithes were a bone of contention between the church and the major communes, the disputes usually ending in the abolition of urban tithe payments. The commune of Parma argued as early as 1219 that the church had no right to the tithes, while after 1233 the commune of Bologna refused to sanction the collection of tithes within the city. What tithes remained, according to Boyd, were rural tithes which were often let to rural communes.[45]

There is reason to believe that episcopal control over tithes was lost considerably earlier than the mid-thirteenth century. The tithes were closely related to the patronage of the rural churches; and the rural communes quite commonly claimed patronage rights by the end of the twelfth century. The rural communes were concerned with the pieve for the same reasons the larger communes wished to control their churches. They had an interest in who was chosen to fulfill the spiritual needs of their communities. In a more practical sense, the local church was the center of their town. As in the larger communes, the markets, money-changers, and notaries usually were located in the piazzas surrounding the church. When the consuls of the rural commune met, or when an assembly of all the men of the commune was called, it was in or near the town's church. Given the role of the pieve in the town it must have been difficult, if not impossible, for the men of rural communes to separate the spiritual power implied by rights of patronage from the civic interests found in any town large or small.

By the mid-twelfth century, rural communes already were litigating with the bishopric and cathedral chapter over the right to select the rectors of local churches. In 1167 and 1168, the men of Fibbialla claimed the right to select the rector of their pieve. Arbiters chosen to hear the case decided that the men of Fibbialla should select their pievano. Then the pievano-elect and the consuls of Fibbialla would appear before the chapter and have their selection approved.[46]

The communes of the jura also exercised rights of patronage. The commune of Montopoli selected a rector for its church of Santo Stefano in 1232 and again in 1293. The commune of Santa Maria a Monte selected a pievano in 1230 and the men of Aquilea chose their own rector in 1294. Selection of the rector of Sesto di Moriano was divided between the commune of Aquilea and the bishop; it took place in the episcopal palace at Lucca in a meeting between the bishop and two representatives of the commune.[47]

In the second half of the twelfth century, the rural communes were also trying to consolidate their districts. Their objectives and their strategies recall the activities of the larger communes such as Pisa and Lucca. In 1156, the communes of Montopoli and Marti both claimed a portion of the corte of Montopoli. The controversy probably concerned the lands between two streams—the Chieccina and the Cecinella—and thus between the two towns.[48] The case was decided by an arbiter chosen by the two communes, a Knight Templar, Truffa del fu Gerardo, who declared that the corte should belong to the district of Montopoli and that the inhabitants of the corte should swear allegiance to that commune.

The commune of Santa Maria a Monte also tried to stabilize its district. In 1120, the commune was litigating with "the men of the corte of Puteo" over rights to Cerbaia, an extensive wooded area between the lake of Bientina and the marshes of Fucecchio. The pertinent document does not contain any information about the litigation or the basis for settlement. It records only that the men of Puteo, in the presence of Bishop Benedetto of Lucca, the judges Fralmo da Ottavo and Ricardo, Gottifredo consul "and many other fideles of the same bishop," ended all claims to the contested lands.[49] In such a litigation, apparently decided by the bishop's men, it is not surprising that the men of the corte lost their struggle with the larger and strategically more important commune of the jura.

On the other side of Santa Maria a Monte, toward Montecalvoli, on the boundary of the Pisan contado, the rural commune does not seem to have had an easily defined border. Both Santa Maria a Monte and Montecalvoli lay beside the Usciana canal, and while Santa Maria a Monte was under episcopal dominion, Montecalvoli was part of the abbot of Sesto's jura. As early as 1146, the abbot of Sesto promised not to litigate with the bishop over episcopal possession of a mill "infra curtem de monte calvoli."[50]

The commune of Santa Maria a Monte quickly followed the bishopric in expanding toward Montecalvoli. Santa Maria a Monte probably would have incorporated Montecalvoli into its district had not the Luccan commune intervened and, in 1183, promised "to defend you [the commune of Monte-calvoli] from those men of Santa Maria a Monte, from all injury, oppression and exactions." The process of incorporation was well advanced by that time since the Luccan commune specifically voided those obligations contained in a document (its date not given) written by the notary Enrico.[51] The Luccan commune may have intervened because it had begun to take possession of the abbot of Sesto's jura, which by the end of the thirteenth century had ceased to exist. Perhaps more important, the Luccans must have feared that Monte-calvoli would appeal to the Pisans for aid in its struggle with Santa Maria a Monte if there was no support forthcoming from Lucca. Despite Lucca's opposition, Santa Maria a Monte continued trying to expand at the expense of its neighbors. As late as 1262, Santa Maria a Monte litigated with the commune of Bientina over fishing rights in the lake of Sesto. Again the com-mune was checked by Lucca, whose judges refused to admit Santa Maria a Monte's claims.[52]

Efforts to consolidate or expand districts led almost naturally to preten-sions toward certain of the episcopal rights. In 1180, the consuls of Monto-poli, Manetto del fu Rolando and Rolandino del fu Rugiero, acting for "the knights and men of Montopoli," asked Bishop Guglielmo I to free the in-habitants of Montopoli from the interdict laid upon the town and its district because the knights of Montopoli, against the bishop's will, had appropri-ated rights to the guida. They returned these rights to the bishop and further promised to abide by whatever the bishop commanded. Guglielmo then in-vested the knights with one half of the guida with the understanding that they would defend episcopal rights and possessions within the district of Monto-poli.[53]

The *guida* was a right to supply safe passage, and in the present context it refers to the *guidaticum* or *guidagium,* the payment made by travelers to insure safe passage through a district. It is closely related to the *pedaggio,* a tax for the upkeep of the roads.[54] By 1207, the collection of the guida had been combined with the pedaggio at Montopoli. In that year, the episcopal advocate, Leonardo del fu Aldobrandino, and Ugolino del fu Galgano, con-sul of Montopoli, appeared before Gottifredo del fu Lamberto Tadulini, an arbiter who had been appointed by Genovese and Opizo, "maioribus lucano consulibus," in a question over the guida and pedaggio collected in the district of Montopoli.[55] Leonardo requested that the rights to the guida, the pedaggio, and their receipts be declared to belong to the bishop and bishopric, except the half of the guida and pedaggio which the knights of Montopoli held as a benefice from the bishop and bishopric. Ugolino contested this claim, citing a convention (the date of which is undecipherable, but probably before 1180) by which the society of knights was formed for the collection of the receipts. He added that the society had been collecting the guida and pedaggio and said, almost as an aside, that the court constituted by the commune of Lucca did not have competence in the matter that the bishopric had brought before it. Leonardo then observed that the bishopric was "in quasi possessione dicte guide et passagii," and he reminded the judge that possession of the guida had been returned to the bishopric in 1180 and that at that time Bishop Guglielmo I had returned only half of the guida and receipts to the knights.

The knights may have gained possession of the guida during the twelfth-century wars between Pisa and Lucca when the bishopric was unable to exercise its rights. The restoration of 1180, which Ugolino of course denied, represented a new compromise between the bishopric and the knights of Montopoli. Although the men of Montopoli obviously felt they should hold all of the guida and pedaggio for their district, the arbiter decided against them. Gottifredo ratified the compromise of 1180, declaring that the knights of Montopoli had no right to the guida, pedaggio, or the profits, except for the one half they held as a benefice from the bishopric.

The bishopric also shared the rights to the pedaggio in the middle Serchio with the rural communes. In 1210,[56] the commune of Diecimo and Bishop Roberto litigated over the pedaggio collected within the district of Diecimo. The consuls petitioned the arbiters, Opizone Colonico and Alberto del fu Gattalioso, who was the bishop's castaldo, that the bishop had carried away their one-fourth portion of the pedaggio. Bishop Roberto, acting for himself and the bishopric, denied that any such thing had been done—though he added that the commune held as a benefice one fourth of all the pedaggio over land and water except for the "pedaggium pecodum," a tax on herds passing through the district. The arbiters decided that the commune should have one fourth of the pedaggio, not excepting that on herds. They added, however, that the commune should pay £55 for the right to receive the benefice, as well as £70 for perpetual possession of the one fourth of the pedaggio.

As in the case of the commune of Montopoli, there are hints of earlier problems at Diecimo which may have caused the alienation of part of the pedaggio. Earlier, in 1178, two brothers, Baccalare and Tornato del fu Falcone, had promised to end all litigation with the bishopric over possession of the castle, district, and curia of Diecimo; for their promise, Bishop-elect

Guglielmo gave them two pieces of land near Diecimo "nomine feudi et bene-fici."[57] There is no known connection with the litigation over the pedaggio though the bishopric may have given the right to one fourth of the pedaggio to the men of Diecimo in return for their support against the brothers. A portion of the pedaggio may have seemed a small price to pay for aid against the brothers in the middle of the twelfth century. The situation probably changed as a result of the popularity of the mountain pastures in Garfa-gnana. One of the major developments in transhumance in the later Middle Ages was the movement of herds of sheep from as far south as the Sienese Maremma to summer pastures in the Garfagnana—the simplest route pass-ing up the Serchio through the episcopate's jura at Moriano and Diecimo.[58]

The rural communes did not just cost the bishopric part of its revenues. They could and did aid it. In 1216, the consuls of Castro di Moriano, Mar-tino del fu Pandulfino of Castro di Moriano, Albertino del fu Rolan-dino of Stabbiano, and Manno del fu Gualfredo of Lama, acting "pro eorum officio consulatus et ex auctoritate et jurisdictione quas habebant pro comuni de [Castro de] Moriano a lucano episcopo et episcopatu," returned to the castaldo of Moriano, Paganello del fu Malatano, episcopal lands on which rents had not been paid. In the same year, the consuls of Castro di Moriano, acting "for the lord [bishop] Roberto and the bishopric," sold a house in Moriano for 29 soldi.[59]

The communes of the jura could provide the legal mechanism for society to function efficiently, but the extent of their competence is unclear. We have no general constitution for the jura as a whole nor any constitution for an individual commune before the middle of the fourteenth century. The earli-est indication of the rural communes' competence is the oath of the podestà or consuls of Santa Maria a Monte, dating from the late twelfth or early thirteenth century. The oath dealt primarily with criminal matters such as assault, homicide, and illegal possession of weapons; in this respect, it re-sembles the late thirteenth-century *constitutiones* for the commune's vicari-ate of Garfagnana.[60] The oath does continue with a more general clause, in which the consuls promised "to rule and to lead and to assemble all the peo-ple of Santa Maria a Monte and its corte and its district in good faith without fraud . . . for the good and the honor and the utility of the lord Luccan bish-op and the good and the honor and the utility of all the people of Santa Maria a Monte." The consuls further swore to observe and enforce any sentences given by the bishop's courts, and to insure that all debts owed to the episco-pate were paid.

The method of selecting the consuls is not known; they were probably chosen at a meeting of the *arenga* or public assembly, held in Santa Maria a Monte outside the bishop's palace. The oath declared that the names of the men selected should be sent to the bishop for his approval and that the terms should begin on All Saint's Day.

We also possess a report of communal rights in the middle Serchio. In 1223, Bishop Roberto, "for the amelioration and the utility of the bishopric," conceded to Conscio del fu Niero, Brunicardo del fu Uberto, Gherardo del fu Guglielmo, Buonaventure del fu Cristiano, Amico del fu Bernardo, Ugolino del fu Buonamico, Guglielmo del fu Stefano, Berlingario del fu Pietro, Buonagiunta del fu Alberetto, and Burichello del fu Benetto, "receiving for [the men] and the commune and the university and each and every family . . . living . . . in the vicinity of the corporation of the pieve of Sesto," full jurisdictional rights over all men living within the territory of Sesto di Moriano.[61] The only exceptions to the rural commune's jurisdiction involved crimes of shedding blood, perversion, adultery, treason of the castle, and appeals. The commune also received a portion of the profits of justice—all fines less than £5 and one half of the fines of over £5. The restrictions on jurisdiction and the division of the profits from justice were essentially the same as at Santa Maria a Monte and at Montopoli. The bishopric further conceded the pedaggio collected on wood being floated through the district of Moriano on the Serchio River. For these concessions, the commune of Sesto promised to uphold and protect episcopal possessions in the curia of Moriano and to pay 12 libre of oil each January to the bishopric or its representatives in Moriano.

This concession, and our knowledge of the rights and privileges granted to other communes, show to what extent the rural communes could act as independent powers. Their right to a large part of the profits of justice (and certainly a majority of the fines must have been less than £5) was a source of income which appears to have been very significant in the early thirteenth century. Even in the large communes such as Pisa and Florence, the profits of justice were the major source of communal income until about 1250.[62] The portions of the guida and pedaggio that the communes held were also significant. Diecimo's right to a quarter of the tax on beasts must have given increasingly high yields throughout the thirteenth and fourteenth centuries when Tuscan cloth manufacturers demanded increasing amounts of wool. The pedaggio on wood moved by water through Moriano also will have brought sizeable returns. Lucca's richest timber stands were in the middle Serchio and in the Garfagnana. The simplest and cheapest way to transport wood for fires and construction to the city certainly was to float it down the Serchio, through the canals on the Luccan plain right to the city walls. Thus, the rural communes had a solid financial base to insure their ability to meet the moderate needs of a small population center.

COMMUNAL LEADERS

An attempt to study the rural communes immediately leads us to investigate the men who controlled the commune. The earliest consuls or men of the rural areas who appeared taking oaths before the bishop almost invariably are called *fideles,* but as Gioacchino Volpe observed,[63] the dependence that the term implies is purely contractual and the fideles are free men in every other respect. This has told us almost nothing about them, however, because the term also could be used to describe those who received a single field or house from the bishopric. The free men may be free only de facto and perhaps originally they had been coloni of the bishopric. During the second half of the twelfth and the early thirteenth centuries, the legally dependent often succeeded in freeing themselves from any hint of servile condition. The very existence of litigation and inquests concerning the personal status of men indicates that the status of individual dependent coloni either was not known or was practically disregarded.[64]

If we examine the individuals who appear in the documents we are slightly better off. At Montopoli, we seem to have an association of nobles who joined with commoners to form the commune. Gioacchino Volpe argued that these nobles may have been rural counts who had been constrained to move into the rural center;[65] I have found no evidence, however, that this *inurbamento* actually occurred. When the commune of Montopoli received one half of the guida in 1180, the consuls were acting "pro omnibus militibus et universo populo illius terre." Essentially the same formula was used in the litigation of 1207.

Very few of the men mentioned in the documents as representing either the knights or the commune of Montopoli appear as officials of the episcopate or as tenants of episcopal lands. One Bernardo received a podere from the bishopric "for the usual rent" and an unusually high *servitio,* or entry fine, of 100 soldi. Another communal representative, the notary Buono, rented a "casamentum seu sedium" in Montopoli for an annual rent of eight soldi. Rubaconte del fu Carnelevare, whose brother, Giova, was a castaldo at Santa Maria a Monte, and who had had extensive dealings with the bishopric, was a consul of Santa Maria a Monte in 1233. What little information we have about the consuls of Moriano is similar. Ugolino del fu Buonamico of Sesto and his sons had extensive holdings of land in the countryside around Sesto. In 1243, he received a lease of 22 pieces of land at Sesto for an annual rent of five stai of wheat, eight stai and one quarra of must wine, and a half staio of chestnuts. In 1254, his sons received a lease of nine more pieces of land.[66]

These few examples that we have of communal officials suggest that the men did not represent any single class or economic group. More likely they are a mixture of noble and non-noble elements including the most important and powerful interests in the area. The lands they rented from the bishopric were for the most part not those types of holdings usually associated with the less affluent members of the community. Nor do we find them holding large benefices from the episcopate. They seem rather to be houses in the towns, or larger holdings in the countryside which presumably would be sublet to others who directly worked the land.

At San Gimignano, Enrico Fiumi found that the earliest consuls were essentially middle class in origin. Even among the wealthiest, noble pretensions were later additions—"they were not truly nobles by blood."[67] The consuls of the jura communes may not have been as markedly middle class in origin as San Gimignano's, because the communes of the jura shared few of San Gimignano's advantages. Santa Maria a Monte never equalled San Gimignano's population. Located on the road along the Arno between Pisa and Florence, it lay in an area contested by Lucca, Pisa, and Florence—not necessarily an advantage for a small commune. It needed episcopal support against the larger communes of northern Tuscany. The other communes of the jura were no better off. Moriano, Diecimo, and Sorbano del Vescovo all lay in an area where to throw off episcopal lordship would have meant almost immediate subjection to the Luccan commune.

The economic resources of the jura were not unlike those of the rest of the Luccan contado. The major activities were agricultural and intended to supply the urban markets, especially at Lucca, Pisa, and Florence. The episcopal lands in Moriano were ideal for production of wine and oil. Leases of lands in the jura also reveal an interest in grain production. This does not mean that the lands were best suited for grain; during the thirteenth century, cereals were cultivated throughout Tuscany, even in areas where grain farming was at best marginal. David Herlihy found that at Santa Maria Impruneta, near Florence, wheat accounted for two thirds of the commodity sales in the last quarter of the thirteenth and the early fourteenth centuries.[68]

The inhabitants of the jura also had some modest industries. The urban markets at Lucca stimulated tanning and iron smelting at Moriano and Marlia, 10 to 15 kilometers above Lucca on the Serchio River. Montopoli possessed a communal brick kiln. Since the brickmaker was required by statute to produce only three batches of bricks each year, we may assume that demand was modest and local.[69] The other artisan industries at Montopoli also seem to have been primarily local. Builders, barbers, butchers all were necessary, no matter how small the town.

The only significant export industry at Montopoli was a modest linen cloth manufactory. According to the statutes of 1360, certain bodies of water were designated for processing flax.[70] In the rest of the jura there is little indication of cloth production though it must have existed. The cloth industry of thirteenth-century Lucca was a cottage industry. Centralized factories did not develop at Lucca before the fourteenth century. Weaving was done in the countryside and was as likely in the jura as elsewhere.[71]

The jura's rural communes demonstrated a certain precociousness during the twelfth century, but unlike the rural commune of San Gimignano they remained dependent on the episcopate. After the 1220s, the consuls of San Gimignano rejected episcopal restraints on their sovereignty.[72] San Gimignano's thirteenth-century independence was based on economic and geographical advantages that the Luccan bishopric's communes lacked. San Gimignano grew rapidly because it was an important station on the Via Francigena. Its geographical position was far superior to that of its mother commune, Volterra. With a flourishing merchant community and ready markets for its saffron and other agricultural products, San Gimignano expanded from a population of about 7,000 in 1227 to a pre-plague population of about 13,000 people in 1332.[73] Politically, San Gimignano benefited from hostility between the bishop and commune of Volterra at the very time that the bishop needed communal support to retain control of San Gimignano.[74]

Santa Maria a Monte is the Luccan rural commune best suited to a comparison with San Gimignano. By 1188, its district was large enough to need regulated weights and measures. In that year Ubertellino del fu Manfredo received from the episcopal castaldo of Santa Maria a Monte the right to certify all liquid measures in the district for an entry-fine of 20 soldi and one pound of peppers each year. He was allowed to charge two denari for each certification. We have an indication of Santa Maria a Monte's population in 1210, when 241 men took an oath to obey the bishop and his envoys. If we can assume that the average family had between three and four members, the population of Santa Maria a Monte would be between 850 and 950— less than 14 percent of San Gimignano's population in 1227.[75]

During the first half of the thirteenth century, we see a few signs that Santa Maria a Monte may have attempted to be more independent. We have only fragmentary examples, but they seem to show that the men of Santa Maria a Monte realized the importance of their position. During the twelfth and thirteenth centuries, as the Pisans continually tried to expand their holdings in the southwestern part of the Luccan diocese, Santa Maria a Monte was a key point in the Luccan defenses. In 1226, the archpriest Tolomeo and the primicerio Ubaldo ordered Franco del fu Maleste and Bartolomeo da Ripa to cease negotiations with Arrigo Tatagna concerning the governance of Santa Maria a Monte.[76] Internal political changes had brought into prominence men whom the bishop did not trust. Franco and Bartolomeo represented a faction inimical to episcopal interests.

The issues were clarified slightly in 1230,[77] during litigation between Bishop Opizone's vicar, Guglielmo, and Buono and Enrico del fu Vitale, Ferrante del fu Ferricane, Gualando del fu Catenazzo, Gandolfo del fu Canino, Magalotto del fu Guanuccio, and Bonaventure del fu Buonfigliolo, guardian for the sons of Bogo. The argument was over control of the bishop's mill at Santa Maria a Monte, which these men, described as the "Lambardi de

Sancta Maria de Monte,"[78] claimed to hold from the commune of Santa Maria a Monte. The vicar, of course, denied this contention and argued that the mill was the bishopric's and all rents were payable to the bishop. The judge Cristiano, delegated by Orlando, podestà of Santa Maria a Monte, decided that the "Lambardi" should pay the rents to the bishopric.

Again, in 1239,[79] the same Lambardi (or their sons) who had held the episcopal mill claimed to hold "in feudum" the right to collect the pedaggio in the district of Santa Maria a Monte. Bishop Guercio, on the other hand, argued that they owed annual rent payments to the bishopric. The arbiters selected by the litigants, the episcopal camerario Baleante and Symonetto del fu Bonensegna "miles de Sancta Maria ad Montem," declared that the pedaggio belonged to the bishopric. They further declared that the Lambardi should pay £28 for each year that they had held the pedaggio and £40 for expenses, and a fine of 40 marks should they again violate the pedaggio.

Santa Maria a Monte seems to have tried during the 1220s and 1230s to end the episcopal overlordship in the same way that San Gimignano escaped the bishop of Volterra's control. These Lambardi probably were a consortium who at some point dominated the commune—their possession of the pedaggio recalls the concessions made to the communes of Diecimo, Sesto di Moriano, and Montopoli. Franco and Bartolomeo, whom the episcopal officials ordered not to interfere with the government, also may have represented this consortium. This faction's domination certainly had ended by 1230 when the judge Cristiano declared that the mill of Santa Maria a Monte was held from the bishopric and not from the commune—Cristiano was, after all, appointed to hear the case by the podestà of Santa Maria a Monte and he had previously represented the commune in litigation with the bishop in 1220. If this faction still controlled the commune, it is doubtful that they would have returned the mill to the bishop so easily.

In 1232, the commune sent Cristiano to Lucca to appear in the episcopal court. An agreement of 1233 indicates an apparent end to the difficulties between the episcopate and its subject commune.[80] Both sides agreed that all arrangements should be as they had been before the last Pisan-Luccan war. The commune agreed that the episcopal castaldo of Santa Maria a Monte should manage the temporalities throughout the curia, that the bishop had the right to amend communal statutes, that the profits of justice would be divided between the commune and the bishopric, and that the consuls elected in a *parlamento* must swear an oath to the bishop. The bishop promised, on the other hand, that he would not interfere with the measure of wine unless fraud had been committed. Finally, it was decided that Arrigo Tatagna, who as early as 1226 had treated with Franco and Bartolomeo over the governance of Santa Maria a Monte, had been elected podestà illegally and would have to make a "concordia" with the bishop. The commune, and probably the Lambardi, must have tried to use Santa Maria a Monte's critical position between Pisa and Lucca to gain increased independence. The agreement of 1233, which resembles the earlier oath of the consuls, indicates that their grasp at autonomy probably had been blocked.

Litigation during the same period stopped another source of the Lambardi's wealth. Even before the decision of 1239, the bishopric had let rights to collect the pedaggio at Santa Maria a Monte and in its district to its own man, the former castaldo at Santa Maria a Monte, Giova del fu Carnelevare, and his sons. Giova received rights to the pedaggio for twenty years, paying an annual rent of £32 and 23 stai of salt.[81] In 1237 we find even clearer proof that the commune's pretensions had dwindled. The ambassadors of Santa Maria a Monte, appearing before Bishop Guercio, presented him with the names of three Luccan citizens and asked him to select one to serve as their commune's podestà for the next year.[82]

By the 1240s Santa Maria a Monte, like the other rural communes of the jura, had given up attempting to claim a greater share of episcopal jurisdiction. The rural communes of the jura, which seem to represent a mixture of noble and non-noble classes, had tried to break free of episcopal control in the late twelfth and early thirteenth centuries, but they never were strong enough to end episcopal jurisdiction.

This was not, however, a complete victory for the bishopric. Revenues, local administration, and appointments of local magistrates were shared with the communes. This was to remain the basic relationship between the bishopric and its subjects through the rest of the thirteenth and fourteenth centuries.

5

The Episcopal Jura
and the Luccan Commune

During the late eleventh and early twelfth-century religious reforms, episcopal interest in amassing rural possessions and jurisdictions was motivated, beyond obvious economic reasons, by a desire to build a power source independent of the Luccan commune. But far from provoking conflict with the Luccan commune, the episcopal move into the countryside inaugurated a period of intense cooperation between bishopric and commune during which both tried to consolidate their holdings in the rural territory surrounding Lucca. The two lordships had to develop a new relationship.

THE CONQUEST OF THE CONTADO

In 1081, Emperor Henry IV rewarded Lucca's "faithful and devoted citizens" for their support during his long and arduous struggle against the papacy and Countess Matilda. He promised the Luccans the right to control their city walls—by which he meant jurisdiction within the walls. He further promised that he would not build a palace within the city or in its suburb; that the Luccans should have the right to free navigation on the Serchio and Montrone rivers; that they should enjoy unmolested passage along the Via Francigena from Luna to Lucca; "that within six miles of the city no castles shall be built and if someone should presume to build [one], it shall be destroyed by our empire and by our aid"; that the Luccans should have, as the Florentines did not, the right to enter the markets of San Donnino and Coparmuli near Parma; that the "consuetudines . . . perversas" imposed by the marquis Bonifacio should be abrogated; that Lucca should be freed from

Lombard judges, unless they were accompanied by the emperor or his son. And as a final recognition of the commune's legal status, he added "that agreements that the marquis or whatever other magistrate [*potestas*] have made with them shall remain valid."[1] The emperor, of course, did not make up the list of privileges, but only conceded to the citizens what they had requested in their petition. The privilege was probably no more than a de jure recognition of de facto appropriations.

Nonetheless the document of 1081 is an accurate introduction to communal interests at the end of the eleventh century and in the early twelfth century. In 1088, reports Tolomeo of Lucca, the castle of Vaccoli along the road over Monte Pisano toward Pisa was destroyed by the Luccans. In 1100, they destroyed the castle of Castagnore—a key fortress in the Freddana Valley along the Vià Francigena between Luna and Lucca. In 1104 and 1105 the Luccans fought the Pisans at Ripafratta—the important ford on the Serchio between Lucca and Pisa. In 1126, they received possession of the district of Nozzano beside the lake of Massaciuccoli. Two years later there were battles at Montignoso in the Lunigiana and at Buggiano in the Valdinievole, on the road to Pistoia and Florence.[2]

The battles recorded by Tolomeo are all along major roads through the dioceses of Lucca and Luna. Possession of these roads gave control of commerce and communications not just between Pisa and Florence, but between Rome and northern Italy. The Pisans recognized the commercial and economic significance of Luccan expansion. Bernardo Maragone, in his *Annales Pisani,* explained the origins of the war that broke out between the Pisans and the Luccans: "For the Pisans acquired the castle of Vorno [on the Luccan side of Monte Pisano] from the son of Soffredo because of injury inflicted upon them [by the Luccans] over the Castel d'Aghinolfo [Montignoso] and over the road of the Franks and the road of the Arno."[3]

The Luccan expansion might at first seem to be wholly motivated by the commercial interests evident in the privilege of 1081, but the city was also trying to subdue independent lordships in the areas to its north and west. When Tolomeo described the destruction of Vaccoli and Castagnore he said that the castle "erat nobilium" or "erat Cathanorum." In 1142, the viscounts Uguiccione and Velter conceded to Lucca half of the fortress of Corvaia (in northern Versilia). In the 1160s and 1170s the commune expanded its aims to include subjection of the "Captains" of Garfagnana. In an attempt to forestall complete Luccan domination of the Garfagnana, Frederick I took the area under his protection, specifically freeing it from jurisdiction and "burdens" claimed by any commune. The burdens claimed by Lucca from the Garfagnana included military service in support of the commune and, most likely, payments of direct taxes based on individual hearths or on the estimated wealth of individuals.[4]

During the twelfth and thirteenth centuries Luccan presence in the Lunigiana, Versilia, and Garfagnana was continuous, if not continuously effective. In 1124, Lucca sent representatives to mediate a dispute between the
bishop and marquis of Luni. Later, in 1140, Lucca mediated a dispute
between the commune of Sarzana and the bishop of Luni. During the rest
of the twelfth century, the wars in Versilia and Lunigiana continued, but by
1206 the podestà of Pontremoli, the marquis Malaspina, and the bishop of
Luni himself had sworn oaths to the commune of Lucca to keep and maintain
the sections of the Via Francigena that crossed their districts.[5] By the third
quarter of the thirteenth century, Luccan claims in the Lunigiana had expanded to include control of episcopal jurisdiction and possession of one
third of the salt tax collected by the bishopric.[6] The situation was much the
same in Garfagnana where, after 1170, the Luccan commune maintained its
jurisdiction despite the attempts of Frederick I, Otto IV, and Gregory IX to
reduce Luccan influence in the area.[7]

Luccan expansion to the north and west seems to have been accomplished
with little active aid from the bishopric. The only role the bishop played was
to allow the commune to use Castro di Moriano, an important defensive
center in the Serchio north of Lucca, as a staging point for the commune's
drive up the river into the Garfagnana. The fact that the bishop controlled
the castles of Sala and Valivo in the Garfagnana was also, of course, to the
commune's advantage, but the castles do not appear to have played a significant role.

In the Valdinievole, however, toward Pistoia and Fucecchio, both the commune and the bishopric were active. By 1107, the consuls of Lucca and the
bishop had been building a *castrum* at Colle San Martino. In 1128 and 1136
the communal army was fighting at Buggiano and Fucecchio, and in 1143
they were fighting along the Arno and at Montecatini. Other than in the construction of the castle at Colle San Martino, there is no clear proof that the
bishopric was working in partnership with the commune of Lucca. Nonetheless, between 1108 and 1130 the bishopric acquired lands and jurisdictions at Uzzano, Fucecchio, Musigliano, Massa Piscatoria, Repezzano,
Villa Basilica and Montecatini.[8]

The acquisitions varied a good deal. At Uzzano, the bishopric apparently
bought only agricultural lands. At Fucecchio, Musigliano, Usciana, and
Massa Piscatoria, the bishopric received parts of castles, suburbs, corti, and
lands from the estates of the Cadolinghi counts. Villa Basilica and its district were ceded to the bishopric by the marquis of Tuscany.

Even after these acquisitions, episcopal control in the Valdinievole was not
extensive. In fact, it is possible that the bishopric was content to let its jurisdictional claims in the Valdinievole lapse to the commune. Only at Villa

Basilica, apparently, did the bishopric exercise jurisdiction in the course of the thirteenth century.[9]

South of the Arno, especially in the Valdera, the commune and bishopric also worked together, but with less success. Tolomeo is silent, but from Bernardo's *Annales Pisani* it is evident that the Luccans were unable, for the most part, to resist Pisan advances. In 1149 the Pisans devastated Montecastello and, recognizing Pisan strength, reports Bernardo, "the castle of San Gervasio and all the castles of the Valdera gave themselves over to the Pisans." By the early thirteenth century, Pisa clearly predominated in this area.[10]

Luccan presence south of the Arno was primarily episcopal: the commune's role was that of an auxiliary. The key defensive points—Santa Maria a Monte, Montopoli, San Gervasio, Montecastello, and Palaia—were all at least partially under episcopal jurisdiction. Conventions, oaths, and purchases of jurisdiction were in the name of the bishopric. When the commune fortified the castle of Palaia, it was understood that jurisdiction and rights to Palaia still belonged to the bishopric.[11]

Lucca's drive to control the surrounding regions was not unusual. Neither was the cooperation between bishopric and commune. But can we really speak of an independent episcopal policy? Did the Luccan bishops, in fact, retain a lordship independent of communal control? In his study *The Italian City-Republics,* Daniel Waley aptly summarized the prevailing opinion among historians.[12]

The earliest submissions of feudatories and villages to the larger towns were often made to the bishop and consuls, or even (on some occasions) to the bishop alone. Such an arrangement was characteristic of a period when the commune had yet to gather full confidence in its juridical status. In the major Tuscan communes (Pisa, Florence, Siena, Lucca) it was only around the middle of the twelfth century that the archbishop or bishop ceased to be the city's major representative on such occasions. Soon he disappeared from them altogether.

Thus the expansion of episcopal lordship would appear to have been little more than an extension of communal policy during the twelfth and early thirteenth centuries. And at Florence, as the commune's sense of its own juridical independence developed, even the previously autonomous episcopal jurisdictions came under communal influence, if not outright dominance.[13]

There is some evidence that this may have occurred at Lucca. According to Davidsohn, the episcopal fortress of Castro di Moriano had passed under communal control sometime before 1209.[14] This fortress was of great importance to the commune since it dominated the road up the Serchio—Lucca's only access to the Garfagnana. That the Luccan commune used the castle as a staging point is certain, but the extent to which the commune had usurped episcopal jurisdiction is not. Davidsohn deduced communal domination of the castle from a series of imperial diplomas that he considered extremely reactionary. "In all his actions," Davidsohn observed of the emperor's Tuscan policy, "Otto tried to revitalize the past while he ought to have created a new order supported by the new reality." In 1209 Otto renewed the privileges granted to Lucca by Henry IV, Frederick I, and Henry VI. Rather than a prize, Davidsohn considered this a refusal to recognize changes that had been occurring in Luccan society over the past century. In support of this he noted that in the same year Otto freed the nobles of Garfagnana from their oaths to the Luccan commune. At the same time Otto took the episcopal castle of Castro di Moriano under his protection and prohibited any noble or commune, specifically mentioning Lucca, from any exactions or exercise of jurisdiction unless it had been customary for the past 48 years. This privilege exempting Moriano from any communal jurisdiction is thus an indication, Davidsohn argued, that until 1209 the castle, like the nobles of Garfagnana, had been subject to communal jurisdiction.[15]

The "new order" that Davidsohn referred to is, of course, the independent commune. Imperial attempts to prop up noble and episcopal lordships were bound to fail as soon as the emperor moved on. Gioacchino Volpe has argued for a similar understanding of the second and third decades of the thirteenth century—that communal power was breaking up episcopal jurisdictions. Even at Lucca in the 1220s, he reported, clerical possessions were attacked as part of a movement aimed at securing the political liberty of the commune.[16]

If the decades after 1210 were so critical, we would expect the commune to reassume control over the castle of Moriano, just as it did resume its policy of exacting submissions from the nobles of Garfagnana and Versilia in the decades after 1209. Tolomeo records, for example, that in 1215 the commune received the submission of the men of Controne "as from the other castles of Garfagnana."[17] From a parchment of 1229 in the archiepiscopal archives it is clear that the commune did retain some undefined rights at Moriano, but there is no mention of episcopal opposition and the document also notes that the communal rights were understood not to interfere with episcopal jurisdiction. The privilege of 1209 was probably much less reactionary than Davidsohn imagined. Since the privilege included a phrase validating exactions customarily collected for the past 48 years, we might guess that the emperor and bishop had in mind a specific agreement that was to remain in force. In that case the privilege of 1209 could be read as a protection against any changes in the episcopal-communal relationship already established by the two lordships.

The events of the 1220s cited by Volpe also seem to indicate something less than a broadly based communal attack on ecclesiastical liberties. The *Gesta Lucanorum*[18] reports that in 1221 "the bridge that was over the Arno at Portasso [near Montecalvoli and Santa Maria a Monte] fell and then was rebuilt from the possessions of the clerics of Lucca and its contado and Lucca was excommunicated for it; and the clergy was abused. That year Parenzio Parente of Rome was podestà of Lucca." In Pope Honorius's view Parenzio deserved most of the credit for the whole affair. In July of 1221 Honorius announced to the Pisans that he was giving the Luccans license "to make a league against P[arenzio], Roman citizen, who is subverting ecclesiastical liberty." Again, writing to the Genoese, Honorius named Parenzio and his followers as the guilty parties rather than blaming the Luccan citizens as a group. In fact the excommunication was lifted in 1222 shortly after the commune replaced Parenzio with a new podestà.[19] This "attack on clerical liberties" was thus at best the policy of a faction. From the beginning Honorius put the blame on one man and asked, most of all, for his dismissal.

The reports are scattered, but it is difficult to believe that the commune opposed an independent episcopal jurisdiction as a matter of policy during the first two thirds of the thirteenth century. Moreover, in the 1250s and 1260s the commune played a key role in the bishopric's retention of its jurisdiction in the Valdarno.

In July of 1252 Luccan troops were badly defeated in a battle near Montopoli by the Pisans, and Santa Maria a Monte was in danger of falling.[20] The Luccan commune stepped forward and offered assistance. A commission of two men selected by the commune and two men selected by the bishopric investigated the threat to Santa Maria a Monte and urged "that the Luccan commune should be held to defend and maintain for the Luccan bishopric the rights which it has in Santa Maria a Monte." The city council of Lucca approved the suggestion in a meeting on August 2. The following day Guidesco da Brescia, the Luccan podestà, appeared before Bishop Guercio and stated that it was "almost common knowledge" that Santa Maria a Monte could be lost during war with Pisa. He asked that the commune of Lucca be allowed to fortify and defend the castle "to the honor and utility of the Luccan bishopric." He also requested that custody of the castle be granted to the Luccan commune during this and all future wars. Bishop Guercio agreed to the commune's request although he underlined that this was in no way to be understood as a concession of jurisdiction or of any episcopal rights in Santa Maria a Monte.

The Luccan commune might promise otherwise, but its custody of Santa Maria a Monte could well have marked the end of episcopal jurisdiction over that rural commune. In late 1255 the new podestà of Santa Maria a Monte,

Bernardino da Montemagno, swore to hold his office "for the honor of the Luccan bishop, Luccan bishopric, Luccan commune, and the commune of Santa Maria a Monte." When the judges of the bishopric of Luni used a similar formula at Sarzana in 1254, it marked the end of an independent episcopal jurisdiction.[21] Sometime during the thirteenth century even the Luccan bishopric surrendered a part of its rights to the commune. In 1229, in renewing an earlier oath, the judge of the Luccan commune confessed to Bishop Opizone that Lucca's custody of the fortress of Palaia (in the Valdera) was not in its own name, "but in the name of the Luccan bishop and the Luccan bishopric. And every acquisition of men and fideles . . . is understood to be made for the Luccan bishop and the Luccan bishopric." By 1308, however, Luccan statutes included a rubric "De non vendendo iura que lucanum comune habet in castro Palarie de Ultra Arnum."[22]

The bishopric did, however, maintain its claim to jurisdiction over Santa Maria a Monte, and that claim seems to have been recognized by both the rural commune and the Luccan commune. On December 30, 1258, Judge Bartolomeo di Gange announced to the episcopal vicars that the commune of Santa Maria a Monte had selected him to be podestà for the next year, and he added "that he did not want the office of podestà unless it should be according to the will of the aforesaid vicars for the Luccan bishop." He announced to the vicars that he had refused the appointment and that he had explained his reasons for his refusal to the ambassadors sent from Santa Maria a Monte.[23]

As a consequence of the Ghibelline defeat of the Guelf forces at Montaperti, Lucca lost control of Santa Maria a Monte until 1276. When the bishopric recovered Santa Maria a Monte, Bishop Paganello again allowed the commune to fortify and defend the episcopal town "according to the terms of the previous occupation agreements between Lord Guercio of good memory, former Luccan bishop, as one party and the Luccan commune and other persons for the Luccan commune. . . ."[24] The commune and bishopric worked together to retain possession of Santa Maria a Monte.

The cooperation was real. In 1284 a sergeant in the Luccan contingent was murdered by a citizen of Santa Maria a Monte. The Luccan castellan of the rural commune locked the murderer in the fortress and consigned the key and the case to the podestà of Lucca. As the case was being heard in the Court of Malefactors in the church of San Michele in Foro of Lucca, the episcopal syndic intervened, arguing that according to imperial privileges jurisdiction belonged to the bishopric. Those delegated to hear the syndic's appeal

all together in general agreement, however with one exception, said and counseled that the punishing of the said malefactors and of the homicide do not pertain to the said lord Luccan podestà, but to the lord bishop's vicar, since the said fortress and the land of Santa Maria a Monte, according to the said privileges, are seen to be of the jurisdiction of the said lord bishop and the Luccan bishopric.[25]

On the one hand the case seems simple enough; however, when we consider that the murdered man was part of the Luccan garrison, we can easily imagine that the commune was sorely tempted to punish the murder itself. That it did not was probably because they could ill afford to alienate either the bishop or his rural commune. Thus the Luccan fortification of Santa Maria a Monte, which according to the agreement with Bishop Paganello took place "at the expense of the Luccan commune," did not end the episcopal jurisdiction, as Luccan participation had in the Lunigiana or in the abbot of Sesto's jura. The Luccan commune was either incapable of or unwilling to oppose the bishop's jurisdiction here.

Was this case unique? Did the Luccan commune choose not to assimilate Santa Maria a Monte only because it feared that this strategically placed rural commune would defect to the Pisans if menaced by the Luccan commune? What was the commune's attitude toward the other communes of the jura in the late thirteenth century?

Other examples are few, but they show that the Luccan commune did allow the continued existence of separate jurisdictions. In an appeal much like that concerning the homicide at Santa Maria a Monte, the episcopal syndic, Ronchino Bottacci, in 1271 successfully intervened when several men of Sorbano del Vescovo brought an action in the podestà's court.[26] The syndic argued that the judges "could not understand or adjudicate between the said [laymen]," but rather, he asserted, "the above-written [men] must be remanded to the court of the above-mentioned bishopric according to the privileges conceded by the Roman Empire. . . ."

During the fourteenth century, the commune's interest in civil and criminal matters in the jura remained what it had been in the thirteenth century. The commune primarily tried to insure that a person could not evade justice by fleeing from one jurisdiction to another—an interest shared by the bishopric and the communes of the jura. The Luccan commune's interests are summarized by a series of actions in 1379. Because of unrest caused by war and unexplained party strife, a group of Luccan citizens complained that they were unable to collect their rents in Moriano. The problem was so serious, they said, that "it did not appear that [the bishop] had the power to be obeyed." The petitioners said that the jura was now a haven for exiles from Lucca, Pisa, and other places, "and by day and by night they go armed with knives and crossbows because they have seen that the bishop cannot punish them." The communal response was less dramatic than one might have expected. The Anziani ordered, first of all, that neither the bishop nor his officials should be impeded by the commune or its officials. They added that the commune's jailer, at the request of the bishop or his officials, should apprehend and return to the bishop all malefactors who had fled from the jura to areas under communal jurisdiction. The bishop, of course, was expected to reciprocate and appoint a nunzio in each commune of the jura who would accompany the Luccan commune's jailer when he entered the jura. And what is probably most significant, the provisions stated "that concerning those malefactors of the said jura and of the Luccan territory, the bishop shall have to observe the statutes of the Luccan commune when imposing personal and monetary penalties. . . ." The commune's interests, therefore, did not seem to require the destruction of private jurisdictions. The Luccan government only desired that laws within the jura not be more lax than those in other areas of the countryside.[27]

TAXES AND MILITARY AID

There was, however, one area in which the commune and the bishopric maintained an uneasy truce: taxes and military exactions. As an independent jurisdiction, the jura theoretically was exempted from taxes and military levies raised by the Luccan commune. Even in the mid-thirteenth century, when the commune levied an estimo on the rural communes of the lower Valdarno, Valdinievole, pieve of Villa, Valleriana, and the Valdilima for the fortification of Santa Maria a Monte, San Miniato, and Montecalvoli, the communes of the jura were not required to contribute funds.[28] These rural communes seem to have paid no direct taxes. The only monies the local communal governments, or the bishopric, seem to have collected in the jura were profits from justice, guida, and pedaggio.[29]

While the communes were asked to defend the bishopric and even bear arms for it, the unique example I have found of their serving in the bishop's host was in 1237, when Bishop Guercio wrote to the podestà of Santa Maria a Monte, ordering him, under a penalty of 200 silver marks, to send two armed knights with horses and necessary supplies to serve with Emperor Frederick II.[30]

By the 1260s this favorable situation for the rural communes had begun to change. The first indication of the altered relationship was an appeal to the Luccan Anziani by Rocchigiano and Portaguerra, notaries and syndics of the bishop and bishopric, and Puccinello Pedrone, syndic and proctor of Diecimo and Pastina, that the communes of the Valdottavo who owed a sum of money for an estimo to the Luccan commune were trying to make the men of

Pastina pay a portion of that sum.[31] The men of Pastina refused to pay since they were part of the curia of Diecimo and under episcopal jurisdiction according to imperial privileges. They asked the Anziani to revoke the tax assessment. They further requested that the commune of Pastina be removed from the books of the estimo of the Luccan commune. They added that if this were not done, they would appeal to the pope. There is no decision recorded, and no other record of action by the Anziani, but since we have no record of an appeal to the pope and since the men objected to actions by another rural commune, it is unlikely that the Anziani risked an interdict in what was essentially a squabble between rural communes.

Luccan communal pressures on the immunities of the jura became stronger during the last quarter of the thirteenth century. In 1276 the commune and the bishopric argued over jurisdiction at Moriano.[32] The commune claimed the right to appoint the podestà of Moriano and to regulate Moriano as it regulated other suburban communities because, it argued, Moriano was within the district of six miles conceded to the city by imperial grant. The episcopal syndic countered with documents showing episcopal approval of the constitutions of Moriano, decisions recorded in the episcopal court, as well as other recognitions of Moriano's special status in the years 1259, 1262, 1263, 1269, and 1275. Faced with such a barrage of precedent, the judge of the Luccan podestà ordered silence on the Luccan commune and its podestà for the suburban communes.

Thus the commune of Lucca was forced, by its own communal courts, to admit that Moriano had a special legal status different from that of other rural communes within Lucca's district. But what exactly did that special status mean in practice? If we examine the series of appeals cited by the episcopal syndic we find that the communes of the jura were exempt from certain military exactions, the millers of the jura could not be regulated by the "captain of the millers of the Luccan city," and the commune of Lucca could not collect any pedaggio at Moriano.

A slightly different picture emerges if we quote the record of a witness who had been asked to testify in court.

Buonamore del fu Benecasani rector or lord of [the church of] San Ansano of Moriano was asked if the said lands served the Luccan commune in the host or cavalcatus and if they paid Lucca according to an estimation or lira of them just as others of the forza [district] of six miles. He said that he believed that the said lands and communes served the Luccan commune in the host and the cavalcatus and that by force and against rights and privileges the Luccan commune compels them to pay the lira and the estimo and that it has compelled them [to pay] for some years, but it is not many years that the Luccan commune has constrained them to pay in this manner. . . . He said that he is seventy years old.

Other witnesses also admitted paying taxes and disagreed only about the length of time that Moriano had paid taxes to the Luccan commune: fifty years, twenty-five years, or "since the death of the late emperor."

The commune may have paid taxes for as many as fifty years. In 1229 Rodolfo del fu Iacobo, consul of Moriano, swore an oath to the commune of Lucca at the request of the castaldi of the Luccan commune for the area beyond Ponte a Moriano.

[The castaldi] said that the consuls and men of Moriano and its pieve for forty years have been accustomed to swear at the command of the Luccan podestà and castaldo beyond Ponte a Moriano for Castro di Moriano, except for the honors and jura of San Martino and of the Luccan bishop and bishopric.[33]

The oath would seem to concern the agreement alluded to in Otto's privilege of 1209 concerning Castro di Moriano. There is no indication of just what rights Lucca had been able to claim in the district of Moriano, but most likely the agreement dealt with the use of Castro di Moriano as a defensive point and staging area in Lucca's twelfth- and thirteenth-century drive to subjugate the Garfagnana. But it may also have been the basis on which the Luccan commune claimed tax revenues from Moriano. Concerning taxes, however, our documentation shows only that by the 1270s the men of Moriano customarily paid some taxes to the Luccan commune, and by 1287 they were listed in the books of the estimo.

Probably as a concession designed to placate the commune, Bishop Paganello ordered in 1287 that the men of the jura should be included under communal regulations for the victualing of the city.[34] In the concession Paganello recognized the importance to the commune of provisioning policies—"without which there can be no life in the city." He went on to allow the judge in charge of provisioning "freely licensed authority and full power in all and against all lay fideles and subjects of the same bishopric's jurisdiction and power over their goods." Hence, the judge could proceed in legal questions against these men and in matters of victualing he was allowed "to do what the bishop can do." The bishop required only that half of all resultant fines should be the bishopric's and that this commission in no way should be understood as an acquisition by the commune of rights in the lands and jurisdictions of the bishopric. Paganello must have recognized that the only way to protect his jura from communal interference was to compromise with the commune on those issues about which the commune felt most strongly.

The commune of Lucca was not entirely appeased, however, and between 1307 and 1309 it renewed its attack on the jura at Moriano by again declaring that the bishopric's jura at Moriano was a part of the Luccan district.[35] Bishop Enrico responded by placing the city under interdict. At the same time the commune began negotiations and sent ambassadors to Pope Clement V. Finally, however, it agreed to whatever the pope or his delegate should order. Clement then ordered the commune to turn over possession of Moriano to his delegate, Stefano, rector of the pieve of Campoli, or to the bishopric, and promised that the interdict would be lifted. The commune lost a good deal of influence in the jura. It specifically had to give up again its claim to the right to appoint the podestà for Moriano.[36]

After its difficult and unprofitable adventure in Moriano, the commune did succeed in claiming the bishopric's jura at Sorbano del Vescovo.[37] The action is recorded in a controversy between the commune of Lucca and the bishopric in 1330. The Minor Sindaco of the commune, ser Federigo of Pistoia, appealed an earlier decision of the commune's Maggior Sindaco concerning the rights to the jurisdiction of Sorbano del Vescovo. Ser Federigo argued that Sorbano was under the jurisdiction of the commune because it was within the radius of six miles and because the commune had exercised jurisdiction there for so long that memory to the contrary no longer existed. As proof he claimed that the men of Sorbano had paid and continued to pay imposts, served in the army, and allowed themselves to be included in the estimo. The bishop's syndic, Simone Tediccione, denied that the men of Lucca ever possessed jurisdiction; if they did, he said, it was "by way of usurpation or against the will of the Luccan bishop and bishopric."[38] Significantly, he did not deny the payments or the fact that the men of Sorbano performed military service for the commune. He also neglected to include in his defense a barrage of precedents like that included by the episcopal syndic in the case concerning Moriano in the 1270s.

Compared to the spirited defense by earlier episcopal representatives, Simone Tediccione's conduct of the case does not appear to have been much more than pro forma. This might lead one to assume that by 1330 it was accepted by all, including episcopal officials, that the Luccan commune had the right to certain aids and services from Sorbano, and perhaps from the rest of the jura. That the agreement was not so general is shown by the actions of Pope Benedict XII.

In 1341 the pope ended an interdict placed on Lucca by Pope John XXII in 1328. The interdict was part of a papal attack on Emperor Louis, his antipope Pietro Rainalucci of Corvaia, and, most of all, Louis' vicar in Tuscany, Castruccio Castracani degli Antelminelli, lord of Lucca, Pisa, and Pistoia. Only Castruccio's inopportune death in September 1329 had saved Florence from falling to his army. When the interdict was raised, we get a few small clues as to the relationship between the commune and bishopric. The Luccans sent proctors to Benedict and they promised

that the aforesaid commune, people, and men will not impose dazi, gabelles, or collections or pedaggios or other burdens . . . [editor's deletion] on churches or the aforesaid ecclesiastical localities and persons against rights, direct or indirect, public or private, nor will they exact imposts, nor will they give aid, counsel, or favor to those imposing or exacting them; hence they will conserve the same churches and ecclesiastical localities and persons in their rights and liberties.[39]

The promise may have been aimed primarily at clerical taxation, but it doubtless acknowledged complaints registered by the communes of the jura over taxation.

During the 1330s the communes of the jura had been included in the estimi, but they do not seem to have paid direct taxes. The bishop did make a convention with the commune in 1334, to the effect that the commune of Moriano would pay £1,500 each year and in return be exempted from all communal taxes except the salt tax.[40] The agreement was probably intended to meet some extraordinary expenses, because it was ended after two years. In 1336, when Lucca was negotiating over ending the papal sentences against the commune, the Anziani of Lucca wrote to the communes of the jura that they would not be made to bear any taxes or other burdens for the Luccan commune for the next year, with but two exceptions. They were excused from the militia unless every other commune of the district was asked to send troops. "And they shall have to accept an impost on salt and for it they shall have to pay to the Luccan commune and the dogana as they presently are accustomed [to pay] and as it is contained in the books of the Luccan dogana."[41]

After Benedict raised the interdict, Lucca itself does not seem to have tried to gain further exactions from the jura, but the communes of the jura were still bothered by communal tax farmers. In 1346 and 1347 the episcopal proctor, ser Spinello Fiorese, complained to the judge of the Gabella maggiore about rapacious tax farmers who were

compelling the communes themselves and the men of the same [communes] to pay the gabelle . . . , that they cannot be held nor do they have to pay . . . since they are not found in the charter of purchase . . . , but expressly were excluded from the sale and the aforementioned gabelle precisely because they are not under the jurisdiction of the Luccan commune. . . .

This clearly was the action of individual tax farmers who saw a way to increase their own profits. There is no evidence that the commune supported their claims, and immediately upon hearing the complaints the court ordered the farmers to cease such practices, return the taxes collected, and retract all penalties.[42]

The commune's attitude toward the tax immunities of the jura changed again in the 1350s. Possibly because of the economic problems brought on by the plague, or continuing military expenses, Lucca tried to increase its tax revenues from Moriano. Bishop Berengario and his fideles in Moriano did not deny that certain taxes had been paid, they simply denied that any new taxes could be added. Berengario emphasized his opposition by abandoning the city; the men of Moriano took the simpler and more direct expedient of killing several communal agents who dared to enter the jura.[43] The problem apparently was settled quickly, for in August of 1351 Berengario announced that he was returning to the city. In 1358, we get a hint of the probable compromise.[44] In that year representatives of the communes of the jura appeared before the city council of Lucca; the council declared that any bans laid against inhabitants of the jura were commuted and that the men of the jura "shall enjoy the benefits and privileges and other [rights] just as other contadini and inhabitants of the Luccan commune's district." In return the communes of the jura agreed to pay a total of £374 16s. 6d. (in addition to the salt tax) each year for the next ten years. All other provisions and regulations which the Luccan commune made for the Luccan contado did not apply to the men of the jura's communes or to their products. And finally, the men of the jura were exempted from any exactions if they held land in a part of the contado outside the jura, just as Luccan citizens who held lands in the jura were not to be molested.

These negotiations indicate the extent to which the financial arrangements had been compromised. The agreement seems to show that after the violent struggle of 1350–51, both the Luccan commune and the communes of the jura had found a basis for cooperation. To emphasize this cooperation the episcopal vicar general, Matteo di Città di Castello, wrote in 1371 to episcopal officials in the curia of Moriano that they were to accompany officials of the Luccan commune sent into the jura for the exaction of the gabelles on salt or whatever other exactions the Anziani should impose. They were further ordered to require a fine of 100 florins from any commune or 25 florins from any individual who refused to cooperate.[45]

COMMUNAL TOLERANCE OF EPISCOPAL JURISDICTION

Aside from the three major controversies in 1307–09, 1330, and 1350–51, the relations between the episcopal jura and the Luccan commune were for the most part peaceful. There seems to have been an extensive basis for agreement about the immunities and the duties of the communes of the jura. On three different occasions the communes of the jura successfully appealed to the communal courts when communal tax farmers overzealously entered the jura and demanded payments from the bishop's men. In 1346, the communes of the jura appeared before the court of the Gabella maggiore and successfully claimed exemption from the gabelles on movables and dowries.[46] One year later the same court ordered Pietro del fu Concione, who possessed

the right to collect taxes on new wine barrels and on other measures, to cease
his illegal collection of taxes within the jura of Moriano.[47] And finally, in
1348, the communes of the jura appealed that they were exempt from the
gabelle on wine.[48] As late as 1379, the Luccan commune still allowed the
communes of the jura exemption from all gabelles except that on salt.[49]

The relations between the bishopric, its jura, and the Luccan commune
during the thirteenth century and at least the first eight decades of the fourteenth century seem to have been fairly stable. While the commune did exact
some taxes from the jura, the bishopric's men remained exempt from a host
of gabelles on wine, bread, and manufactured goods that Lucca did exact
from other areas surrounding the city. Episcopal jurisdiction at Sorbano was
lost, but the commune never completely destroyed the bishopric's jura.

The communal attitudes toward the bishopric's special jurisdiction resemble in some respects the situation that Marvin Becker has reported in
Florence. Before the 1340s Becker found what he called the "gentle *paideia.*"
That is, the commune accepted without much question the special jurisdictions and immunities held by the Florentine church and many old magnate
families. In the 1340s the commune responded to a series of crises, mostly
financial, with legislation,

culminating in the formation of the territorial state of the late *trecento,* that repressed
recalcitrant patrician, obdurate magnate, and overly expansive corporate bodies.
In the course of this process traditional forms of government intimately associated
with the era of the medieval commune dissolved, while successive regimes replaced
private immunities with public law.[50]

If, as Becker suggested for Florence, economic and political pressures led
to a change in communal attitudes toward special jurisdictions, then one
would expect to find such a change at Lucca during the early fourteenth century. Castruccio Castracani's attempt to establish hegemony over northern
Tuscany had bankrupted Lucca. Shorn of political independence, ravaged by
almost continuous war, Lucca should have experienced the same kind of
reaction. And by the mid-fourteenth century the jura did contribute men and
money to the commune and communal law did extend into the jura. But the
process had begun during the mid-thirteenth century and it was not a continuous development. The experience of the Luccan episcopal jura seems to give
partial confirmation to Becker's observations. But it is also true that the
communal attitude relaxed when the commune was no longer so hard
pressed. The increased communal influence in the jura was accomplished by
a series of crises followed by compromises that gave the commune a part of
what it wanted. Lucca encroached upon episcopal immunities, but it never
ended them. Controversies over taxes in the fourteenth century were not over
the commune's right to collect taxes from the jura, they were "taxpayers' re-
volts" against increasing taxes already paid and the imposition of new ones.

The arguments between bishopric and commune over the episcopal jura were in no sense conflicts of "Church and State." The rights claimed by the bishopric were always imperial concessions, and further, the commune does not seem to have objected to the separate jurisdiction in principle. The commune did not need to fear an independent jura because the bishop resided in the city and at times needed communal support, including its assistance to maintain order in the jura. Without the commune's aid the bishopric could not have retained possessions in the Valdarno as long as it did. That the "jura vescovile" continued to exist until 1726 is proof that the bishopric and the commune looked upon each other not as enemies, but as partners in providing uniform laws and government throughout the countryside.

6

Sources of Wealth

Italian bishoprics, like civil governments of the Middle Ages, constantly found themselves needing more revenues to carry out their work. Expenditures must have been many and varied but only the most fragmentary information about their nature remains. Whereas there are numerous partial or complete inventories of possessions, no similar records or registers of expenditures have survived—and it is doubtful that they ever existed.

Episcopal financial administration never developed a bureaucratic structure comparable to that of the communes. Relative to communal government, the episcopal bureaucracy remained small. While communal officials served a defined term (usually six months), episcopal officials served at the pleasure of the bishop. While communal officials were required by statute to undergo an audit at the end of their terms, episcopal scrutinies seem to have analyzed only income. Lacking the accounts of expenditures, it is impossible to evaluate the areas, or measure the impact, of episcopal expenditure.[1]

The fragmentary reports remaining in the archive indicate that episcopal expenses included many expenditures that today would be considered the responsibility of secular governments. The bishopric had to pay for the construction of castles and defensive works. It contributed troops to the communal army. In times of need the bishops could feel called upon to provide grain. As early as the eighth century, the bishopric transported grain and salt from the Maremma to provision Lucca. In the twelfth century the bishops on occasion still would supply grain. During the famine of 1180, Bishop Guglielmo I found it necessary to pawn parts of his treasure in order to alleviate the misery in the city.[2]

Payments were also made to churches and religious corporations within the diocese, but of this only indirect evidence remains. In 1180, the bishop gave his portion of the tithes of five pievi to the hospital of San Jacopo of Altopascio for the nominal rent of three libre of wax. The bishop may have aided other hospitals by similar grants at comparatively low rents. Twenty-eight of the 30 hospitals recorded in the *Martilogio* of 1364 were making small payments like that of San Jacopo.[3] By the end of the twelfth century both the cathedral chapter and the canons of San Frediano had received rights to tithes from the bishop.[4]

The bishopric also had to make a variety of payments to support the Roman church and to send proctors to the Holy See.[5] The papal tithes of the late thirteenth and early fourteenth centuries are only the most famous of these payments.[6] Early in 1260, the bishopric and the rest of the diocese had to pay an estimo to the papacy for the expenses of the bishop of Monopoli who had served as papal legate in Lucca.[7] In addition, the bishopric made annual payments to the papacy, among them the 50 soldi it owed for possession of the pievi south of the Arno.[8] The total amount of these exactions as well as the normal administrative expenses must have been significant. In no case do we know the cost of the bishop's official family, although the expenses necessary to maintain notaries, castaldi, proctors, and nunzios could not have been minor.

Added to these annual expenses, the bishopric had to bear some of the costs of warfare. The Pisan-Luccan battleground during much of the eleventh, twelfth, and thirteenth centuries was in the middle of the bishopric's jura south of the Arno. Bishop Guercio's concession of the defense of Santa Maria a Monte in 1254 suggests that hitherto, the episcopate had borne the costs of defending its territory in the Valdarno.[9] Added to these direct costs of warfare were significant indirect costs. Episcopal pedaggio revenues were certainly adversely affected by reciprocal agreements between the members of the Tuscan League of 1282 to lower road taxes paid by the citizens of the various jurisdictions.[10]

The bishopric usually met its expenses without too much difficulty. It did, of course, have to take occasional loans to meet expenses, but only in the early years of the fourteenth century is there any evidence of large loans. In 1301, Pope Boniface VIII gave the Luccan bishop permission to pawn lands in order to raise 3,000 florins necessary to expedite unspecified matters before the Holy See. In 1306, there was a record of a 1,000-florin loan to the episcopate, and in 1308, Betto of Coreglia, acting for the bishopric, gave in pawn for two years lands paying annual rents of £750 to several Luccans in return for a loan of £1,050 to the bishopric![11]

The bishopric's sources of income were as varied as its expenses. It received payments for essentially religious activities, such as the selection or ordination of rectors of churches or hospitals, or abbots for monasteries.

These payments appear to have been largely nominal in value. In the *Martilogio* of 1364, the larger of two payments noted as being made "at the time of the confirmation of a new rector" was only two libre of wax.[12] Other occasional payments were made when new churches or hospitals were founded.

The secular revenue sources such as road taxes and income from urban properties, mills, and agricultural lands are more significant and better documented. These are the revenue sources upon which my investigation concentrates.

A study of the revenues of a single Italian bishopric could help us to understand several historical problems, for example the decline of the thirteenth-century Italian bishoprics. After taking a lead in the reconstruction of Italian society in the eleventh and twelfth centuries, the bishops tended to become, in effect, "rural lords" dependent upon their agricultural lands. The reasons for the shift are in part political, but we must attempt to ascertain what economic forces contributed to the change. What were the results of this process that has been called "il feudalismo di ritorno"?[13] The problem is one of how the bishopric chose to utilize its financial resources during the thirteenth and fourteenth centuries.

The explication of the bishopric's problems also involves wider issues which affected all levels of Italian society. We must examine certain basic changes which were occurring in Italian agriculture, such as the formation of new farms called *poderi*. To what extent did the bishopric take part in this fundamental restructuring of the Italian countryside? Closely related is the question of the effects of the so-called economic decline of the late Middle Ages. When did it begin and how did it affect the episcopate's exploitation of its agricultural resources?

Our ability to deal with these questions hinges, of course, on the extant documentation. The restrictions are in many ways similar to those encountered in studying the jura. Surviving leases seem to be only a fraction of those which at one time existed. We cannot consider them a properly random sample, however, since they seem to form geographical and chronological clusters.[14] I have record of only 20 contracts from the second half of the twelfth century. On the other hand, there are 30 contracts from the Valdarno dated between 1211 and 1220—most of them from the curia of Santa Maria a Monte. There is another concentration of leases for the same area in 1266-67, but almost no leases after 1267. Again, though the *Martilogio* of 1364 indicates extensive holdings in the middle Serchio region, we find only occasional leases from that area, except for the 30 years between 1231 and 1261. The situation in the Valdera is the same, a high concentration of leases from the late 1250s, a lesser concentration in the early 1320s, but almost no mention of the Valdera in the *Martilogio* of 1364. Thus we cannot hope for complete coverage of the various geographical areas.

We face equally serious problems when we try to establish just how the individual tenants cared for their lands. Sub-leasing and perpetual loans appear to have been common, but the archiepiscopal archives tell us next to nothing about the nature of these leases and loans. We also know little about commodity prices and nothing at all about agricultural technology— both essential subjects if we are to determine the state of the Italian peasantry at the end of the Middle Ages.

The leases often lack the very information we could most likely expect them to contain. The lands being let may be described only by the name of the former tenant, or perhaps simply as a podere without precise information about the number of pieces of land or their size. Many place names have changed or disappeared completely. It is often impossible to establish just what type of land was let. The district of Moriano, for example, included bottom lands along the Serchio River and low hills of 200 to 500 meters, as well as mountain lands. The description of the land (when we have it) is generic. "Terre cum arboribus et vitibus" were not necessarily wooded vineyards. Many times the rents from such lands were to be paid in grains. These lands were probably much like the fields in the modern Luccan countryside—small fields with trees and vines planted around the edges.

Thus the leases were spare practical documents including only the information which the inhabitants of the area could not be expected to remember—the term of the lease and the rent owed for the lands. Whether the rent had changed, or whether the land was a grain field or a meadow was of little consequence in writing a lease.[15] With these limitations in mind, however, we can still trace the major changes which affected the financial resources of the Luccan episcopate.

MINOR SOURCES OF WEALTH

By the fourteenth century, episcopal wealth was primarily in rural lands, yet the bishopric still retained other less important sources of income. Some of these may have been significant in the eleventh or early twelfth centuries, where we have almost no documentation, but by the late thirteenth or early fourteenth century they had declined in value. We must consider such topics as market dues, tithes, mills, road taxes, and urban housing. In most cases our information is fragmentary, although we may find suggestions of why these revenue sources remained minor or disappeared altogether.

MARKET DUES

Dues from markets were very important in the eleventh century when, according to Cinzio Violante, "a very numerous [group of bishoprics] acquired the right to found and supervise urban markets and to collect the customary taxes."[16] At Lucca, the market of the spice dealers and money changers was in Piazza San Martino, the medieval "court of St. Martin," in front of the cathedral. The oath of the money changers was inscribed on the front of the cathedral of San Martino in 1111: "to maintain the justice of the court of the church of St. Martin"; we can interpret this to mean that then, at least, the rights of the market belonged to the bishopric.[17] Unfortunately, imperial and papal diplomas do not specify what market rights the bishopric possessed, saying only that the episcopate shall have the "curte Sancti Martini."[18]

The only other market the episcopate definitely possessed was at Forcoli in the Valdera. This market was probably very old, although it is first mentioned in an agreement in 1227 between the bishopric and the commune of Forcoli for the construction of a market in an area called "mercantale." One half of the rights to the market was the bishopric's, the other half belonged to the commune.[19] The bishopric at one time must have had similar rights at Santa Maria a Monte, Montopoli, and Moriano, though the rural communes probably had taken control of those markets by the late twelfth or early thirteenth century. Thus, in the later Middle Ages, market rights were a very minor revenue source for the bishopric.

TITHES

Tithes, too, seem to have been unimportant during the thirteenth and fourteenth centuries. The bishopric's portion of the tithes was often in the hands of the local parish or rural commune. The bishopric may have virtually alienated the tithe payments, either because of local opposition to tithes or because it was inconvenient to collect them. The tithe payments to the bishopric seem to have been largely symbolic—usually a few libre of wax.[20]

WATER MILLS

Water mills provided a more significant source of revenue. At Lucca, they powered fulling mills for the cloth industry and mills for making flour and crushing olives. On the episcopal lands, the mills were used almost exclusively for milling grain and crushing olives. Mill rights were, in origin, signorial rights deriving from possession of manors and jurisdictions. The earliest mention of water mills owned by the bishopric is in a contract of 874 for the reconstruction of a mill at Teupascio in the Maremma.[21]

During the eleventh and twelfth centuries, water mills were built throughout the diocese. In the eleventh century, the cathedral chapter bought two mills near the city of Lucca. During the twelfth century the chapter, the monastery of San Pietro of Pozzeveri, and laymen were all involved in mill construction.[22]

In a provocative essay, Marc Bloch[23] argued that the proliferation of water mills during the Middle Ages was related to the possible revenues available to the rural lords who held the milling rights. Hand mills, according to Bloch, would have been more economical. It is unlikely that the Luccan mills were built for this reason. Although the episcopal mill at Teupascio was a part of a manor, as were some of the mills belonging to the chapter and San Pietro of Pozzeveri, a number of the twelfth-century mills were very near Lucca or large communes. Further, Tuscan communes encouraged the construction of flour mills as part of their general policies to provision their expanding populations.[24] Hand mills may have sufficed for low manorial populations, but large urban centers required larger mills.

Probably because it was expensive to construct the runs and the mill itself, the first twelfth-century mention of mills on the episcopal lands is a lease of mill rights in the district of Moriano: in 1115, the bishop gave the milling rights to three men from Sesto di Moriano for an annual rent of six stai of wheat.[25] In the early twelfth century such a lease of mill rights may have seemed profitable, but in fact the greatest profit was to be found in ownership of the mill itself.

That the bishopric also was constructing mills is seen from an agreement of 1141 between the bishopric and the abbot of the monastery of Sesto concerning possession of the episcopal mill on the Usciana canal.[26] The location of the mill "infra curtem de monte calivoli" meant that the episcopate had built a mill within an area under the secular jurisdiction of the abbot—which made such an agreement absolutely necessary. The mill probably served the episcopal lands at Santa Maria a Monte and the nearby town of Montecalvoli. The abbot promised that he would not build a mill along the Usciana canal without the express permission of the Luccan bishop.

Litigation between the rector of the pieve of Santa Maria a Monte and the episcopate gives a clear indication of how the mill was constructed. In 1215, the episcopal advocate, Giova del fu Carnelevare, before Uguccio Arlotti who had been chosen as arbiter by the litigants, asked the clerics of the pieve for unpaid rents and interest on a mill in the Usciana. Giova said that the rector of the pieve had received two "sepes" (possibly a type of wing dam or canal in or along the Usciana) for the purpose of constructing a mill. The clerics of the pieve were to pay two moggi of wheat and all large fish, lampreys, and eels taken from the canal.[27]

This was not the only episcopal mill in the district of Santa Maria a Monte, for just two years after the litigation, in 1217, the bishopric let one eighth of another mill to one Buono del fu Buono for an annual payment of six quarre of grain, 28 eels, and an entry-fine of seven soldi.[28] Buono may have been a speculator rather than a miller, as it is unlikely that a miller would have been content to share operation of the mill. Further, Buono also received leases of five pieces of land, two of them in the center of the town of Santa Maria a Monte, all of considerable speculative value.²⁹ A series of litigations between 1222 and 1230, between the bishopric and a consortium known as the Lambardi of Santa Maria a Monte or Colle, confirms the suspicion that the bishopric let the mill to individuals who did not directly operate it. These men, who very probably had controlled the commune during the early thirteenth century, had combined possession of the mill with their control of the pedaggio in the district of Santa Maria a Monte.

The Lambardi returned the larger mill to the bishopric in the 1240s. The bishopric continued to have trouble collecting its rents from the men who possessed the mill. Episcopal officials finally became more careful about who held the mill. When we next hear of it, in 1274, the custodians of the episcopate let the mill to Giunta del fu Buonacurso. Giunta had been the episcopal castaldo at Santa Maria a Monte in 1265–66 and in the lease document he was called a "*converso* [i.e., a layman who followed monastic discipline] of the aforesaid bishopric." The lease gave Giunta the rights to the pedaggio as well as the mill. He must have been chosen simply because the men who formerly held the pedaggio and mill had not made the required payments to the bishopric. The officials went on to appoint Giunta "syndic and proctor" for the recovery of the pedaggio revenues from Ricomano di Ciassarino and his associates and the mill revenues owed by Bellagatto Mungnio.³⁰ Giunta was to turn over whatever he collected for the mill to the bishopric; the document does not mention any remuneration for Giunta. He probably received financial support as a converso. In 1294, the bishopric again let 9.5 out of 12 parts of the mill for a specified rent of 36 stai of wheat, 200 dried eels, and all large fish valued at more than 12 denari.³¹

In the early fourteenth century, political affairs continuously affected mill revenues. In 1317, when the Pisans again gained control of Santa Maria a Monte, the bishopric gave Giovanni del fu Guglielmo Amati, a Pisan citizen, a 29-year lease of the mill for an annual £60 rent. The conversion to a money payment must have occurred because the Pisans would not allow the bishopric to export grain from what was then considered part of the Pisan contado.³² The change to a money rent was probably an economic blow to the bishopric, because wheat was generally a better protection against changes in the economy than a money payment.

The mill was then within another commune's jurisdiction and the episcopate's ability to profit from it was restricted. Just how restricted is shown by a lease of the mill in 1354.³³ The mill was let to a group of men from Santa Maria a Monte: Lippo del fu Giunta received one half and Duccino del fu Giorgio, Jacopo del fu Selmo, Michele del fu Talucce, Tomeo del fu Turrello, Dino del fu Niero, and Niccolao del fu Rainuccio received the other half. The men were given the mill for 29 years for an annual rent of £48 and 50 salt-cured eels. What was significant about the lease was that it contained a provision for renegotiating the rent if the mill was damaged during a war or if the Florentines prohibited milling (by 1354 the Valdarno had been incorporated into the Florentine state). Perhaps the Florentines preferred to restrict milling in the countryside, hoping that the grain would be brought to Florence and only ground when it was needed for consumption there. The other possibility is, of course, that the restriction of milling was a way to force the bishopric to accept the Florentine conquest of the jura in the Valdarno. The clause probably was meant to take into account problems that had already arisen. In 1343, the Anziani of Lucca had written to Pope Clement and to the lord of Florence, Duke Walter of Athens, asking that the Luccan bishopric's rights in the Valdarno be recognized. The Anziani complained to the pope that the Florentines had interfered with the bishopric's revenues as well as with its jurisdiction.[34]

Placing restrictions on milling could be a valuable tool for negotiating with a recalcitrant bishop. The Luccan commune probably was not above using it too. In January of 1346, the episcopal mill at Marlia was enjoined from milling grain "pro mallo lucani communis." Our information comes from a document by which an earlier lease of 1342 was voided without further explanation. Literary sources do not mention the incident, though we might guess that it involved matters of taxation since that was a continuing issue between the bishopric and commune. In any case, eight months later the mill was again in operation.[35]

The question remains as to how valuable the mills were to the bishopric. Unfortunately we can only guess. We cannot estimate, for example, the value of the fish and eels which were part of the rent paid at Santa Maria a Monte. If we assume that the fish, eels, and grain paid by the major mill at Santa Maria a Monte were worth £60 in 1260 (the money rent paid for the same mill four decades later), then that mill represented almost two percent of the bishopric's estimated wealth of £3,500.[36] The total value of the mill revenues still escapes us. If, however, we consider that the bishopric had a large mill in the Valdera at Padule, and others at San Gervasio, Marlia, Sala di Garfagnana, and San Pietro di Valdottavo, as well as the two mills at Santa Maria a Monte, we must conclude that the total value was great.[37]

URBAN RENTS

Another source of income which we might assume to be important was urban rents. Since the bishopric was an urban organization, we would expect it to exploit its urban revenues to the fullest. The thirteenth-century cathedral chapters at Gaeta and Amalfi did have large urban holdings.[38] Evidence of urban rents is strangely lacking, however, in the thirteenth-century records of the Luccan bishopric. We must consider why this was so and the extent to which the bishopric actively exploited the urban lands it did hold.

During the eleventh and twelfth centuries, the reform bishops busily attempted to recover properties lost during the previous centuries. As seen earlier, a part of this energy was expended in forming territorial curie in the countryside. To follow this policy, the bishopric needed liquid capital, money, and jewels or other valuables with obvious market value. In this period of episcopal revival, urban properties represented an easily marketed form of real capital.[39]

At Lucca, the bishop owned properties in several areas within or very near the city walls. According to papal and imperial diplomas the episcopate's urban lands were the corte of San Martino, comprising the piazza of the cathedral and the surrounding area, the meadow of San Columbano, and the lands surrounding the church of San Pietro Somaldi.[40] As the city grew, demand for houses and shops created a sure market for lands within the city walls. At Milan, Cinzio Violante found examples of houses selling for £24-30 in the first half of the eleventh century.[41] Eleventh-century prices in Lucca were lower, reflecting perhaps the less precocious urban development in Tuscany. We have two indications of the cost of houses in eleventh-century Lucca: one house in Lucca was valued at £12 and another at £11.[42] Low as these prices are, they are higher than prices for rural lands. At Milan, ecclesiastical institutions tended to let urban lands at symbolic rents in an attempt to raise capital and yet escape provisions that church lands were not alienable.[43] The revenues thus raised could be used to repossess or buy rural lands, which were cheaper to keep up and—in the eleventh century at least—seemed to offer a safer investment.

Although we have little or no evidence of it, the Luccan bishopric may have followed a policy of alienating urban properties in order to amass rural lands during the twelfth century. At least a part of the episcopate's urban holdings was used to house episcopal officers and the cathedral chapter. In the mid-eleventh century, Bishop Giovanni gave part of the corte of San Martino to the chapter for the construction of a *canonica,* a house where the chapter could follow common life. Later, in the thirteenth century, there is evidence that one of the palaces in what is now Piazza San Martino was reserved for the layman who acted as the episcopal advocate. Members of the bishop's official family also received board and room and thus accounted for other of the bishopric's houses.[44]

In actuality, there is little evidence that the bishopric ever held much urban property. A rental agreement indicates that in 1165 the bishop owned a house in Lucca near the gate of San Donato, but the annual rent of one floor of the house was a mere six denari. Giuseppe Matraja's study of Lucca in the year 1200 indicates that the bishopric held only one house within the Luccan walls—at Posterule Malestafa.[45] The amount of urban lands listed in the *Martilogio* of 1364 as held by the bishopric is not significantly greater than that found earlier. In addition to the house at Posterule Malestafa, the *Martilogio* lists 12 other houses at San Columbano, San Pietro Somaldi, and Fratta—areas outside the walls in 1200 and thus not included in Matraja's study. We look in vain for any indication that the bishopric owned any shops —one of the most profitable kinds of urban property—in Lucca.

Our sporadic information about urban houses seems to show a rather dramatic rise in rent. A single house rented for 6s. 6d. in 1232. In 1257-59, one house in Piazza San Martino rented for 40 soldi while another at Fratta rented for 18 soldi. These figures probably do not represent realistic rent figures. Even higher average rents of £4 8s. paid between 1300 and 1319 might be half of what some lay landlords received.[46] Between 1250 and 1270, the Castracani family let houses for annual rents of £3, £4, £5, £7 10s., and £8.[47] The few bills of sale we possess indicate that the bishopric's rents rarely if ever amounted to more than 3.6 percent of the market value of the houses. In 1257, one house located near the episcopal palace and owing to the bishopric an annual rent of 40 soldi was sold by one layman to another for £55. In the early fourteenth century another house near San Pietro Somaldi was sold for £36; its annual rent to the bishopric was only 11 soldi (1.5 percent).

The profits were even lower in the rural centers. At Montecatini in 1201,[48] the bishopric had 51 houses in the old castle and the surrounding suburbs. The bishopric apparently alienated many of these houses in much the same way that the Milanese churches alienated their urban properties. Twenty-three of the houses were held as benefices and owed no rent.[49] The rents collected for the other 28 averaged just under three denari a year. Average rents paid in other towns in the countryside appear to have been almost as low as at Montecatini. The rents averaged two soldi between 1200 and 1220 and remained fairly constant throughout the thirteenth and fourteenth centuries. Although the number of extant contracts is very small, our evidence suggests that the rents may have continued to average about two to three soldi. The highest payment was 20 soldi and the most common payment during the thirteenth century was two soldi.[50] During the same period even the bishopric's urban rents at Lucca rose dramatically. It seems either that the bishopric was not interested in increasing the house rents in the country or, perhaps, that the demand for houses in the rural centers was declining.[51] Given the nature of our sources, our only firm conclusion is that the bishopric does not seem to have profited greatly from urban properties whether in Lucca or in the surrounding rural centers.

AGRICULTURAL LEASES

The situation is significantly different when we consider the bishopric's agricultural lands, its most important source of wealth. Agriculture's primacy is evident in a variety of ways. Agricultural leases constitute a major part of the extant parchments in the archiepiscopal archive. A cursory glance at the *Martilogio* of 1364 shows that a majority of the payments recorded were for agricultural leases. And officials of the bishopric were found dealing most often with agricultural matters.

The three primary concentrations of episcopal lands before 1000 were near Massarosa (in Versilia), on the plain of Lucca, and to the northeast of the city. In the twelfth and thirteenth centuries, however, the lands in Versilia were transferred to the chapter, leaving the bishopric to concentrate on lands on the Luccan plain, in the middle Serchio, and in the Valdarno.[52] The medieval pattern of crops was already established by the ninth and tenth centuries, since at that time grain, olive oil, and wine were appearing as commodity rents.[53]

By the eleventh century, the bishopric's exploitation of its agricultural lands seems to have been indirect. Demesne lands, the *res domnicata* worked by slaves and servile day laborers, were the exception rather than the rule. The preferred form of agriculture was to let lands to peasants on perpetual leases for a payment in money or commodities.[54] The lands held by the peasant, often called his *masseum,* were of indeterminate size; scholars generally define the masseum as the amount of land necessary to fulfill the needs of a single family.[55] The continued use of words like *masseum* probably indicates that there was a continuity of settlement patterns from our earliest documentation in the seventh and eighth centuries until about the year 1000.

During the tenth and early eleventh centuries, the system of dividing land among the various heirs and an expanding rural population combined to break up these traditional holdings. The results of David Herlihy's ingenious study of land trades and sales, noting the proportion of divided homesteads, show that this parcelling of lands reached its height about the year 1000:

From about 1000, however, certain elements within the depressed agrarian community, those with resources superior to their neighbors, began a vigorous effort at agricultural reorganization. That effort consisted importantly in an effort to buy up scattered pieces of land and marginal farms, to restore the "congruity" of holdings, to "reintegrate" estates too widely scattered—to make use of the language of the contemporary texts.[56]

Lucca's reformed bishopric of the eleventh and twelfth centuries seems to have followed Herlihy's pattern, with one important difference. The episcopate was interested in gaining or regaining control of jurisdictions. Through-out the period, the bishopric concentrated on acquiring castles and corti and the jurisdiction over these territories. Of the 13 purchases or donations that I have found dated between 1000 and 1050, only three could be considered "scattered pieces of land"; the rest include manorial jurisdictions and castles. Between 1050 and 1100, there were only five purchases of specifically agricultural land out of a total of 24. In the entire twelfth century, there are only 45 such acquisitions out of a total of 115.[57] These sales and donations of pieces of demesne lands or "omnia ex omnibus casis . . . tan domnicatus quam et massariciis," do not represent a new rationalization of tenures. At most, they probably represented a change of landlord for the farm tenant. As Elio Conti[58] noted of monasteries in general, this expansion was haphazard and ill-planned and the purchases did not represent fundamental social changes. "For the most part, it was a conquest of a juridic and not an economic character."

The social and economic change in Luccan agriculture is to be found in the leases made in the second half of the eleventh and in the twelfth centuries. The Luccan bishops restricted the number of leases given to magnates and others who were not required to work the land directly. In contracts given to magnates the bishopric had previously required only that the lessee see that the land was worked. This change in policy may have occurred as early as the episcopate of Giovanni II; it was defined by Pope Alexander II (Bishop Anselmo I) in an undated bull directed to the Luccan church. After blaming earlier bishops for their largesse in giving church properties to their own families and other powerful people (unnamed), Alexander ordered that no future Luccan bishop

shall endeavor to alienate, carry away, or give by any contrivance castles, *mansi,* lands, and possessions which we now have in our possession or which in the future the Church itself shall have gained by the gift of God [donations by pious laymen?] and from the creation of properties [possibly a reference to land clearance or other reclamation projects], unless he trades it in pawn for understandable necessities and without evil intention at the time . . . so that no one in the future shall presume to give as a benefice or concede as a livello or contribute in whatever manner the aforementioned goods of the Church except to farmers and laborers paying an account to the bishop himself or his envoy or his minister . . . .[59]

Such a prohibition was not uncommon in Italy during the reform period, and it was probably no more effective at Lucca than elsewhere. Even Alexander found it necessary at times to violate his own directive.[60] In the twelfth century, the bishopric occasionally conceded what appear to have been sizable holdings for moderate rents. In 1103, Rangerio, another reform bishop, let one fourth of all that pertained to the bishopric in Santa Maria a Monte for an annual censo of two soldi.[61] In 1181, Bishop Guglielmo gave by perpetual livello to Alberto del fu Ansaldo all of the episcopal possessions at the villa of Perignano (in the pieve of Triano south of the Arno) for an annual rent of 20 soldi. The amount of land given was not stated although Perignano, its castle, lands, and jurisdiction were part of a purchase made by the bishopric in 1158 for £150.[62] All this was let for very little more than the 12 soldi Bishop Anselmo I had received for the rent of a single vineyard a century earlier.[63]

Although there were such cases of leases to men other than farmers or laborers, it seems that the bishopric attempted to restrict its leases to those who worked the land. Documentation is scarce, but the extant leases indicate that the properties were small holdings usually described only as "pieces of land" rather than corti.[64]

The decline in the number of leases of large holdings given to affluent men also seems to coincide with a change in the name of the leases. Before the mid-twelfth century, the leases were called *libelli* or *livelli*. The new leases were called *tenementa* or occasionally *locationes*. A similar change occurs on the cathedral chapter's lands. "In general," concludes Philip Jones, "they were rustic leases, imparting a new name to the peasant *libellus,* with some of its older characteristics revived. . . ."[65]

These tenementa, like the earlier livelli which had been given to peasants, included the obligation to live on the land, to till the soil (or sometimes to have it tilled), to improve the land, and to pay rent and give services. Unlike the livelli of the tenth and early eleventh centuries, the tenementa did not include the duty to appear at the bishop's court for justice—a sign of servile status.[66]

The significance of the obligation to improve the land is not exactly clear. Philip Jones seems to overemphasize the duty to develop the land both in the livelli and the tenementa when he states that "the conventional instrument of improvement was the individual lease of land, by private lords or communes, *ad meliorandum* or for clearance."[67] In the Luccan episcopal leases the phrase states that the peasant shall remain on the land, till it, improve it, and not allow it to decrease in value. Even in the chapter's leases the phrase is always "detinebunt suprascriptas terras ad meliorandum et non peiorandum."[68] When actual improvements were to be required, they were specifically named in the lease. As early as 982, when the bishopric gave a libellus for 42 years in the Sienese Maremma, it required that the ruined mill on the property be rebuilt.[69] Comparable specific improvements were recorded in the eleventh, twelfth, and thirteenth centuries. One Gerbaggio del fu Buono received land "that was a vineyard and now is overgrown with brambles [*ster-*

petum] in Vallebuia" for an annual rent of 12 denari the first year and 4 soldi in successive years. In 1208, the bishopric required that a house be built in Buggiano.[70] Most of the leases did not include any requirement to drain, deforest, or alter the productivity of the land. In almost every case I have found, when specific improvements were required the lease called for the construction or repair of buildings.

Improvements not specifically required by the lease remained the property of the tenant. Countless documents record the purchase of the "melioramentum" from the tenants when the lease had expired or was being renegotiated. In 1246, Barbiero del fu Buonino of Marlia received £10 from the bishopric "pro melioramento" of the lands he held from the episcopate. Because of their sale Barbiero agreed that the annual rent would be raised by four stai of wheat. He previously had paid five stai of wheat, one and one half stai of barley, five denari, and half a rooster every four years, "mediam operam ad claudendum prati de Marlia," one fourth of a cart of wood, and half a cart of hay.[71] A lease contract of 1240, between the bishopric and Bianco del fu Guido of San Terenzio of Marlia and his wife Buonaventura, included a clause specifically stating the tenant's right to the improvements: "The said couple shall not have to sell the improvements of the said land to any person or place or to the bishopric, nor shall they have to make any inquisition concerning the improvements for the Luccan bishopric or for . . . him who *pro tempore* is bishop."[72]

The major reclamation projects at Lucca, as in most of Italy, were not accomplished by means of individual leases. As early as the mid-eleventh century, Pope Alexander II could claim to have sponsored a major project. In the list of episcopal possessions in his bull of the 1060s he included "the land which is called Cerbajola [Vallebuia] that we have caused to be returned from wilderness to fecundity."[73] How this was accomplished and at what cost is unknown. From the series of leases Alexander gave at Vallebuia it seems that the land was cleared, vines planted, and the land divided and let to individual proprietors.[74] Other improvements, such as the terracing of hillside vineyards and the construction of grape arbors, both of which are mentioned by the late thirteenth century, must have been the work of individual farmers, because we have no record of episcopal participation in such improvements.[75] Late thirteenth- and fourteenth-century documents describing lands "cum pergulis" offer the only indication of arbors in episcopal documents.

Large projects of drainage and flood control must have been attempted by both the Luccan commune and the bishopric. We have only scanty references to such projects and no information on the costs, organization, or technology involved. For the commune we have a terse note in the *Annales* of Tolomeo of Lucca that in 1182[76] the commune of Lucca completed a large reclamation project that included draining lands around the swamps of Buggiano and Sesto and along the Usciana canal and in the area along the Arno called Cerbaia. Similar communal projects must have continued throughout the fourteenth century. A levee was built at Saltocchio to protect Lucca from one branch of the Serchio, and in 1342 the city council of Lucca directed the Anziani to supervise annually repairs made on the Luccan defenses against the river. Controlling the waters of the Serchio was the aim of San Frediano's "miracle" and it remained a problem for the commune throughout the Middle Ages. Until the completion of dams on the Serchio in the twentieth century, Luccans called any great expense "as expensive as the Serchio to the Luccans."[77] Our only evidence for the bishopric's involvement in hydraulic projects is one lease at Moriano in 1234, which described the property as land "that the bishopric recovered from the river."[78] As with Anselmo's land clearance in the eleventh century, we have no information about when, how, or at what cost this reclamation was accomplished.

RENTS

The change in the rural landscape increased the potential profits for the episcopate but, as we have seen, it had to buy improvements from the tenant if rents were to be increased. Similarly, the bishopric could not arbitrarily raise rents even if no improvements were involved. Philip Jones has reported that on occasion, lay lords may have tried to evict tenants or raise rents by denying that the tenant held the land "per tenementum vel libellum."[79] When the bishopric tried this in 1218,[80] Buonconte del fu Buonello appealed the additional rent of eight stai of must wine which was added to his normal rent on the maseo he held from the bishopric. The tenant argued that his rent had been only two stai of must wine—the same as his father had paid. The episcopal advocate did not deny that the rent had formerly been two stai, but he asserted that the bishopric had the right to change the rent. The arbiter, without explanation, sustained Buonconte's appeal and ordered the bishopric to end this suit and any further litigation over the augmentation of the rent.

This affirmation of traditional rights is further supported by the history of a "podere seu maseum" at Diecimo.[81] A document of 1274 records that in the 1230s the late Ugolino Martinelli and his late brother Gerardo of Legnano had received from the archdeacon Opizone and the primicerio Ubaldo a lease of a podere of 22 pieces of land at Diecimo. Later (the document does not say how much later), the brothers alienated one of the pieces back to the bishopric and their rent was reduced by 28 stai of wheat. Then, in 1274, the castaldo of Diecimo restored the piece of land to the widow Guardata, Ugolino's daughter, for an annual rent of 28 stai of wheat. This contract indicates a surprising stability in the thirteenth-century countryside. That a piece of land could be reincorporated into a farm after forty years is amazing, but that the rent remained the same is even more so. These two cases illustrate the problems the bishopric had to face in trying to utilize to the fullest its agrarian resources.

Still, the bishopric occasionally did manage to raise rents. Both Philip Jones and L. A. Kotelnikova observed that by the late twelfth century, rents were being increased on the cathedral chapter's lands. The Russian scholar found that the new rents might be as much as eight times the previous rents. The related change from money to commodity rents was more than just a simple conversion—"sometimes a significant augmentation of rents in general happened."[82]

The conversion from money to commodity rents has been the subject of a long debate which is still far from settled. Unlike northern Europe, Italian agricultural rents had been, for the most part, paid in money during the tenth and early eleventh centuries. Far from indicating a "barbarization" of the economy, the conversion to commodity payments occurred in Italy at a time of growing urban markets and a revived economy.[83] The change to commodity rents is first noticeable during the eleventh century, and it continued through the thirteenth century. Near Mantua, it was only in the early thirteenth century that payments in commodities became more common than money rents.[84]

Explanations of the conversion are varied, and not entirely convincing. The simplest is that many of the religious bodies controlled the urban markets and therefore had a ready-made outlet for their commodities. Though logically sound, there is little documentary evidence to support it. Both Rosario Romeo and Cinzio Violante have sustained this view, but in reaction to it, L. A. Kotelnikova observed that the thesis is constructed basically on a single rubric of the twelfth-century Milanese constitution.[85]

According to a second, monetary, theory, a deterioration and shortage of money during a period of rapidly rising prices in the eleventh and twelfth centuries caused the change. There is little evidence of a "monetary crisis." According to a clause in a single lease contract, the value of Luccan money declined by half during the last thirty years of the twelfth century.[86] Such a theory is weakened by several factors, including the symbolic nature of many of the land and commodity prices quoted and the scarcity of documentation. Many of the money rents, such as two-denari rents, were so low that they could hardly be considered remunerative. Thus the rent actually may have been symbolic, the land in reality having been alienated. Land prices recorded in documents also may not reflect the land value. What appear as sales may often hide transfers of properties as pawns for loans, or restitution of mortgaged properties when the loan was repaid. In these cases, the price probably represents a sum lower than the actual market value of the property.[87]

Cinzio Violante, in objecting to a purely monetary explanation for the conversion to commodity rents, suggested that the transformation was a part of the revolution in outlook associated with the Gregorian reform.[88] The change was more apparent than real since, according to Violante, the small proprietors had always paid in commodities. The only real change was that the religious houses and the episcopates ceased renting lands to the wealthier classes who did not directly work the land.

While Violante's thesis has the advantage of linking the conversion of payments to easily dated and certainly profound economic and political changes, it is not completely acceptable. The payments owed by small landholders were never paid exclusively in commodities. When the pope-bishop Anselmo (who forbade leasing lands to all except farmers and laborers) let his newly cleared lands at Vallebuia, he specified payments in money and not commodities.[89] An 1187 inventory of all payments to the bishopric in the Valdarno indicates the continued importance of money payments.[90] The sheer numbers give some indication: 181 of 296 payments were made exclusively in money. If we compute the frequency of payments in money we find that nearly 62 percent of the payments were in money; only 27 percent were paid in wheat, barley, or other grains. Lest we overemphasize the absolute value of the money payments, we should note that the average money payment was just under 14 denari per person. While money payments may not have predominated on episcopal lands in absolute value, they represented 20 to 40 percent of the recorded payments to the bishopric through the first quarter of the thirteenth century.[91] The results of L. A. Kotelnikova's attempt to establish the absolute value of money and commodity rents shows that between 1075 and 1120, money rents still represented about 32 percent of the total value of rents paid in the Luccan countryside. Even as late as 1200, money rents accounted for 11 percent of the total value.[92] The money payments, though they were occasionally symbolic, continued to be included among the agricultural rents in the fourteenth century. Thus the change from money payments would seem to be more than just a shift away from leases to middlemen.

A part of the change seems rather to represent a change in the structure of Italian agriculture that goes deeper than renewed ecclesiastical vigor or a revaluation or possible shortage of coin. A growing urban population is more dependent on good harvests than a rural population. Cities often found themselves at the mercy of the market and consequently grain prices could fluctuate wildly. There is abundant evidence that during the thirteenth and fourteenth centuries communes attempted to regulate the grain prices and the movement of grain within the areas they controlled. There is, however, no evidence of regulation at Lucca in the eleventh or twelfth century.

In the second half of the twelfth century, fragmentary reports of wheat prices show a variation from three denari to eight soldi per staio. "In that year [1181]," reports Giovanni Sercambi,[93] "there was such a great famine that the staio of wheat cost seven soldi." The following year, he adds, wheat cost one soldo more. Lower, more normal (though still fluctuating) prices were recorded in 1193 (3s. 4d.) and 1195 (1s. 3d.).[94] Clearly profit was not to be found in taking a fixed money rent when the price of grain could fluctuate so rapidly and when the urban population was continuing to expand.

The conversion from money rents to commodity rents occasionally may have worked to the advantage of the tenant. While he lost the profit to be made in the years of high prices, he was protected against low prices.

The question remains as to how the conversion to a commodity rent or a rent increase was accomplished. Given the traditional nature of the peasant leases and the tenant's ownership of the melioramentum, any changes in rent had to be a quid pro quo arrangement.

The five earliest documented rent increases all indicate that the episcopate had to pay for the right to increase rents.[95] In 1137, Vivano del fu Moretto sold for 55 soldi, "nomine pignoris," a piece of land he held from the bishopric. The land was returned to him for a rent increased by eight stai of must wine and seven soldi. The second documented rent increase in the thirteenth century was in 1223, when the bishopric paid £6 for an annual payment of three libre of oil. The transaction occurred because Martino del fu Niero of Corciano needed money for the expenses of his daughter's marriage.[96] In 1242,[97] Gerardo del fu Vitale of San Terenzio of Marlia returned his podere to the bishopric and received it back at a rent eight stai of barley higher than the previous rent. For this he received £4 10s., "which denari the same treasurer [acting for the episcopate] has to pay for the debts of Gerardo himself to those creditors to whom he [Gerardo] obligated his land."

We would like to know more about the reasons for the indebtedness and why the tenants were willing to sell their melioramenta and perpetual rents on their properties. In some cases the money probably was used to buy plow animals, fertilizers, and other supplies necessary for increasing yields. Yet, Martino's declaration that he needed the money "for the honor of God and the marriage of his daughter Agnese" might be closer to the realities of peasant life in the thirteenth century. Other students of Tuscan agriculture have observed that the peasant often lived just at the subsistence level.[98] To possess only a marginal farm and to be cursed with several daughters who needed at least moderate dowries, might be just the combination that drove a peasant to accept higher rents. Improvements and new tools could be put off if there were no money, but a dowry and marriage expenses represented a social obligation which eventually had to be met. In mid-fourteenth century Florence, even a portion of the funded public debt was set aside for small investors who needed funds for dowries.[99] The only other case where we know why rents were changed concerns six men from San Terenzio of Marlia who, in 1239, returned to the bishopric their lands which owed "certas redditas et certa servitia."[100] The bishopric then returned the lands to the six for rents of between 11 and 24 stai of wheat and an oath of fidelity. The notary added that they were not to be considered *coloni* or of a servile condition "but shall be held to be just as other free men." The six had accepted higher rents so as to free themselves from their servile condition.

We have only 40 examples of raised rents (or indications that rents had been changed). Where we have record of the bishopric making a payment for the right to raise rents, it would be useful to be able to compute the bishopric's percentage return on the investment. That, unfortunately, is almost impossible. In a few cases where we can interpolate a commodity value, the percentage return varied dramatically. In 1246,[101] the episcopate paid £10 for a rent increase of four stai of wheat. In the same year wheat sold for only 1s. 7d. per staio, which meant that the bishopric received a return of only 3 percent on its investment. If the higher wheat prices of 1243 (6s.) or 1255 (4s. 9d.) were more normal, the bishopric's return was 9 to 12 percent. Conversely, in 1242, the bishopric paid £4 10s. for a rent increase of eight stai of barley (valued in 1243 at 3s. 4d. per staio), which would have meant a return of about 30 percent![102] In the few cases between 1223 and 1259 in which we can estimate the bishopric's return,[103] it seems to have been about 6 to 9 percent (remembering that the return varied according to commodity prices). This would indicate that the bishopric's return was relatively high, though not nearly so great as the rent returns of Pistoian businessmen of the late thirteenth and fourteenth centuries whose "thinly disguised usurious contracts," according to David Herlihy, "wrung from the peasant rates usually as high as 20 per cent and sometimes as high as 50."[104]

With but one exception the rent changes all come from the area of the Luccan plain or middle Serchio.[105] The changes are also chronologically restricted: the first 28 of the 40 examples occurred before 1260, 21 of them between 1223 and 1259. We might speculate that the need for cash was more keenly felt on the Luccan plain—the lands closest to the profitable urban markets. This explanation is not entirely satisfactory, because these rich plain lands within easy carting distance of the city ought to have been more profitable for the peasant, making outside sources of investment capital less necessary. It is more probable that the bishopric chose to invest its capital in this region. Diecimo, the most distant of these agricultural centers, was only 15 kilometers from Lucca and located on the Serchio. Episcopal lands in and beyond the Valdarno were all over 25 kilometers from Lucca in an area of almost constant turmoil because of the Pisan-Luccan wars. Hence, a decision to concentrate investments in the closer and presumably safer areas to the east and north of Lucca would be both reasonable and politic.[106]

As the bishopric attempted to increase its revenues by raising rents, it also required a payment called a *servitium* on the issuance of some leases. The servitium, according to Philip Jones, was simply the equivalent of the entry-fines often collected by English landlords—a payment necessary for the assumption of leases.[107] The English entry-fines often were collected from lands owing labor services to the lord. The entry-fine, then, occasionally could be a fee for the commutation of labor or other services. In other cases, the entry-fine was paid for possession of lands owing no rent or extremely low recognition-rent. Evgenni Kosminskiĭ cites fines twelve times the value of the annual rent and implies that this was not unusual.[108]

Collection of entry-fines at Lucca seems to have begun in the twelfth century, although I have found only seven examples of the episcopate collecting servitia payments before 1200.[109] The payments seem to have been collected most often in the second through the fifth decades of the thirteenth century. There are only two examples of entry-fines after 1250.

The economic significance of the servitia is difficult to establish. Philip Jones, in his study of the Luccan chapter's lands in the twelfth century, cites only three examples of entry-fines paid to the cathedral chapter.[110] There are 76 such payments to the bishopric recorded in lease contracts during the twelfth and thirteenth centuries (out of a total of over 500 extant contracts). These entry-fines are peculiar because they were collected almost exclusively from lands in the southern part of the diocese—at Santa Maria a Monte, Montopoli, and San Gervasio. Of the 77 servitia payments, only 12 were for lands located outside the Arno and Era valleys.[111] The entry-fines also differ from the English model since they were not collected only upon the renewal of hereditary leases, but when lands were let to a tenant who seemingly had no previous claim to the land. One common feature of many contracts in which servitia were recorded was that the rents specified were quite low, as little as a single denarius.[112] Rent payments of 12 denari or less represent 29 percent of the 63 cases where we know what rents were required for the lands. The most common rents collected on all contracts at Santa Maria a Monte were from one to ten stai of wheat—rents double or triple the highest rent payments in money for agricultural lands.

The contracts usually state that the entry-fine was paid so that the contract would be perpetual.[113] The formula recording the entry-fines paid to the cathedral chapter explains that the payment was made for the right to possess the lease.[114] The notarial form of the chapter's payments differs from the formula used in the episcopal records. Probably because the chapter's payments were made in the twelfth century—before the notarial formula was set—they are recorded in a much simpler style, for example, "Corsus dedit servitio sol. v predictis canonicis pro suprascripta libellaria acquirenda."[115] In this respect the chapter's payments are like those made by English tenants—payments asked for the possession of a lease.

The question remains as to why the entry-fines were paid almost exclusively on lands in the area of the Valdarno. Was population growth and competition for land greater in this area? Were these entry-fines a form of commutation of labor services?

Perhaps a single money payment was easier to exact than small annual payments in commodities. It is also possible that labor services were of little value to the bishopric in this area where its holdings were relatively scattered. There is evidence that during the twelfth, thirteenth, and fourteenth centuries, the bishopric retained some labor services in the Valdarno in the area of the middle Serchio at Diecimo, Moriano, and on the Luccan plain at Marlia, where episcopal holdings were larger and where the bishops customarily spent their summers. In the Valdarno, the bishopric could claim 35 labor or service payments. According to an inventory composed in 1187, the bishopric could collect 348 work days in the Valdarno. In most cases this was just a number—from one to 48—of days to be worked. Other common services were hauling or mowing duties during harvests. In one case three men owed five soldi for horses whenever the bishop travelled to Rome.[116] At Domazzano, near Diecimo, the bishopric gave a perpetual lease of a podere in 1232, requiring that the traditional rents and services should be paid.[117]

If the servitia were collected, in part, as commutations of labor services, this might explain why they were found when and where they were. As we noted earlier, the lands in the Valdarno were in an area of turmoil where the close supervision necessary to employ laborers was often impossible. Whatever labor services were owed for lands probably were more difficult to use effectively. Thus, the commutation of labor services could yield a greater return than the labor services themselves. In 1248, the bishopric converted the services owed by a *colono* in Aquilea (Moriano) into a rent of six libre of oil.[118] Thus, the entry-fine may have been required in place of services where the services owed were minor, or where rent collections were sometimes difficult. In other areas the servitia could be commuted into sizable rents.

The justification of the entry-fine originally may have been the commutation of labor services, but the documents show that entry-fines were also collected in areas where it is unlikely that services would have been owed. In five cases, the bishopric received the payments for leases of houses at Marlia, Santa Maria a Monte, and in the Luccan suburbs.[119] The bishopric in addition collected fines for a lease of the mill of Santa Maria a Monte (at Piedi-ripa) and for a lease of the revenues owed to the bishopric by four men at Montopoli.[120] In four other cases, the word *servitium* was not even used. The leases simply stated that the payment was "pro suprascripta locatione" or else "nomine intrate."[121]

Thus it appears that the servitia may have been, in most cases, a commutation of labor services, but that the payment could be collected because of the competition for lands. In a competitive market, the bishopric could change labor services of little value into entry-fines. During the twelfth century, when there were lands to be reclaimed, entry-fines were unusual. In the few twelfth-century contracts we have, there are scant notices of labor services, but our evidence from the Valdarno should alert us to the probability that such labor servics were owed at Marlia, Moriano, and Diecimo, where the Luccan episcopate had extensive manors. These services may have disappeared temporarily while the total acreage under cultivation was expanding and when there may have been a relative shortage of laborers. Although there is little direct evidence of such a labor shortage, such a situation in the twelfth century would conform to the English experience under similar conditions. In the early thirteenth century, after the plain and marshes had been drained and reclaimed, the commutation of services and collection of entry-fines was more common.[122] The cessation of entry-fine collection may indicate an end of the competition for lands.[123]

THE FORMATION OF PODERI

At the same time that the bishopric was converting and raising rents, changing labor services to commodity rents, and charging entry-fines, the Italian agricultural landscape was changing profoundly as larger agricultural units were formed. We must now attempt to assess the extent to which the bishopric influenced, or was influenced by, this movement.

During and after the twelfth century, Italian agriculture adjusted itself to a new base. The former foundation had been the *mansus,* a holding large enough to support a family. The mansi had been destroyed by population growth and a concomitant parcelling of lands. During the twelfth and thirteenth centuries, with the movement of many families onto newly reclaimed lands and into urban centers, larger agricultural units, the *poderi* or farms, took shape.

The formation of the poderi is a process as yet imperfectly understood. The podere is easily visible only in the early fourteenth-century tax records, but by then the new agricultural units were well established. In most of Tuscany, documents offer examples of poderi by the early twelfth century.[124]

Two scholars studying Florentine agriculture have provided essentially contradictory theories of the formation of the podere. Emphasizing the "tidy pattern" of the poderi, Philip Jones draws attention to the landlord. "It appears in a deliberate policy, forecast already in the twelfth century, but pursued most assiduously from the mid-thirteenth, of systematic resumption of customary land."[125] Jones argues that there was an evolutionary process, an obvious and rational goal toward which the landlord, lay or ecclesiastic, must have worked. Elio Conti does not seem as convinced that such a "tidy pattern" existed. "The birth of a podere was usually a slow, discontinuous operation, not always destined to succeed. It was rarely the definitive conquest of a single individual."[126]

The development of the podere is difficult to follow on the Luccan bishopric's lands. By the end of the twelfth century, the documents have ceased to speak exclusively of *sorte* or *mansi,* but they continue to describe leases of "pieces of land" not always defined as having buildings. Even though the notarial formula is vague, it is unlikely that these pieces of land were large enough to be considered a single agricultural unit capable of supporting a family.[127] The rents collected seem to point in the same direction. Many of the contracts required low rents of a staio of wheat or a single libra of oil, or a few denari in money. If we consider the number of pieces of land let in each contract (Table 4),[128] we find that at the end of the twelfth and in the early thirteenth centuries, the average contract was for only about two pieces of land. In the course of the thirteenth century and the early fourteenth century, the average number of pieces let in each contract increased rather dramatically. During the period 1221-40, the average number of pieces was slightly over three. The number remained fairly stable until 1280-1300, when the average number of pieces let by a single contract had jumped to slightly over four. The number of pieces per contract continued to increase in the early years of the fourteenth century.[129] Our survey at first seems to support Philip Jones's description of landlords trying to end customary holdings and his reports of attempts to merge various holdings into larger (and presumably more economically viable) units.

If, however, we consult the extant tax records from Moriano, a different picture of the formation of the podere begins to emerge. According to the tax records at Aquilea for 1286-87,[130] the 57 men who owed rents to the bishopric held an average of 9.2 pieces of land; one man held as many as 47.[131] The reason for their almost doubling of the number of pieces held by the individual farmer is that episcopal contracts have told only a part of the story. Twenty of the 57 men at Aquilea paid rents to more than one landlord. Some of the payments were separate rents for melioramenta, or a perpetual loan,

TABLE 4

Average Number of Pieces of Land per Contract

	Number of Contracts	*Pieces of Land/Contract*
1181–1200	7	2.00
1201–1220	39	1.97
1221–1240	142	3.24
1241–1260	187	3.00
1261–1280	68	2.95
1281–1300	15	4.20
1301–1320	58	7.50
1321–1340	39	5.42
1341–1360	6	2.50

NOTE: The figures include only those contracts in which the number of pieces was specified. Documents describing a "maseo" or "podere" without specifying the number of pieces of land have not been included in these figures.

but it remains likely that many if not most of the extra payments represented an attempt by the tenant to increase the amount of land he held. For the 20 tenants owing more than one rent, the average number of rents owed is 3.4. The average number of rents paid by all 57 men is 1.8.

If we expand our inquiry to include all the lands in the Luccan district (which comprises all the episcopal lands except those in Diecimo, Garfagnana, and the Valdarno) included in this *Estimo,* we find a similar situation. Throughout the Luccan district, those holding lands from the bishop held an average of 6.15 pieces of land. Throughout Moriano, an area of hillside vineyards and olive groves, the fields were smaller and each tenant held more pieces, averaging 7.7. The bishop and bishopric could claim little credit for this accumulation. On the Luccan plain at Tempagnano (ca. 4 kilometers east of Lucca, near Lunata), five men held an average of 28 pieces of land each, but an average of only four each from the bishopric. Of those people throughout the district who paid more than one rent, the average number of rents paid was nearly four (3.93).

The *Estimo* of 1286–87 from Moriano has given us clues that perhaps the bishopric was not a central force in the formation of the podere. If we consider the documents in which the notary chose to refer to the lands being let as a podere instead of as "petia de terra," we do not find an increased use of the term during the thirteenth century to describe the land being let by the bishopric (Table 5).[132] I find it used about five to ten times per decade between 1220 and 1280.

TABLE 5

Poderi Mentioned in Episcopal Contracts[133]

	Number of Poderi	Number of Extant Contracts
1221–1230	9	39
1231–1240	11	97
1241–1250	9	57
1251–1260	6	137
1261–1270	5	73
1271–1280	3	10

The bishopric also did not succeed in ending long-term leases—a policy which Jones argued was essential for the maximization of agricultural profits.[134] Instead, the bishopric continued to grant leases for 29 years or "in perpetuum." If we graph the number of leases for periods of less than 29 years (Graph 1), we find that these "short-term" leases were not more prevalent in 1250 than they had been in 1200. Nor does the number increase during the second half of the thirteenth century. In 1258–59, out of a total of 79 contracts (Graph 2), 23 were for less than 29 years—29 percent of the total. Only 53 of the 483 pieces of land recorded in the *Estimo* of 1286–87 had been let for periods of less than 29 years—only 11 percent of the total. Our evidence from Lucca seems to indicate that the bishopric in fact was moving away from leases of less than 29 years! Similarly, documents from the first half of the fourteenth century do not show a marked rise in such contracts. The bishopric does not seem to have followed a policy of centralizing holdings—or, if it wished to follow such a policy, it was unable to do so.

Although information from episcopal sources is only fragmentary, it appears that early in the thirteenth century, economic momentum began to pass from the episcopate itself to laymen. In 1227 and 1232, Martino, the son of one Orlando, received perpetual leases of six pieces of land in the area of Montopoli.[135] Later, in 1265, Barone, the son of Guido, received four leases of a total of 22.5 pieces of land at Montefoscoli (near Santa Maria a Monte). The bishopric did not think of these 22.5 pieces of land as a single farm, for the leases were given over the course of almost two months. Barone also did not consider the lands to be a farm: he sold his rights to one of the pieces almost immediately.[136]

Episcopal tenants sold or leased their rights to lands held from the bishopric and to the melioramenta they possessed on these lands. In 1192, two brothers, Roberto and Perfetto del fu Manniade, sold for £18 12s. a piece of

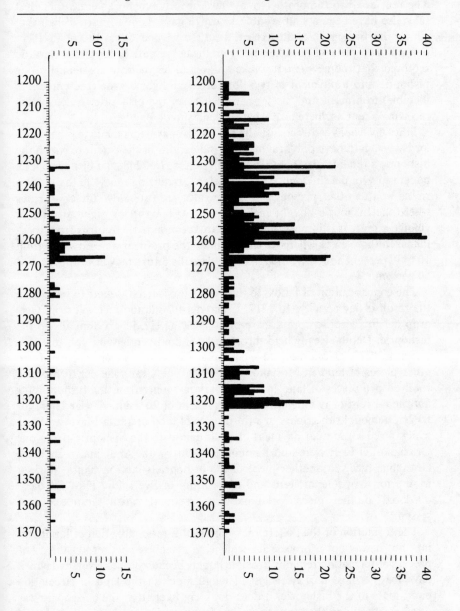

land at San Columbano (in the Luccan suburbs) which owed an annual rent of eight stai of wheat to the bishopric and four stai of wheat to themselves.[137] The rent owed to the brothers may have been for melioramenta, though it may also have been a simple sublease which gave them a return of half that which the bishopric could expect. In 1216,[138] one Gerardo del fu Piero Scroppi let a piece of land he held from the episcopate in Moriano. Gerardo required that the new tenant make an annual payment of six denari to the bishopric and a payment of two libre of oil and some wine (the amount is illegible) to himself and his son. In their case, the bishopric obviously was receiving a rent nowhere near what the land should pay.[139]

Since episcopal contracts usually did not list payments made to other landlords, we again have only fragmentary indications of the extent to which the bishopric's tenants also held lands from others. In 1248, the bishopric let a podere to Vita del fu Donuccio of Musciano, requiring rents "to the bishopric as well as other persons."[140] These sales are probably similar to cases where the bishopric bought melioramenta or bought the right to raise or change a rent. It is impossible to more than estimate the returns from these loans. In those cases where we can estimate the profit, it was anywhere from 10 to 18 percent annually, though in one case the return may have approached 50 percent.[141]

The concentration of lands, to the extent it occurred, seems to have been the result of lay activity. In 1217, Debio del fu Baldino received from Gerardo del fu Piero Scroppi a lease of land owing six denari annually to the bishopric. Debio already held three pieces of land contiguous with this one. Later, in 1223, Debio received a perpetual lease from the episcopate of two other pieces of land in Moriano.[142] In 1219, one Grandone del fu Moretto received two pieces of land in Santa Maria a Monte from the bishopric for an annual rent of two denari and a servitium of 20 soldi. A year later, for £6 2s., he bought the rights to a third piece of land in Santa Maria a Monte which owed an annual payment of eight denari to the bishopric, from one Graziano del fu Relfere and his mother, Schierlatta. And finally, in 1223, Grandone received another piece of the bishopric's land in Santa Maria a Monte for a two-denari rent and a servitium of five soldi. This last piece bordered another piece, presumably a freehold, which Grandone possessed.[143]

The formation of the podere may represent a rationalization of landholding, but it was not a process for which the bishopric was responsible. The process of formation remains invisible largely because leases given by laymen have for the most part been lost. Though much of the land in circulation owed rents to the bishopric, it does not seem likely that the episcopate was directly involved in the formation of the larger agricultural units. A policy of enlarging holdings would have required more control over the lands than the bishopric could exert. The inquests into landholding done for the bishopric in several areas are an indication that the bishopric continued to have difficulty knowing exactly who presently held episcopal lands.[144]

Nor were foreclosures on tenants effective. As Robert Brentano has observed in another context, medieval Italian courts always preferred compromise.[145] In suits involving unpaid rents, the Luccan communal courts or arbiters selected by the litigants usually tried to collect the unpaid rents, but preferred not to return the lands to the bishopric.[146] Such a policy almost always allowed the tenant to retain possession of his lands, and thus formation of poderi was possible only when those who held the land chose to do it.[147]

DECLINING EPISCOPAL PROSPERITY

During the course of the thirteenth century, the bishopric's efforts to control its agricultural lands may have declined, possibly because the policies which had been effective in the first half of the thirteenth century could not succeed in the second half.

While there are no reliable quantitative data available, there are hints that the Luccan countryside was not as prosperous in the second half of the thirteenth century as it had been earlier. There was a dramatic change in the distribution of churches. According to the *Estimo* of 1260, there were 750 churches, monasteries, and cult centers in the diocese of Lucca. The number recorded in the tithe payments of 1276–77 was 515.[148] If we examine the regions where the bishopric held its lands we find, for example, that San Gervasio had 25 subaltern churches in 1260, but only 12 were considered wealthy enough to pay a tithe in 1276–77. Santa Maria a Monte showed a similar though less precipitous decline: only 11 of its 19 subaltern churches paid the tithe in 1276–77. The decline appears in all parts of the diocese—at Marlia (from 7 churches to 5) and at Diecimo in the lower Garfagnana (22 to 13). Pietro Guidi, a church historian writing during the interwar period, assumed that the differences only represented errors made by the collectors of the papal tithe—an error of over 31 percent![149]

The exclusions from the tithe lists were not just random errors. In San Gervasio's district it was the subaltern churches in the small rural centers that did not pay. The churches in Montecastello, Forcoli, and Gello—the rural centers of some size in the district—did pay the tithe.[150] Similarly in the district of Santa Maria a Monte those churches not paying the tithe were outside the rural population centers such as Santa Croce, Castelfranco, and Montecalvoli. Many of the rural churches within Santa Maria a Monte's district that did pay the tithe in 1276–77 had been transferred into the rural centers sometime after 1260. A marginal note in the *Estimo* of 1260 records that the church of San Martino di Catiana "hodie est in Castrofranco." Notes appended to four other place names also indicated the transfer of a rural church into a larger rural center.[151] We must suspect that the lower number of rural churches recorded in the tithe receipts of 1276–77 represents a basic change in the makeup of the Luccan diocese.

This readjustment of rural churches may in fact indicate a demographic decline. David Herlihy[152] has found such a decline in rural population at Pistoia beginning in the second half of the thirteenth century. His figures show the number of rural communes in the Pistoian contado dropping from 124 in 1244 to 108 in 1255, to 64 in 1344, and to 53 in 1383. His figures indicate a rural population decline of 23 percent, from 31,220 in about 1244 to 23,964 in 1344. This decline, Herlihy found, "was in fact accompanied by a shift of major dimensions in the pattern of rural settlement": people tended to move away from the areas he designated as "the middle hills," districts at 200–500 meters above sea level. Such a shift would, of course, bring about the very changes we have observed in the Luccan pieve's relative wealth.

Our earlier findings also seem to suggest the beginnings of economic (and possibly demographic) regression at mid-century. When we investigated episcopal policy toward raising rents, we found that two thirds of the examples occurred before 1259. House rents in rural centers were stagnant throughout much of the thirteenth century. Similarly, servitia payments ended about 1250—there are only two extant examples of servitia payments after 1248. And the bishopric made few purchases of lands in the second half of the thirteenth century.[153]

If we consider that the bishopric did not seem to be an active partner in the formation of the new poderi or in changing agricultural technology,[154] we can conclude that there may have been less competition for farms and, possibly, that episcopal officials saw little reason to hope for high returns. If there were fewer farmers, it would be more difficult to exact entry-fines. Lower entry-fines have been used as key evidence of economic decline in fourteenth-century English agriculture.[155]

Our investigation, however fragmentary, shows a change in agriculture on the episcopal lands after the mid-thirteenth century. The reasons for this seem to be linked to fundamental economic and demographic problems in the Luccan countryside rather than to Luccan episcopal administrative policy. There is little evidence of less vigorous administration. Elio Conti has found that the religious houses lost control of their lands in the eleventh and twelfth centuries because these possessions were widely spread and acquired mainly piecemeal through pious donations which made efficient centralized administration difficult if not impossible.[156] This may be true for monasteries and hospitals, but there is little evidence of pious donations made to the bishopric after the early twelfth century. Further, its landed wealth seems to have remained stable throughout the thirteenth century.

The bishopric attempted to increase its profits from agriculture during the eleventh, twelfth, and early thirteenth centuries. But it never controlled its lands by means of short-term leases of fully developed poderi. The bishopric, unable to oust middlemen who were raising rents, was left with its traditional profits from the "locatio perpetua." Thus de facto control of the episcopal lands seems to have passed from the bishopric into the hands of those laymen who invested heavily in agriculture.

7

Tuscan Bishoprics in the Middle Ages

The temporal lordship of the Luccan bishopric in the Middle Ages had a long and varied history. At different times the bishop and episcopal officials found themselves involved in major problems of church reform, of papal and imperial diplomacy, of communal growth and expansion, and finally of economic and social change. In summing up the Luccan experience we must consider the extent to which it was unique.

Comparison with other Tuscan bishoprics is difficult because there are few studies of episcopal temporal lordships. With but one exception,[1] studies have treated the bishoprics only tangentially. Economic historians such as Philip Jones and David Herlihy have studied ecclesiastical lands primarily as exempla of more general economic trends.[2] Urban historians, on the other hand, use episcopal sources to illuminate earliest communal origins. Enrico Fiumi dedicated but a few pages to the place of episcopal policy in the formation of the commune of San Gimignano. Gioacchino Volpe, even while calling for more studies of the areas under episcopal temporal jurisdiction, had in mind only studies of the rural communes.[3] Our summation therefore will be incomplete. None the less we can evaluate the Luccan bishop's place in medieval Tuscany.

The structure of the episcopal temporalities changed dramatically during and after the eleventh-century reforms. "Every initiative of reform," observed Cinzio Violante, "found one of its primary and most important accomplishments in a vast program of recovery, organization, and expansion of what was considered the *res sacrae,* namely, of the ecclesiastical patrimony."[4] Where previously large parts of episcopal possessions had been held by magnate families, the reformed bishops resumed control of properties and purchased other lands and jurisdictions from hard-pressed rural lords; the bishops themselves became in effect rural lords. Luccan episcopal lands

116

and jurisdictions were concentrated in territorial curie primarily at Sala di Garfagnana, Moriano, Sorbano del Vescovo, Santa Maria a Monte, Montopoli, San Gervasio, and Forcoli. Similar decentralization occurred at Pisa, Pistoia, Florence, and Volterra, where episcopal jurisdictions were found in many parts of the diocese. An exception to this rule is Siena. Its *vescovado* was a unified territory some five to ten kilometers south of the city.[5]

At Milan, reorganization of the episcopal patrimony included a shift from possession of both urban and rural properties to an almost exclusive concentration on landholding in the countryside. The rural properties, according to Violante, were more desirable because improvements and upkeep of rural property entailed less capital outlay than urban land and also because of a "grave financial crisis" among the rural proprietors. We have already noted the lack of urban holdings at Lucca, and the same generally is true in other Tuscan towns. The cathedral of Santa Maria of Pisa traded suburban lands for partial possession of the castle of Piombino in 1115.[6] At Luni, Volterra, Pistoia, Siena, and Florence, there is little indication that the bishops retained appreciable amounts of urban land in the twelfth and thirteenth centuries.

The change was dramatic. During the first half of the twelfth century, the patrimony of the Pisan church, observed Gioacchino Volpe, "grew enormously."[7] At Luni, Volterra, and Massa Marittima, the bishops similarly expanded their patrimonies by purchase of lands and jurisdictions in the second half of the twelfth century. At Pistoia too, episcopal purchases were common in the late eleventh and the twelfth centuries. "It is certain, however," Sabatino Ferrali argued, "that the most common types of growth of the ecclesiastical patrimony were donations or bequests *pro remedio animae* and feudal oblations."[8]

The growth of the patrimony, according to Cinzio Violante and Gioacchino Volpe, was most common after the 1060s and especially during the twelfth century. Reform bishops used the accumulated treasures of their churches to expand landholdings of their churches. The result, Violante said, was "the formation, after the middle of the eleventh century, of new territorial unities as a result of the reunification in the hands of a single lord, of the shares—formerly divided [among several lords]—of individual castles or individual *curtes* to which powers of jurisdiction and district were connected."[9] The purchases of jurisdiction were often the results of a fruitful association between the early communes and the bishops. At Pisa, before the commune received imperial recognition in the mid-twelfth century, the archbishop often would act as a legal *persona* representing the commune. Similarly, at Florence and Siena the bishop on occasion acted for the commune.[10]

David Herlihy agrees that a fundamental change was occurring in Italian society, but he argues that it was more closely related to population growth and the fractioning of inheritances than to episcopal or communal policies. The phenomenon also occurred earlier than either Violante or Volpe thought. The economic impact of the purchases "reaches a sort of climax in the pontificate of Gregory VII (1073–1084)."[11] Herlihy's chronological difference with the two Italians may well derive from his unusual method of research. He attempted to arrive at the percentage of land held by the church by measuring the percentage of church land bounding fields mentioned in all the north-central Italian and southern French donations, bills of sale, trades, and inventories he had been able to find. To make his sample more representative he did not count references to anyone mentioned as a principal in the document. This, he argued, would produce an unbiased sample of land ownership. But most ecclesiastical institutions tended to buy or trade lands in order to build up concentrations of land in selected areas.[12] Thus, as twelfth-century episcopal purchases were more and more concentrated in territorial curie, the sample might indicate a lower percentage of ecclesiastics as "contiguous owners" even while actual episcopal purchases continued to increase. The sample could be considered representative only for the late twelfth century, when a larger proportion of documents originated from more completely random lay sources.

The purchases of rural lands and jurisdictions in the eleventh and twelfth centuries also played a major role in securing the *libertas ecclesiae* that had concerned the reformers. In addition to insuring the church's continued wealth, Tuscan bishops may well have been reacting to growing urban pressures for autonomy. Attempts at religious reform at Lucca eventually became enmeshed in the struggle between the lay leaders of Lucca and their secular lord, Countess Matilda. Bishop Anselmo's flight from Lucca to his rural castle at Moriano may have convinced later bishops that no longer could they expect to remain autonomous without rural centers in which they could take refuge, or from which they could expect aid. Pietro Santini observed that there were few controversies between the bishops and commune at Florence during the twelfth century because the bishops surrendered their urban prerogatives for a privileged position among the rural feudatories, guarantees of ecclesiastical liberty, and communal protection of episcopal properties. Significantly, it is at Pistoia, Volterra, and Massa Marittima—precisely those towns where the bishops attempted to retain significant urban prerogatives—that violent struggle between commune and bishop was most common.[13]

"Il feudalismo di ritorno" was Cinzio Violante's phrase to describe the rural outlook and interests of thirteenth- and fourteenth-century central and north Italian bishops. The change occurred when the bishops ceded their urban lands to laymen. At the same time, cathedral canons, sons of these same lay magnates, successfully challenged the bishop's control of the diocese. As at Lucca, the chapters at Pistoia, Volterra, and Sarzana aligned themselves with the commune and served as a check on episcopal pretensions.[14]

By the early twelfth century the reformed cathedral chapter at Lucca held tithes and patronage over some churches in the diocese as well as its own independent jurisdiction in the countryside. Beyond this, the twelfth-century chapter secured the right to select the bishop of San Martino, to administer a vacant see, and to participate with the bishop in the selection of rectors for a good number of the churches in the diocese. At Orvieto, in 1209, and at Siena, in 1081, the chapters received "gifts" from the bishops which, according to Vincenzo Natalini, were in fact divisions of the episcopal patrimony.[15] These concessions, as at Lucca, probably accompanied a chapter reform which included an acceptance of collegial organization.

The chapters consulted with bishops concerning appointments. They regulated ·the cathedral, oversaw building programs, and generally played a larger role in church life than did north European cathedral chapters.[16] In 1264, Orvieto's chapter even litigated successfully with the bishop over the proposed location of Orvieto's new cathedral. Orvieto's chapter, like Lucca's, provided the most important members of the episcopal bureaucracy and assumed control over the temporalities during a vacant see.[17] Capitular powers were similar at Pistoia, Florence, Volterra, and Siena. At Massa, where the bishop and the commune continued to struggle for control of the town during the thirteenth century, communal officials claimed the right to control the temporalities during a vacant see.[18]

In response to the stimuli of the eleventh and early twelfth centuries, the Luccan bishopric began to seek a strong administrative foundation for its spiritual and secular activities. But similar bureaucratic expansion is not apparent in all the Tuscan bishoprics. The mid-thirteenth-century bishop Guglielmo of Luni had little or no bureaucracy. When he needed a representative he chose members of the Luccan cathedral chapter who served on an ad hoc basis. It is not unlikely that Luni rather than Lucca is closer to the realities of the medieval Tuscan, if not the Italian, church. We can only guess, however, since no other Tuscan episcopal bureaucracies have been subjects of recent scholarship.[19]

The eleventh-century reforms brought about the active participation of the chapter in episcopal administration. Until the death of Bishop Guercio (1256), the chapter supplied the most active of the episcopal officials. The office of treasurer may, in fact, have been borrowed from the chapter. In the first half of the thirteenth century, the chapter members served increasingly long terms as proctors, vicars, and treasurers of the episcopate. Cathedral canons were especially evident in episcopal administration between 1231 and 1236 when the primicerio Ubaldo and the archdeacon Opizone were vicars for the vacant see. Between 1231 and 1256, only four of the fifteen clerics who served as episcopal officials were definitely not chapter members. As at Lucca, most Tuscan chapters did have the right to administer during vacant sees. But only Arezzo's chapter could, like Lucca's, claim the right to appoint episcopal vicars.[20]

The first half of the thirteenth century seems to have been when the functions of episcopal offices were defined. The first officer to appear regularly was the treasurer, who in the 1230s and 1240s could be found conducting inquests and leasing lands throughout the diocese. The office of vicar general and the division of the diocese into vicariates also probably dated from the first half of the thirteenth century. The first vicar of whom I have record was found in 1245. By about 1256, the diocese had been divided into vicariates, probably under the influence of the Luccan commune's division of its contado into vicariates—a system of organization that had begun by 1218. These vicars were primarily judges in the bishop's local churches, and thus in function too they resembled the commune's vicars. Lucca's use of vicars who served for specific terms and in specific areas was, according to Robert Brentano, unusual:

In the thirteenth-century Italian church the bishops were represented, and also sometimes aided, by vicars. The vicar might act for a short time, for a specific business, or he might be a continuing administrative assistant. The latter sort of vicar appears for precisely those dioceses, like Città di Castello [and Lucca], and those provinces, like Milan, where in general the ordinary's attitude towards his diocese, the metropolitan's toward his province, was most continuously administrative, most like the attitude of English prelates.[21]

The vigorous, well-defined administrative structure developed at Città di Castello, Brentano suggested, because it was of moderate size and close enough to progressive papal administrative models to find some inspiration, but far enough away to keep from being overwhelmed by the papacy. Lucca may have learned of the importance of administrative reform from the ex-papal secretary Guercio dei Tebalducci, who was bishop of Lucca from 1236 to 1256. We lack information about the clerical members of other Tuscan episcopal families, but it seems unlikely that their administration resembled that of "exceptional" dioceses like Lucca and Città di Castello.

We are better informed about lay members of the Tuscan bishops' official families. Between 1220 and 1240 the noble Avvocati family, which had held the visdominate of the Luccan bishopric (possibly since the late tenth century), acted as episcopal advocates. They may well have attempted to add hereditary control of the advocate's office to their control of the visdominate. After 1241, however, the Avvocati disappeared almost completely from episcopal administration and the offices were usually filled on an ad hoc basis, usually by the notaries.

In broad outline, the history of the Avvocati family very much resembles the experience of other Tuscan visdomini. At Massa, Volterra, and Luni, the offices of the advocate and the visdominate were combined permanently. The Visdomini family of Florence in fact was more successful than the Visdomini at Massa and the Avvocati at Lucca. They managed to retain their prerogatives, including the rights to temporal offices in the episcopal rural communes. At Massa communal pressure aimed at keeping the Visdomini out of episcopal administration. By the 1220s the family members no longer styled themselves "Episcopal" but instead "Vicedomini massane civitatis."[22]

The change in title was obviously related to communal pressure on the Visdomini. At Lucca too, the fall of the Avvocati and the subsequent rise of the notaries may be related to political changes in Lucca. By 1252, the Luccan commune had been captured by the *popolo* and the magnate families such as the Avvocati were proscribed from participation in communal magistracies, and possibly from positions of influence in the episcopal government.

The structure of episcopal administration in most Tuscan dioceses is unknown and unstudied because it has largely been overshadowed by the history of temporal jurisdictions. The struggle between secular and religious governments was not as acerbic or as long-lived in Tuscany as it was in the North. The reason is not hard to find. In Tuscany, only the bishops of Luni, Volterra, and Arezzo were comparable to the Lombard "count-bishops." In twelfth- and thirteenth-century Tuscany, episcopal jurisdiction over cities was usually based on a pro tempore appointment as podestà—lasting only long enough to end internal factional disputes. Between the twelfth and the early fourteenth centuries bishops at Luni, Massa Marittima, Pistoia, and Arezzo served short terms as "rector" or podestà.[23]

Episcopal competition with secular governments in Tuscany was usually based on dynastic interests rather than religious issues. In the twelfth century, Bishop Goffredo degli Alberti of Florence increased episcopal wealth by extending his fiscal and jurisdictional claims over the various religious bodies in the diocese. Perhaps the most significant use to which he put his ecclesiastical power was to force Florence into a war in support of Alberti claims to parts of the Cadolinghi estates.[24] The most famous of the thirteenth-century dynasts were probably the Pannocchieschi counts who controlled the bishopric of Volterra and used it to further their dynastic ends. At Pistoia, the Guidi counts had relatives in the episcopal see during much of the eleventh and twelfth centuries. To them, the cathedral was little more than a tool to control the nascent commune. Hence, most of the problems at Pistoia during the twelfth century involved the conquest of rural nobles rather than the destruction of urban ecclesiastical privileges.[25] Where there was less friction between the church and commune it was often because noble families could not dominate the cathedral. At Lucca the bishops did not follow any recognizable dynastic policy before the late thirteenth century, and even then they exhibited no more than a moderate nepotism. At Pisa and Siena too there is little indication before the fourteenth century of any family domination of the episcopal sees. Perhaps noble families could not capture these episcopates because of the strong interests of the cathedral chapters in the twelfth- and early thirteenth-century episcopal elections.[26]

Lacking urban pretensions, Tuscan bishops contented themselves with temporal jurisdiction over rural centers constructed during the eleventh and twelfth centuries. This brought them into conflict with the rural communes which developed on episcopal lands during this same period.

It is still unknown to what extent episcopal policy itself was responsible for the growth of rural communes. Cinzio Violante has argued[27] that the formation of rural curie (whose administrative centers often later became rural communes) resulted from the episcopal policies of building rural centers which could serve as economic and demographic *foci* for the flowering Italian society. Enrico Fiumi reversed the relationship between episcopal policy and the economic and social changes.[28] The bishop of Volterra, he said, did overcome lay feudal classes and he did increase his patrimony and temporal jurisdiction. But the revolutionary change, according to Fiumi, was the formation of a "territorial unity that graviated toward San Gimignano" and away from Volterra and its bishop. No person or group could take credit. San Gimignano "was an expression of an irresistible economic and demographic force." Pisan archiepiscopal policy also emphasized a judicial reorganization of the countryside. From the tenth through the twelfth centuries the archbishop collected rights and prerogatives and destroyed the power of the rural lords. The result, as at San Gimignano, was the growth of rural communes. But Gioacchino Volpe observed that the communal formation should be credited to the growth of associations of free men—the men who would become the consuls of the rural communes. By forming associations the free men, and even some serfs, were able to protect themselves against the powerful rural lords who had previously controlled the countryside.

It is a question . . . of the full triumphant development of the principle of free association, of contract, where formerly there had been a complete dependence according to fully developed private signorial rights. This transformation happened earlier around Pisa, on the patrimonial lands of the archbishop, because of the lack of an armed force there to defend the interests of the lords.[29]

Depending on the area, each of these explanations seems inviting. At San Gimignano, Prato, and even at Pescia, in the Luccan diocese, demographic and economic forces probably account for the rise of powerful rural communes. But other rural centers in the Luccan diocese, such as Santa Maria a Monte and Montopoli, owed their prosperity to their positions as administrative centers for the bishopric. The famous imperial stronghold in the lower Valdarno, San Miniato al Tedesco, on the other hand, probably remained a power in the southern part of the Luccan diocese during the thirteenth century because of its powerful communards. San Miniato resisted the pressures of such economic rivals as Fucecchio and such political rivals as the Luccan-subsidized San Genesio and remained the most important center in the southeastern part of the diocese. Thus in various parts of Tuscany, in different economic, social, or political situations, rural communes seem to have owed their prosperity to no single factor. For each rural commune we must investigate its situation to isolate those factors most responsible for its development.

Episcopal rights within these rural areas were fairly uniform throughout Tuscany in the twelfth and early thirteenth centuries. Typically, bishops had the right to appoint (or approve the rural commune's selection of) podestàs, to approve statutes, supervise justice, and collect revenues. Payments often derived from signorial rights to mills, carting or guard duties, profits from justice, and road taxes. Usually the bishops shared most of their taxes, signorial revenues, and fines with the rural commune or with a dominant group within the territory. In the Volterran diocese, however, taxes collected within episcopal castles in the early thirteenth century were shared with the commune of Volterra. The archbishop of Pisa divided the pedaggio of Ricavo (in the Valdera) with the "Lambardi" of the same place, while the commune of Forcoli (also in the Valdera) possessed a portion of its market from the archbishop of Pisa and the bishop of Lucca.[30]

Most Tuscan bishops maintained their jurisdiction only with the aid of the larger citizen communes. At Florence, as at Lucca, the bishop could use citizen magistrates to hear cases originating in areas under episcopal jurisdiction. Communal judicial officials could not initiate action, but only heard cases at the bishop's pleasure. At Pisa, Volterra, and Siena, communal interest in episcopal jurisdiction was less passive. If episcopal officials had not already initiated action in episcopal courts, communal officials could initiate action in communal courts. At Pistoia in the first decades of the thirteenth century episcopal officers needed communal force in order to enter the episcopal communes of Lamporecchio and Orbignano and in order to make their judgments stand.[31]

After about 1250, the relationship began to change. By the 1270s Archbishop Federigo Visconti of Pisa complained that the Pisans

have established that the jurisdiction of all lands must devolve to the Pisan commune; they say that this must be understood whether the jurisdiction over the lands pertains to the Pisan archbishop or to laymen; they say, furthermore, that since the statute is general, no one's jurisdiction may be exempted.[32]

It was a period, Gaetano Salvemini observed, of "attempts to free society from the ecclesiastical fetters of the Middle Ages and to give it a perfectly lay form."[33]

Overstated, perhaps, but episcopal jurisdictions did have to admit more communal interference in the second half of the thirteenth century. The bishop could never have won a contest with the large urban communes. As Robert Davidsohn observed, they had no completely reliable lay officials. The Florentine bishops, he said, "could not call anyone to such offices if not Florentine nobles who, not wishing to risk their own lives or those of their relatives, dared not do anything against the commune's wishes."[34]

At Lucca, the commune dominated relations with the bishopric, but thirteenth- and fourteenth-century developments indicate a partnership in both theory and reality. Lucca fortified and defended the bishop's rural commune of Santa Maria a Monte. The Luccans declared, however, that the rural commune should remain under the bishop's jurisdiction "since the said bishop [Guercio in 1252] has not made nor shall be understood to make any gift or concession to the Luccan commune of any of his or the bishopric's rights in the previously mentioned castle."[35] Even the homicide of 1284 was returned to the bishopric's court after the episcopal advocate objected to the Luccan communal claim to jurisdiction over the matter.

The major conflicts between the commune and the bishopric in 1276, 1309, 1330, and 1351 seem to have concerned tax revenues and attempts to bring the laws of the jura into congruence with Luccan communal law. Except for the case of Sorbano del Vescovo in 1330, the controversies seem to have ended in compromise. In 1287, the jura was placed under Luccan victualing regulations; in 1334 and 1335, the communes of Moriano paid £1,500 each year for exemption from all taxes but the salt tax. In 1358, the communes of Moriano agreed to pay almost £375 in addition to the salt tax for the next decade. If, in fact, these conflicts between the commune and bishopric represented attempts to negotiate higher fiscal contributions, there is no reason to believe that the concession of tax revenues represented any great constitutional change. Even in southern France during the age of Philip IV, when the monarchy claimed taxes for the defense of the realm from all Frenchmen, it received money from the nobility with the understanding that the king had no constitutional right to the payment. Exactions were paid in lieu of taxes. That these taxes were the subject of negotiation and not of royal right is shown by the reaction against royal claims after the death of Philip IV.[36]

Other Tuscan bishoprics do not seem to have been quite as fortunate as Lucca's. At Arezzo and Volterra, impoverished bishops sold jurisdictions to the communes to pay debts. In 1241, the bishop of Florence paid the dazio for his men of Monte di Croce; from 1257, the men of the bishop's jurisdiction paid communal taxes as a matter of course. By the beginning of the fourteenth century, according to Robert Davidsohn, the independent jurisdiction of the bishop of Florence had, for all practical purposes, ceased to exist.[37] Throughout the first two thirds of the thirteenth century, the Sienese continuously interfered with episcopal jurisdiction over its Vescovado. Only after 1271 did the commune agree not to send its podestà into the Vescovado. In the late thirteenth and early fourteenth centuries, the Sienese commune seems to have abandoned attempts to collect the contado gabelle from the episcopal jurisdictions.

Even within the individual diocese, the communal-episcopal experience was not without contradictions. What both Gioacchino Volpe and Gaetano Salvemini described as an all-out fight for "laicization" of Italian society was never complete in either theory or practice. Even Federigo Visconti, who had bitterly decried Pisan interference with his signorial rights, complained about the commune "carrying away from us jurisdiction over our lands although everyone has sworn to defend the rights of the archbishopric."[38] Communal governments did not necessarily destroy independent episcopal jurisdictions, but they did demand that these regions contribute to the common defense, follow local legal custom, and contribute to communal finances. Episcopal jurisdiction, on the other hand, was never completely ended. Even as late as 1500, the bishop of Volterra could still claim, however dubiously, that "the church of Volterra, by right of ancient privileges both from emperors and popes, always has exercised jurisdiction *inter laicos* [on lands in the Val di Cecina] without opposition; and I, bishop of that church already for twenty-two years, have always exercised it."[39] Luccan bishops could have made a similar statement as late as the early eighteenth century.

The bishoprics' varying experiences probably reflect the geographical and political differences between their situations. At Lucca, bishops were not nearly so closely identified with the old feudal magnates as they were at Pistoia, Luni, Massa Marittima, or Volterra. Sienese communal-episcopal rivalries may well have reflected Siena's Ghibelline foreign policy before the battle of Montaperti. Under the later, Guelf government of the Nine, communal-episcopal relations more nearly approximated the Luccan or the Florentine experience.[40] The communes also may have been willing to compromise with the bishop if the area in question was particularly strategic. Hence the Pisans rarely interfered with religious jurisdiction at Piombino or even at Ricavo in the important Valdera; the Luccans interfered with episcopal jurisdiction only at Sorbano del Vescovo or Moriano, both close to Lucca. In the Valdarno, the commune was careful to support the bishop. Nor did it care to press the rural communes too harshly in an area where they might easily go over to the Pisans, or later to the Florentines.

As in political affairs, economic developments in the course of the thirteenth century did not all work to the advantage of the Tuscan bishops. The Luccan bishops' attempts to increase their wealth focussed on exploiting agrarian resources fully. Land reclamation along the Serchio River and on the Luccan plain and a policy of building or authorizing construction of mills increased the worth of episcopal possessions. At the same time leases of agricultural land were granted almost exclusively to men who worked the land themselves.

This concentration on agrarian revenues was not unusual. Of the Tuscan bishoprics, only that of Massa Marittima received a significant income from other sources—the mines in the Maremma and on the island of Elba. In the rest of Tuscany rural, mostly agrarian, revenues were the rule.[41]

Increasing competition for land in the twelfth and early thirteenth centuries also increased the potential returns from land. Beginning in the 1220s, the bishopric of Lucca raised rents, especially on lands located on the Luccan plain and in the middle Serchio regions, by repossessing lands and by buying the melioramenta. Where the bishopric had to buy the melioramentum or a perpetual rent, we find a rather wide variation in the possible returns on the investment. In one case it could be as low as 3 percent, in another as high as 29 percent. The normal return seems to have been about 6 to 9 percent, less than half of the 20 percent Pistoian investors received on similar contracts. Over half the rent increases occurred between 1223 and 1259.

During the same period the bishopric did not try to increase rents on its lands in and around the Valdarno. Rather its officials exacted entry-fines on the issuance of contracts. The entry-fines occur in the same chronological period as the rent increases. Almost none are found after 1250, which seems to indicate that after mid-century the demand for agricultural lands had declined. Other indirect evidence gives the same impression. The number of subaltern churches in the pievi of San Gervasio, Santa Maria a Monte, Marlia, and Diecimo declined between 1260 and 1276-77. For whatever reasons, the Luccan countryside appears to have been less populous after 1250-60 than it had been previously.

Scholars studying other Tuscan bishoprics have reported similar situations, but interpretations of their significance vary widely. Gioacchino Volpe, studying the bishopric of Luna, and Brunetto Quilici, studying that of Florence, found what they considered a rationalization of revenue sources. Between 1150 and 1250, there were remissions of servile dues and collection of servitia (a money payment in lieu of labor or other services) in order to fix annual rent payments in kind.[42] Philip Jones has agreed in part, but he would add:

In Tuscany, by 1200, many churches were afflicted with heavy debt, and because of debt, in certain cases, were obliged to sell their freedom to dependent cultivators. Most acts of manumission, in fact, and many charters of franchise, were in some measure contracts of sale and exchange, which could easily be read as evidence of a general crisis of fortunes on ecclesiastical and feudal domains.[43]

There is even less agreement on the question of economic decline in the second half of the thirteenth century. Brunetto Quilici noted an end to servitia payments by 1250, but generally considered the bishopric economically sound. Gioacchino Volpe and Giovanni Cherubini found the economic position of the bishops of Volterra and Arezzo to be extremely weak in the second half of the thirteenth century. For the other Tuscan bishoprics there is little indication of their economic position.[44]

After our short, schematic survey of other Tuscan bishoprics, the Luccan bishopric at first appears exceptional. But no doubt in part this is because the Luccan episcopal records are exceptionally well preserved. In general, the bishopric of Lucca faced the same problems faced by other Tuscan bishops. That the results were sometimes so different may well owe more to political, economic, and social conditions in the various towns than to the vigor of individual bishops.

Luccan Bishops, ca. 1000–ca. 1350

The bishopric of Lucca was governed by 26 different bishops between 1000 and 1350. The following list is a summary for convenient reference. The materials in this survey are from Ferdinando Ughelli, *Italia Sacra* (10 vols., Venice, 1717-22; rpt. Nendeln, Lichtenstein, 1970), I, cols. 789-823; Umberto Nicolai, *I vescovi di Lucca* (Lucca, 1966); and Guerra, Guidi, *Storia ecclesiastica lucchese*.

GHERARDO II, 991-1003   The son of Inghilfredo and thought to be a member of the noble Soffredinga family, the so-called lords of Anchiano (near Diecimo).

RODILANDO, 1005-1014   Nothing is known of him.

GRIMIZZO, 1014-1022   He is thought to belong to the noble Tegrimi family.

GIOVANNI II, 1023-1056   The son of Gottifredo and the first of the Luccan reform bishops.

ANSELMO I, 1057-1073   A member of the noble da Baggio family of Milan and one of the leading Italian reformers. After 1061, although he also served as Pope Alexander II, he retained control of the Luccan episcopate.

ANSELMO II, 1073-1086   A nephew of Anselmo I, he was sent to Lucca to serve with his uncle. At one time he was Matilda of Tuscany's confessor. He adopted the Benedictine habit, and presumably joined the order, in a period of crisis when he had resigned from the Luccan see. He did return to the see at the urging of Pope Gregory VII.

GOTTIFREDO, 1091-1096   Between 1086 and 1091 a schismatic pseudo-bishop controlled the diocese. Gottifredo was selected as bishop by Pope Urban II. The beginning of his episcopate marks the reconciliation between the papacy and Lucca at the end of the Investiture Contest.

NOTE: Throughout the Appendixes and the Notes, all archival citations, unless otherwise indicated, are from the Archivio arcivescovile of Lucca, Fondo diplomatico. The parchments of the Fondo are organized under four major divisions: ++, +, *, and A; the divisions are subdivided into series by letters of the alphabet and numbers, 1-100, e.g., ++ A 1, ++ A 2, A 1, AB 1, AC 1, etc. Quotations from unpublished sources have been reproduced exactly as they appear in the original documents, except that abbreviated words have been written out in full. Irregularities of spelling and syntax have been noted or corrected only in exceptional cases.

RANGERIO, 1097-1112   Probably of French birth, Rangerio was a Benedictine and the author of the metric life of Anselmo II.

RODOLFO, 1112-1118   We know nothing of his origins.

BENEDETTO I, 1118-1128   He had served as archdeacon of the cathedral chapter during the episcopate of Rodolfo.

UBERTO, 1128-1135   A cathedral canon and a friend of St. Bernard and St. Norbert; we know nothing more of his origins.

GUIDO II, 1135-1138   He was a cathedral canon and the only bishop between 685 and the present who has not left a single extant document.

OTTONE, 1138-1146   We know nothing of him or his origins.

GREGORIO, 1146-1164   He was a subdeacon and canon of the cathedral before his selection as bishop.

PIEVANO, 1164-1166   He was a native of Pescia and a member of the cathedral chapter. After his death, the diocese remained four years without a recognized bishop.

GUGLIELMO, 1170-1194   He was a member of the Guinitinghi family of Lucca and former primicerio of the cathedral chapter.

GUIDO III, 1194-1202   He was of Milanese origin and former archpriest of the cathedral chapter.

ROBERTO, 1202-1225   A member of the Leccomolini family of Lucca, he had been a cathedral canon before his election.

RICCIARDO, 1225   A cathedral canon before his election.

OPIZONE, 1228-1231   A canon before his election, he was constrained to abandon the city when Gregory IX placed Lucca under interdict and suspended the diocese. The quarrel was over possession of the Matildine lands in Garfagnana claimed by both the Luccan commune and the papacy.

GUERCIO, 1236-1256   He was a member of the Tebalducci family of Siena and a member of the pope's official family until he was selected by Gregory to be the Luccan bishop.

ENRICO I, 1257-1267   He was a cathedral canon and a member of the noble Rodalinghi family of Lucca.

PIETRO III, 1269-1274   A Dominican, he was a member of the Luccan Angiorelli family and the first non-chapter member selected as bishop by the chapter itself.

PAGANELLO, 1274-1300   He was a member of the Luccan Porcaresi family.

ENRICO II, 1300-1323   He was a Franciscan and a member of the Ligurian De Carretto family. He was provided to the see by Pope Boniface VIII.

GUGLIELMO II, 1330-1349   A former proctor general of the Dominican order and a member of the Sienese Dolcini di Montalbano family. Guglielmo was provided to the see by the Dominican Pope John XXII.

Acquisitions or Repossessions of Properties and Jurisdictions by the Bishopric, 1100–1310

Included here are the acquisitions or repossessions of lands, jurisdictions, corti, castles, tithes, and churches. They were gained by purchase and donation. Lands returned to the bishopric through the actions of the communal courts have not been included. Most of these court actions were to recover pieces of land because of nonpayment of rent, and most often the land was returned to the same tenant at the same rent; thus, they do not represent an extension of episcopal wealth. Perpetual rent contracts and purchases of melioramenta (on their significance see Chapter 6) have been included, since they required a new investment by the bishopric and they increased the episcopate's economic potential.

1. 31 May 1102. Norte del fu Lamberto of Paterno gave to the bishop and the episcopate "pro anime mee remedio et pro solidis centum sexagenta . . ." 30 pieces of land between the Usciana and the Arno rivers near Santa Maria a Monte.   + F 93.

2. 6 June 1102. Counts Ugo and Raniero, sons of the late count Guido, with the consent of their mother, Lena, traded to the episcopate their one-third portion of the castle, curte, and district of Capannoli "qui fuit qd ranieri comitis. . . ." Bishop Rangerio gave them "meritum anulum unum argentum pro ipsa tradictione . . . et pro solidis duo centum bonorum . . . de moneta de luca. . . ."   AC 54; AC 56; + K 3.

3. 11 June 1102. Tabulio del fu Roberto and his wife, Samartana del fu Benedetto, "pro animibus nostris remedio" offered to Bishop Rangerio and the episcopate the pieve of Santa Reparata of Bozzano and all its possessions.   * O 56.

4. 13 September 1102. Uberto del fu Uberto gave to the episcopate "omnia ex omnibus terris et rebus meis" which he possessed within the castle and corte of Palaia and in the "loco petriolo prope flumine Arni" except for his slaves whom he had freed. + + L 16.

5. 29 March 1104. Baroncione del fu Sighinulfo returned to the episcopate a piece of land "cum cassina super se . . . et curte et ortale . . . foris civitatem lucensem prope ecclesia Sancti Petris que dicitur Somaldi" which he had held from the episcopate. He received "meritum unum aureum pro ipsa finitione et refutione."   + L 9.

131

6. 6 April 1104. Ugucione del fu Frigiano returned to the episcopate possession ". . . de cassina et re massaricia" in Sorbano del Vescovo for a "meritum anulum aureum."   + + L 99.

7. 30 March 1105. Ugucione del fu Ildebrando sold to the episcopate "omnia ex omnibus . . . in loco et finibus Coselle" [near Vorno on the western edge of the Luccan plain] for a "meritum anulum unum argentum a Sigismundo clero et vicedomino pro persona tua qui est Rangerio episcopo."   + + K 52.

8. 22 June 1108. Ranerio del fu Ildebrando "pro anime mee meorumque parentum remedio" gave to the episcopate all his possessions within the castles and corti of Palaia and Pava except for "securitate quam Uualfredo qd item Gualfredi feci de illa portione tantum quam ab ipso recepi per comutationem . . ." and also reserving that which he possessed in the castles of Casallia and Bibboni.   + K 3.

9. 4 November 1108. Bernardo and Rolando del fu Sigismondo gave to the episcopate "pro anime nostre remedio" 4 moggie of land "in campo de Pescia" which pertained to "curte nostra de othano" [Uzzano near Pescia], for which they received "meritum anulum aureum."   + + G 65.

10. 5 November 1108. Ermanno del fu Rolando, having received "launechilt meritum anulum unum aureum" from Bishop Rangerio, "Sigismondus clericus et vicedominus . . . pro persona tua qui est Rangerius," renounced any claim he or his family had had over two pieces of land "infra monte et poio de Othano."   * L 11.

11. 1 March 1109. Ugolino del fu Atione and his wife, Imelda del fu Martino, traded to the episcopate "pro animarum nostrarum nostrarumque parentum remedio . . . unum sedium prope castello de palaia" and one piece of land in the same area.
* K 25.

12. 19 August 1109. Count Ugo, son of Count Teudicio, ceded to the episcopate "in nomine pignoris" one half of the castles of Barbillo and San Pietro (in the Valdera) in order to secure continued possession of the episcopate's lands between the Cecina, Ursario, and Monte Verde (in the diocese of Volterra).   *Mem e doc,* IV, ii, No. 113; + K 3.

13. 3 November 1114. Count Guido del fu Guido and his wife, Inmilla di Rainaldo, traded to the episcopate one half of their portion "de poio seu castello qui vocatur Salamarthana [south of the Arno] cum ecclesia et curte et sala super se habente sicut circumdatum est per fossas de subta . . ." for "launachild meritum anulum a fralmo."
       + K 1; + 41.

14. 1114. The notary Alberto del fu Villano and Wilicione del fu Rustico and Biagolino del fu Count Ugo as executors of the late count Ugo [degli Cadolinghi] traded to the episcopate one half of the "poio et burgo et curte de Ficiclo," one half of the castles and corti of Musigliano, one half of the corte of Visciana (Usciana), one half of Massa Piscatoria, one half of Cerbaia and Galleno, one half of the corte of Montefalcone, one half of the corte of Valdarno, and one half of the corte of Ponte di Arno, for which they received a meritum worth £300 of Luccan denari.   *Mem e doc,* IV, ii, App., No. 98.

15. 30 May 1117. Ghisolfo del fu Fontino and his son, Binello, sold to the episcopate for a meritum which they received from "Gerardo qd. Danielis pro solidis viginti pro persona vestro q. s. Rudolfo Episcopo, . . . omnes illas terras cultas et incultas . . . [quas] nos nomine feudi ditenemus a te ipso episcopo et ab Ecclesia Episcopatus Sancti Martini." *Mem e doc,* V, iii, No. 1811.

16. 1 August 1118. Rainerio del fu Guido and his wife, Adalascia del fu Gerardo, sold to the episcopate the "montem et pogium seu castellum qui dicitur riocavo sicut fossis et carbonariis circumdatum esse videtur . . ." for "meritum unum aurei a benedicto archidiacono pro soldis mille. . . ." + + F 55.

17. 11 February 1119. Frediano del fu Frediano returned to the episcopate "unam petiam de terra que est in loco et finibus suburbum que dicitur piscopi que est campus cum arboribus et paliaretto insimul" for a payment of 44 soldi, 26 stai of wheat and 26 stai of favas "pro predicta refutatione et sponsione." * G 39.

18. 1 March 1119. Ghisolfro del fu Fontino, Guidone del fu Briscio, and Carbone del fu Fusco, having received from Bishop Benedetto 20 soldi, declared to the bishop that they no longer had any claim to the tithes formerly held by one Folcardi over lands in Carpinetta, Dardagna, and Aquilea (all in the district of Moriano). + H 31.

19. 1 August 1119. Buiamonte del fu Schiatre, Rilevante di Mizzano, and Guido del fu Germando sold their portion of a "podere" at Calezano (near San Miniato al Tedesco) held by the sons of the late Dato to "Anconevollio qd Palmieri . . . procuratorio nomine pro beati martini lucensi" for 45s. 9d. + M 79.

20. 24 January 1120. Abbot Ugo of the monastery of Santa Maria of Serena "causa utilitatis et meliorationis predicti nostri monasteri" traded to the episcopate one half of all its possessions "a flumine cecine usque ad fluminem Arni nominative in loco ad montem de castello, et infra ipsum castellum et curtem in loco vicinatico, in loco ponte gundi, et infra castellum et curtem de collecarelli, et in loco laviano, et infra castellum, et curtem de furcule, et infra castellum et curtem de capannule, et infra curtem de Sancto Pietro, et infra curtem de morrona in loco antiqua, et infra curtem de pirignano, et infra castellum et curtem de cummula, et infra castellum et curtem de sancto petulo, et per alia loca et vocabula ubicumque habere et possidere visum sum ex parte suprascripti monasterii nostri. . . ." For which the abbot received a meritum from the episcopate. AD 79; AD 80.

21. 10 July 1120. The brothers Martino and Baroncio del fu Stefano of Sorbano del Vescovo returned to the episcopate "omnes terras, casas et cassinas, prata et pascua, paludes et piscationes, buscaria et omnia super predictis terris vel in illis habentia, . . . que essent vel pertinerent de suprascripto episcopatu lucensi sancti Martini." Fedor Schneider, "Nachlese in Toscana," *Quellen und Forschungen aus Italienischen Archiven und Bibliotheken,* 22 (1930–31), No. II.

22. 5 September 1120. Gerardo and Guido del fu Lamberto and Gerardo's wife, Matilda, and Guido's wife, Gemma, gave to the episcopate "integram tertiam portionem illius collis et montis qui vocatur plenetule [Pianezzoli, northeast of San Miniato al Tedesco]" and all their possessions between the "Ficu" and the Arno for a meritum "a vicedomino pro persona tua." * H 48.

23. 30 September 1120. Uberto and Guadardo del fu Ildebrando and Ghisla del fu Ursico, his wife, gave to the episcopate one piece of land in Sorbano del Vescovo; in return they received another piece of land in the same area and 60 soldi.   + C 12.

24. 19 April 1121. The monk Lanfranco di Ugo sold to Bishop Benedetto the one-fourth portion "que mihi pertinere videtur per illa comutationem seu deganium quam fecit Rolando Abbas ecclesie et monasterio Sancti Salvatoris [of Fucecchio]", that is, one fourth of one half of the castle and corte of "Repethano" as well as one half of all that pertained to the castle and corte, for 100 soldi.   * F 91.

25. 25 May 1121. Count Guido Malaparte del fu Count Guido received £36 from the episcopate for his portion of the castle and district of Ricavo.   + C 82; + B 20; + + R 92.

26. 24 August 1121. Corrado, marquis of Tuscany, ceded to the episcopate Villa Basilica and its district.   *Mem e doc,* V, iii, No. 1815.

27. 13 April 1122. Guglielmo del fu Rainerio and his wife, Parentia del fu Ardingo, sold to the episcopate their house between the Uscina and the Arno at Santa Maria a Monte, and they received 280 soldi from the bishop's representative (unnamed) at Santa Maria a Monte.   + + L 93.

28. 27 April 1122. Ugo del fu Ugo sold to the episcopate for £1,600 his possessions, "omnibus casis et cassinis atque casalinis simulque terris et rebus meis cultis et incultis, donicatis, massariciis, agrestibus et padulibus [*sic*] et aquariis et piscatonibus quas habeo infra judicaria de plebe Sante Marie a Monte fini a flumine Arno usque ad paludem de Sexto et a catiana usque ad blentinam et in bibiano et poio robertingo."   + + K 75; + + S 1.

29. 5 May 1122. Moretto del fu Uberto sold to the episcopate two pieces of land in Marlia "prope ecclesia S. Marie" for 180 soldi.   + + N 97.

30. 9 May 1122. Guido del fu Moscaro sold to the episcopate his one-fourth portion of the curte and villa of Valivo (in Garfagnana) and one fourth of the castle of Sala for 200 soldi.   AE 29.

31. 22 May 1122. Mabilia del fu Raimundo, widow of Guido, with the consent of her son and "Mundualdo" Raimundo, sold to the episcopate her portion of the castle and corte of Valivo di Sopra (Valico di S.) for a "meritum" worth 120 soldi from one Malciabato.   + N 17.

32. 26 May 1122. Imelda del fu Raimundo, the widow of Opizone, with the consent of her son and "mundualdo" sold to the episcopate her portion of the castle of Valivo di Sopra, for a payment of 120 soldi.   + + R 95.

33. 3 June 1122. Itta del fu Raimondo, widow of Rodolfo, with the consent of her sons Armando and Enrigone sold to the episcopate her portion of the castle of Valivo di Sopra for a meritum worth 120 soldi paid by Rotomento del fu Rolando "pro persona tua [the bishop's]."   *Mem e doc,* IV, ii, No. 100; + G 8; + + S 90.

34. 11 July 1122. Orso del fu Raniero and his wife, Masaia del fu Pincione, "pro animabus nostris et nostrarum parentum remedio" gave to the bishop and the episcopate 13 stiori of land in the district of Vinciano.   + + S 92.

35. 11 December 1122. Bartolino del fu Leone and his wife, Sindiga del fu Rodolfo, called "Inganna the Elder," sold the episcopate all his lands "in curte de castello quod dicitur Usiliano, et in curte et castello quod dicitur colliule, et in curte et castello quod dicitur cerrito, et in curte et castello quod dicitur pratillione, et per alia loca et vocabula . . ." for "annulum aureum unam pro solidis ducentum lucensium denariorum. . . ."   AD 76; AD 77 (Bartolino's mother agreed to the sale).

36. 13 June 1123. Benno and Rustico del fu Ugone gave "nomine pignoris" their one-half portion of the castle and corte of Colcarelli (in the Valdera).   * K 87.

37. 15 August 1123. Biacca del fu Alberto, widow of Gerardo, with the consent of Martino del fu Berno, her mundualdo, sold to the episcopate two "cassinas et res massaritias" at "Villa" in the district of Moriano near Aquilea and her "Morgincap" (one fourth of three pieces of land) for 500 soldi.   + + G 50.

38. 23 February 1125. Lamberto del fu Gerardo "pro anime mee remedio et pro remedio anime predicti patri mei et mater mea et pro remedio anime qd Guidi germano meo" gave to "God and the episcopate of San Martino" 3.5 parts of 9 parts of one piece of land at "pianetore."   * K 40.

39. 26 September 1125. Two widows promised not to molest or litigate with the episcopate over lands they had sold to the episcopate for 300 soldi. There were four mansi "cum casis et rebus masaritiis cum fundamentis et omnibus edificiis in loco demethano [Domazzano] et novangaio et aquilea. . . ."   + + B 30.

40. 3 March 1129. Giovanni, prior of the church and monastery of San Tommaso "sita in territorio Pistoriensi," sold to the episcopate the corte of San Vitale and all the monastery's lands between the Nievole and the city of Lucca for 480 soldi. *Mem e doc,* IV, ii, No. 119.

41. 28 July 1129. Opizone and Tancredo del fu Guido restored to the episcopate the castle of Lavaiano and its district for an unspecified meritum.   + + M 15-19.

42. 24 March 1130. Gerardo del fu Franile sold one piece of land "cum casa" to the episcopate for 80 soldi.   + + D 34.

43. 13 July 1130. Count Ugolino del fu Count Guido and his wife, Gema, traded to the episcopate "integram nostram partem de perignano cum omnibus rebus ad predictam nostram portionem pertinentes vel aspicientes" for a meritum of unstated value.   + + R 15.

44. 6 August 1130. Pietro del fu Rolando returned to the episcopate the episcopal lands he held in Marlia and received 25 soldi.   * F 75.

45. 8 October 1130. Count Ildebrando del fu Alberto, for himself and his son Guido called "Bargongnone," returned to the episcopate one half of the castle and corte of Monsummano and its lands in the Valdinievole, and having received a "merito auro pro solidis mille" promised that he and his son would not contest the episcopal possession of Monsummano.   + B 69; + R 17.

46. 28 May 1131. Guido called "Maleparte" del fu Count Guido traded to the episcopate his portion of the castle and corte of Forcoli, for which he received a meritum

worth 145 soldi from Zicione del fu Mathulino "pro persona tua q. s. Uberto Epis."
Mem e doc, V, iii, No. 1817.

47. 30 September 1132. Count Ugo del fu Count Guido traded to the episcopate
"pro hanc carta pignoris" his portion "de castello et poio de forcole cum omnes sua
pertinentia," for which he received 240 soldi.   * Q 38.

48. 10 March 1134. Mencuccio called "Bocca" del fu Pepe sold "loco pignoris" the
"jus et actionem" of one piece of land that he held from the episcopate in Moriano
near the mill at Castro di Moriano, for 20 soldi. Mencuccio promised to buy back
the land within a year for 20 soldi and a "soma" of wine.   * K 85.

49. 20 November 1135. Cenamo del fu Rodolfo and his wife, Iolitta, offered to the
episcopate one half of the castles and corti and borghi of Toiano and Brento (on the
northern edge of the diocese of Volterra?).   *Mem e doc,* IV, ii, App., No. 103.

50. 23 August 1137. Lamberto del fu Gerardo and his son Merallare, and his wife,
Teberga, and Pozione and Tancredo del fu Guido sold to the episcopate "omnia
quecumque nobis pertinent aliquo jure seu aliquo modo in castello et curte de Lava-
gnano," which is in the Valdarno near Santa Maria a Monte.   + + M 15–19.

51. 11 July 1140. Presbyter Lamberto, monk of San Michele of Quiesa, and his
mother, Berta del fu Pagano, gave to the episcopate their portion of one piece of land
in the pieve of Bozzano.   + 39.

52. 23 July 1140. Bendelmanno and Viviano del fu Adimare returned "in manu
Johannis d. g. presbytris recipientis domino Ottone" all they held from the episcopate in Marlia, for which they received 90 soldi.   + F 4.

53. 7 May 1141. "Sisemondus sacri palati comes et domini Imperiis missus," acting
for his nephews Rolandino and Ugolino del fu Malaparte, sold to the episcopate their
portion of the castle and corte of Forcoli for 62 soldi "pro paterno debito solvendo."
         * Q 13. Transcribed in Schneider, "Nachlese in Toscana" (No. 21 above),
No. IV.

54. 6 July 1141. Damiano del fu Damiano returned to the episcopate his possession
"de omnibus videlicet casis et cassinis et casalinis simulque terris et rebus cultis et
incultis, donicatis et massariciis . . . [which] habuit vel detinuit per beneficium et
feodum a suprascripto episcopatu Sancti Martini in loco et finibus spardaci, et in
loco et finibus Sorbani Episcopi, et in loco et finibus Ducata, et in loco et finibus
Mugnani prope ecclesiam Sancti Michelis ubi dicitur inter ambas aquas vel in aliquibus aliis locis vel vocabulis. . . ." For this, Bishop Ottone gave Damiano a meritum
worth 200 soldi "ad confirmanda suprascripta."   AC 89.

55. 5 August 1141. Pietro del fu Gerardo, Bonacurso del fu Giovanni, and Ubertilot-
to del fu Roberto Pisciatini sold to the episcopate all the rights they had received
from Viviano del fu Moretto over one piece of vinea in Vallebuia which Viviano had
"per tenimentum ab episcopatu et tempore vivianus ea nobis pignoris nomine obliga-
vit pro omni suprascripto debito . . ." for a price of 74s. 6d.   + F 12.

56. 8 September 1141. Pepe, Guido, and Tezicio del fu Count Ugo traded to the episcopate "omnia ex omnibus casis . . . atque terris et vineis" that the brothers possessed

in the castle, corte, and borgo of Forcoli. For this trade they received a "lunechild" worth 70 soldi.   + B 11.

57. 30 May 1142. Guiduccio del fu Cenamello gave to the bishop and the episcopate "omnes res meas mobiles et immobiles" in Palaia.   + + L 16.

58. 16 December 1142. Godefredo del fu Martino sold to the episcopate "omnes jus et actionem et directum" in two pieces of land in Sorbano del Vescovo for 60 soldi.   + + D 57.

59. 10 February 1143. Dragncino del fu Alberto and his wife, Villana del fu Cecio, sold to the episcopate "omnia ex omnibus casis et cassinis seu casalinis atque terris et vineis . . . in loco de vicinattico seu in loco montecastelli et in tavernule et in eis finibus" which they held as Villana's "Morgincap" for a "meritum" which they received from Alberto del fu Bernardo.   * R 17.

60. 27 March 1143. Balduino del fu Brunello, acting for his minor son Count Luterio and with the consent of his wife, Countess Orabile, "per hanc cartulam pignoris nomine" traded to the episcopate his one-fourth portion of the castle and corte of Vivio and one fourth of the castle and corte of Santa Lucia and "quartam portionem una cum omnibus castellis et curtibus atque villis . . . mihi qua est Orabilis et supra-scripto Luterio comiti filio meo aliquo modo pertinentibus a fluvio era usque mare excepto curte de Morrona . . . ," for a price of 1,160 soldi.   AD 65; AD 68.

61. 9 May 1143. Udalrico, marquis of Tuscany, invested the episcopate "per feu-dum" with one half of the "poio de Fontana" and one half of the corte of Bientina.   *Mem e doc,* IV, i, No. 18.

62. 22 February 1144. Ereppaldi del fu Orlando and his sons Ildebrando, Daliotto, Mascatto, Diudaldo, and Bastone, and Malafronte del fu Alberto restored to the episcopate their portion of the "actione, melioramento, et censu atque omni jure" of the corte and villa of "casale," for which they received a "meritum anulum aureum ad confirmandum." [On the reverse side, in a later hand, "Donatio de melioratico casalinis et aliis rebus facta episcopatui in agro Florentino," possibly Casale di Cer-taldo in the Valdelsa near Castelfiorentino?]   + + N 23.

63. 30 July 1144. Mezzolombardo del fu Gerardo and his wife, Eugenia del fu Gu-glielmo, sold to the episcopate their one-half portion of the castle and district of "Mustorno" and all that pertained to the castle "pro quibus a Truffa lucano consule pro te recipimus meritum argentum pro pretio quinque mille solidis. . . ."
+ E 82.

64. 21 August 1144. Count Rainerio del fu Guido promised to liberate the "Castrum de colcarelle cum omni suo pertinentia et aiacentia atque curia" for the episcopate from the sons of the late Opizone and the late Ubaldo within the next year. For this, Rainerio received £100.   AC 93; + I 87.

65. 18 December 1146. Count Tedicione del fu Count Ugone traded to the episco-pate all that pertained to him "in curte et districto Capannule," for which he received "mastrucam unam" worth 60 soldi.   AC 62.

66. 10 July 1147. Tezicio called "Tinioso" del fu Lamberto of Lucagnano and his wife, Poma del fu Giandulfo, sold to the episcopate "omnia ex omnibus casis et

casinis seu casalinis atque terris et vineis cultis et incultis quas nos habemus in loco et finibus seu castello que appellatur Sancto Pietro tam intro Castello quam et deforis." For this they received a meritum from the priest Aldibrando, pievano of the pieve of Santa Maria di Suvilliano, worth £30.   AD 51.

67. 1147. One Buonadeo sold the "jus et actionem et melioramontum" of one piece of land in Prato di San Columbano which he had held from the episcopate for 60 soldi.   + + L 10.

68. August 1149. Count Pepe del fu Count Ugolino sold to the episcopate 16 pieces of land between the Era and Rogio rivers for £6 10s.   *Mem e doc,* V, iii, No. 1818.

69. 1149. . . . sold to the episcopate one piece of land in Marlia for a meritum. + + O 86.

70. 18 January 1150. The brothers Ildebrando and Enrico del fu Lamberto sold to the episcopate one field in Vico Moriano for 32 soldi.   * K 55; * K 85.

71. 11 February 1150. Raimundo and Oddo del fu Pietro traded to the episcopate "alodium et omnem jus et actionem et derictionem . . . et usum que nobis pertinet de aliquibus terris . . . in plebe sancti pancrati et in plebe de marlia," and in return they received a garden in the area of Miliaciatico.   AD 35.

72. 22 August 1150. Andrea del fu Pietro and his son Maggio sold to the episcopate one piece of land in Domazzano for which they received "meritum argentum a Martino qd Carbonis . . . pro solidis sex."   + E 84.

73. 4 November 1150. Ildebrando del fu Uberto, having received a "meritum argentum" from "Alexio diacono qd Raineri pro Gregorio lucano episcopo," promised that he would pay 12 denari annually to the episcopate for one piece of land at Sorbano del Vescovo.   + P 96.

74. 15 January 1153. Gerardo called "manaiola" del fu Gerardo "manaiola" invested the bishopric with his rights to one fourth "de omnibus terris et aquis in loco ercti in loco et finibus cappiani" near San Miniato al Tedesco.   * Q 6.

75. 28 January 1153. Soveno and Selvagno, sons of Ciardo, sold to the episcopate two pieces of "silva" at Diecimo for 40 soldi.   + + P 91.

76. 12 April 1153. Guido del fu Ugone and his wife, Gallita, sold to the episcopate one third of the castle and corte of Forcoli for 600 soldi; 420 soldi of the sale price remained with the episcopate since Guido's father had obligated a portion of the castle to the episcopate for that sum.   *Mem e doc,* IV, ii, No. 127.

77. 18 January 1154. Tasca del fu Adimaro sold to the episcopate his one-twelfth portion "de castello de Pedoni ['Castello' in the Val Pedogna near Diecimo] cum curte et turre et fortia et districta" plus six other pieces of land at Motrone and "Gricciano" for £147 16s. 3d.   + 47.

78. 4 February 1154. Tuccio and Lamberto di Ugo and Lamberto's wife, Adalecta, sold to the episcopate their half of the Castle of Pedogna "cum curte et turre et fortia" for £73 18s. 3d.   + 48.

79. 27 February 1154. Guerra del fu Pietro and his wife, Berta del fu Pietro, with the consent of her son Corsetto sold to the episcopate their one-third portion of one piece

of land "cum oliviis super se que est in burgo de castello de Palaia," for which they received 2 soldi from the bishop's castaldo Bernardino.   * K 25.

80. 14 May 1154. Caccialupo del fu Guerra and his wife, Stroppia, sold to the episcopate all their possessions "in loco et finibus curtis de castello de decimo" for a meritum worth 150 soldi which they received from Carbone del fu Menco.   * G 5.

81. 14 May 1154. Guerriscio del fu Roberto and his wife, Semirella, sold to the episcopate one piece of land at "Rio cavo" at Diecimo, receiving a "meritum argentum a Carbone qd Menchi pro solidis quadraginta."   + E 97.

82. 23 July 1154. Atto, the abbot of the monastery of Sesto, sold to the episcopate a one-eighth portion of the monastery's castle "quod nuncupatur colcarelli videlicet a fosse sive a pede carbonarie solummodo ad sumitatem montis, toto riservato predicto monasterio quod extra corporem predictum predicti castri ei pertinet." For this sale he received 100 soldi.   AC 90.

83. 7 June 1155. Beldie del fu Rosso with the consent of her husband, Guidotto del fu Gerardo, traded to the episcopate her portion of two pieces of land in Moriano for a meritum worth 8 soldi.   AD 48.

84. 24 June 1155. Uberto and Lamberto del fu Omodei and his wife, Redora del fu Enrigetto del fu Martino, sold to the episcopate one piece of land, "illa que est isola que esse videtur in finibus Moriano ubi dicitur 'ala puta' " for which they received a meritum worth 8 soldi.   + P 22.

85. 14 July 1155. The brothers Guiscardo, Ugone, Luteringo, and Bene, sons of Rotthetto, and Luteringo's wife, Vissa del fu Rainero, sold to the episcopate their one-eighth portion of "de castello sicut designatis per carbonaria et per fossa de colecarelli" for a price of 100 soldi.   AC 99.

86. 30 November 1155. Count Pope del fu Count Ugone and his wife, Ermina, sold to the episcopate their one-ninth portion of the castles, corti, and districts of Forcoli, Capannoli, and Padule and whatever belonged to them in the castle and district of Alica, for £55.   AD 66.

87. 8 September 1156. Countess Galiana, widow of the late Count Malaparte, with the consent of her sons, Ermanno and Rolandino, "per hanc cartulam nomine pignoris" gave to the episcopate the one-half portion of the "casa et res massaricias" that pertained to her in the pieve of Padule. The land, measuring 24 stiori, was located near Fegataia, and she received 200 soldi for the pawn. The repurchase price was to be set by extimatores at the time of repurchase.   AD 67.

88. 19 March 1157. Abbot Guido of the monastery of Santa Maria of Serena "per hanc cartulam nomine pignoris" obligated to the episcopate the lands and rents of eight men for a meritum worth £10.   AD 62.

89. 19 January 1158. Count Rolandino del fu Count Malaparte sold to the episcopate all his possessions "ad eram [sic] usque ad roghio in curte di Padule et di Fegataia et in eos [sic] finibus," for £10. A repurchase clause was appended stating that Rolandino or his heirs could buy back these possessions for £10 plus 4 denari per pound for each month that the episcopate held the lands (annual interest rate of 13.2 percent).   AD 59.

90. 16 February 1158. Counts Ermanno and Rolando del fu Count Guido Malaparte sold to the episcopate their portion (2 stiori) of one piece of land at "amuriccio" (beside the Era River), for which they received 27 soldi "a Tancredo vicedomino pro persona tua qui est Gregorio."   + K 58.

91. 28 May 1158. Guiciardus del fu Buonfiglio del fu Guido gave to the episcopate "pro se et Monte nepote suo tutorio nomine . . . pro remedio anime sue suorumque parentum" all rights over a podere of seven pieces of land in the area of Tempiano. AE 35.

92. 28 November 1158. Abbot Guido of the monastery of Serena traded to the episcopate the monastery's portion "que est medietas in integra de podio et castello et curte de monte de castello" and all that pertained to it "a Cecina usque ad Arnum et usque ad Elsam scilicet in curte de Colle Carelli et in loco et curte de Taurerle et in curte de Padula et in curte de Capannule et in curte de Sancto Pietro, et in curte de Camulliano et in curte de Ceule et in curte de Perignano et in curte de Lucagnano, et in castello et curte de Lavaiano et in curte de Milliano et in curte de Aqui et in curte de Morrona et in Castello et curte de Teupetoro, et in castello et curte de Cumolo. . . . Pro pretio scilicet centum quinquaginta lib. luc. den." The abbot further confessed that he surrendered any right of repurchase of the other half of all this property that he had previously given in pawn to the episcopate.   AD 63; * F 6.

93. 3 April 1159. Count Ermanno del fu Malaparte sold to the episcopate all his possessions in the area between the Era and Roghio rivers in the corti and districts of Capannoli, Padule, and Fegataia for a price of 100 soldi paid by the bishop's castaldo at Padule, Guglielmo.   AD 56.

94. 16 February 1160. Counts Ermanno and Rolando del fu Count Malaparte sold to the episcopate the lands held from them by one Fariseo of Padule for a price of 51 soldi paid by Tancredo visdominus.   AC 64.

95. 18 March 1164. Viviano and Alberto del fu Patto "pro paterno debito solvendo" sold to the episcopate one piece of land "que est vinea et olivetum" at Moriano for 50 soldi. The land was then returned to them for an annual rent of four lib. of olive oil according to the *libra venditoria* of Moriano.   * K 85.

96. 9 May 1165. Iacopina del fu Bruno "pro anime sue salute" returned to the episcopate one moggio of "vinea" in Vallebuia, for which she received "anulum aureum ad confirmanda."   * D 86.

97. 4 November 1174. Forcone del fu Sesmundillo and his wife, Niera, sold to the episcopate one piece of land in Moriano "ad Marno" which they held from the episcopate. The sale price was 180 soldi.   * K 85.

98. 9 June 1179. The episcopate bought the "jus, actionem et melioramentum" of one piece of land in Moriano for 40 soldi. (Document is badly damaged). + + B 44.

99. 24 August 1183. Pandolfo del fu Guarnerio and his mother, Lutteringa, sold to the episcopate a piece of land which they held "per libellum tenimentum" from the

episcopate for an annual rent of 9 stai of wheat. The sale price was £36. Pandolfo noted that he collected annual rents of 2 stai of wheat and £1 8s. 1d. from the land. ++ F 59.

100. 28 September 1183. Lamberto del fu Seghiero of Toiano sold to the episcopate two pieces of land in Toiano, the first "regitur per . . . ghetum massarium" and the second "per Bonfilium massarium," for which Lamberto received 31 stai of wheat and barley "et alios redditos" for a price of £(?) 13.   + S 85.

101. 1 April 1185. Pepino del fu Diotisalvo and his brother Cinzello returned to the episcopal castaldi of Santa Maria a Monte, Guido Tediccione and Francesco del fu Bernardo, possession "de omnibus terris et vineis et rebus quas tenent Riccus qd Ciaceri, filii qd Gualturii et Bruno qd Cicii et filii qd Verracli" in the district of Santa Maria a Monte for 700 soldi each.   ++ C 75.

102. 4 August 1187. Cecio, son of Enrico, and the brothers Ermannetto, Enrico, and Bonaventura del fu Cecio sold to the episcopate their two portions "de castello et pogio de plancthra et pogio qui dicitur castellum Vecchium et castello et pogio qui dicitur Sancta Maria Vallepone" for 450 soldi. Vallepone is near Montecatini and Planectule is near San Miniato al Tedesco.   ++ I 50.

103. 1187. Ranuccio and Peroscio del fu Ildebrandino and Rainerio and Ildebrando di Rainuccio and Guerriero di Peroscio, Santo del fu Ranuccino, Santino di Rainuccio and Gargozzo and Rainucino del fu Giurico sold and returned to the "iurisperto" Tinioso del fu Martinaccio of Montecatini for the bishop and the episcopate possession "de omni jure et actione et derictu et proprietati vel feudo seu beneficio eius . . . ," for which they received £210.   * R 82.

104. 9 February 1189. Servado del fu Corbiccione and Proficatta his wife sold to Benedetto del fu Pietro Rofredi, proctor for the episcopate, their possessions in the cappelia of San Geminiano di Saltocchio (on the northern edge of the Luccan plain), from which they received annual rents totalling 6 libre of oil, for a sale price of £6 10s.   ++ B 90.

105. 14 October 1189. Rustichello di Bonissime sold "tibi Benedetto qd Petris Rofredi procuratorio nomine accipienti pro Guilielmo divina gratia lucano episcopo . . ." two pieces of land in Prato di San Columbano for £14.   * G 3.

106. 17 June 1190. Ciarino del fu Malafrante, Bonacurso del fu Pandolfino, and Gottifredo acting for Bono di Ciarino sold to the episcopate two pieces of land at Sorbano del Vescovo for £14 which they received from Arrigetto del fu Guglielmetto. + R 43.

107. 13 March 1191. Bellomo del fu Manno of Corciano sold to the episcopate all "jus, actionem, et melioramentum" that he held from anyone, for £1.   * H 53. (See below, Nos. 128 and 134, and App. 7, No. 67.)

108. 8 April 1191. Bondo del fu Baroncietto of Corciano sold to the episcopate "omnem meum alodium et omnem jus et melioramentum" that he held, for 20 soldi. Bishop Guglielmo then returned these rights to Bondo for an annual payment of 1

libra of oil in addition to whatever else he might owe to the episcopate for whatever reason.   * D 61.

109. 22 April 1191. Penato del fu Rustichello of Corciano sold one field located at "vinea Marliatica" in Corciano to Bishop Guglielmo and the episcopate for 40 soldi.
    * I 99.

110. 31 May 1191. Bondo of Corciano sold to the episcopate "omnes jus et melioramentum quod habeo in aliquibus terris quas teneo in Corciano vel alibi et omnem meum alodium . . ." for 20 soldi. The lands were then returned to Bondo for an annual rent of 1 libra of oil.   + + I 52.

111. ca. 1192. Picchio del fu Ciquale and his son Buonacurso sold to the episcopate one piece of "campus" at Rimuotule in Compito (east of the lake of Bientina) for 20 soldi.   + + M 72.

112. 5 April 1193. Benetto del fu Mincurcio of Sesto Moriano and Bello, his son, sold to the episcopate for £3 the "jus et melioramentum" of all lands they held from it, and then they received the same lands back for an annual rent of 3 libre of oil.
    + + R 27.

113. 28 January 1195. Count Ugo del fu Malaparte made a refutation of any claim to the lands which the episcopate held "in pignore" in the area of Padule and Capannoli, for which he received £14 from the episcopate's advocate Normanno according to the terms of a laudamento between Ugo and the episcopate.   AC 67 (see the "lis et controversia" AC 66, 68; and the pawns by Ugo's brother and his mother recorded above, Nos. 87 and 89).

114. 4 July 1195. Ildebrandino del fu — and his wife, Sibulina del fu Lupicino, and Ildebrandino's brother Ermanno and his wife, Ervina del fu Alberto, and Everardo del fu Gerardo and his wife, Ghisla di Ugo, traded to the episcopate their portions of three mansi in Domazzano, for which they received 1,000 soldi.   + E 83.

115. 8 October 1197. Avvocato del fu Tancredo degli Avvocati sold to the episcopate the "terras cultas et incultas atque agrestes casas et casinas et res masaricias" of three men who paid rents totalling 6s. 2d., for a price of £25.   + + A 14.

116. 28 December 1200. Corso del fu Bruno sold to the episcopate two pieces of land "prope ecclesie Sancti Viti ubi dicitur in Campo Sancte Marie [forisportam]" measuring 4.5 cultre. Corso would continue to hold the lands, paying annually 4 moggie of wheat and millet, for "Tancredo de Mologno et eius consortibus de Mologno de Terris de Mologno . . . pro feudo et beneficio lucani Episcopi et lucensis Episcopatus."   + E 79.

117. 15 March 1201. The brothers Ugucione and Lamberto del fu Buonaguida sold to the episcopate "omnes res et massaritias et manentes et fideles et vassalos et omnia jura et actiones et rationes et placitum et districtum et banna et jure patronatus ecclesie Sancti Andree et quicquid nobis modo vel ingenio pertinet . . . in castro et podio de palaia. . . ." (south of the Arno) for £40.   + + L 11; + N 19; + R 11.

118. 11 January 1202. Enrigo del fu Cencio and his wife, Leritia, sold to the episcopate's castaldo Guido del fu Tediccione (acting for the episcopate) "unam nostram integram casamentum casam solariatum" at Planetere for 340 soldi.   AE 91.

119. 31 August 1202. Benedetto and Tancredo, rectors of the bridge over the Uscine (near Santa Maria a Monte) sold to the episcopate "causa reedificandi et faciendi" 16 pieces of land at Montignano for a price of £3 9d. per stiora of land.
    ++ E 3.

120. 6 October 1202. Monaco del fu Inselmino and his sons Cuiscardo and Guido sold to Saparello del fu Parente (acting for the episcopate) one piece of land at "Bucca de Riva de Soglano" in the area of Pratiglione for £13 7s.   ++ S 44.

121. 11 September 1204. Ciaffarmo, deacon and rector of the church of San Terenzio of Marlia, traded to the episcopate the payments owed and the lands held by three coloni at Marlia, for an annual rent of 5 stai of wheat paid to the church of San Terenzio.   ++ Q 93.

122. 20 February 1209. Rustichiello del fu Inalciato sold the episcopate his portion of a piece of land (measuring one stiora) at Santa Maria a Monte in Montignano for £(?) 20s. 6d.   ++ E 15, 16.

123. 28 March 1223. "Martino del fu Niero of Corciano in the pieve of San Pancrazio, confessing to be a fidelis and colonus and manente of the lord Luccan Bishop and of the Episcopate, and concerning the Bishop's allod upon which he resides at the will of the above-written bishop, sold to the Luccan bishop, he himself receiving [payment] for the episcopate, [a rent of] three libre of oil annually in perpetuity . . . for a price of £6 of Luccan denari which the same Lord Luccan Bishop gave to the same [Martino] for the honor of God and for the marriage of his daughter Agnese. . . ." Martino further promised 3 stai of must wine in years when he could not pay in oil.   * H 53.

124. 15 July 1223. Ghibertine del fu Buono and his wife, Belladetta, "pro remedio animarum suarum" gave "to God, the church of San Paolo, and the episcopate of San Martino" one piece of land along the Via Meçhane just outside the Luccan city walls.   * G 75.

125. 17 March 1231. According to the will of the late Franco del fu Moletto, the episcopate received one piece of land (measured 1.5 stiori) located in the curia of Santa Maria a Monte near the "prato del Vescovo."   ++ E 91.

126. 23 November 1231. Cecio del fu Villano and his sons Bonaventura and Villano sold to the episcopate one piece of campo in "Anghaia" (?) from which they received annual rents totalling 4 stai of wheat, for a price of £10.   * G 74.

127. 25 November 1231. The same Cecio and his sons traded to the episcopate their one-third portion of two "masei cum suis pertinentibus" at Caregnana and received in return one piece of land "cum vitibus et semitula" near Picciorano (all lands located near Lunata on the Luccan plain).   * H 50.

128. 27 November 1231. Bellomo del fu Manno and his son Marcovallo of Corciano agreed to pay, in addition to their usual rents, 1 libra of oil to the episcopate. For this promise they received 25 soldi from the episcopate.   * H 53 (see also No. 107 above, No. 134 below, and App. 7, No. 67).

129. 27 February 1232. Vitale del fu Moriano of the cappella of San Geminiano (on the northern edge of the Luccan plain) sold to the episcopate one piece of land at

San Geminiano for 28 soldi. The land was then returned to Vitale on a perpetual lease for an annual rent of 1 libra of oil.   + + B 86.

130. 16 March 1232. Buonassemina of Marlia, the wife of Orsello, with her husband's consent sold to the episcopate "campus cum arboribus in confinibus Cappelle Sancti Justi de Marlia," which owed an annual rent of 2 denari to the episcopate, for £6. The land was returned to Buonassemina and Orsello for an annual rent of 2 denari and 3 stai of wheat.   + + N 83.

131. 26 March 1232. Recchisciano, son of Supprinello, with his father's consent sold to the episcopate one piece of land ("ortus cum arboribus super se") in the prato of San Columbano from which he received annual rents totalling 12 stai of wheat, for a sale price of £12.   + + A 63; + + N 68.

132. 1 April 1232. Caromo del fu Viviano of Sorbano del Vescovo and his wife agreed to pay annually 2 stai of wheat (in addition to their usual rents), and for this they received £4 10s. from the episcopate.   + + D 57.

133. 4 April 1232. The episcopate bought 21 pieces of land in Diecimo for £70 (the document is badly damaged).   + + A 63.

134. 22 June 1232. Bellomo del fu Manno and his son Marcovallo of Corciano promised to pay the episcopate 12 stai of must wine annually and to do this "pro pretio" of £4 5s. that the episcopate had paid to Bellomo. "Hec omnia facta sunt salvis aliis reddititbus et servitiis que ipsi episcopatui faciunt de maseo episcopatus . . . et salvis aliis xxiv stariis vini musti et duobus libris olei . . . et uno stario grani et uno ordei ad affictales et denariis xvi pro pensione et una opera ad pratum de duobus annis unum in claudendo pratum et pollastro de duobus annis uno et una gallina de quattuor annis unum. . . ."   * H 53. (See Nos. 107 and 128 above, and App. 7, No. 67).

135. 28 December 1232. Guiento del fu Rusticuccio of the cappella of San Geminiano of Saltocchio sold to the episcopate one piece of land (vinea) at San Geminiano for £3 15s.   + + B 87.

136. 4 January 1234. Ubertello del fu Fabre returned two pieces of land at Santa Maria a Monte to the episcopate and received a meritum of unspecified worth. + + D (an unnumbered roll).

137. 27 February 1235. Guido del fu Giovanni and his wife, Mardora, of Casore in the pieve of Valliano sold to the episcopate two pieces of land at Casore, "vinea cum olivis et ficibus," for £3. The land was returned to Guido for an annual rent of 1.5 libre of oil.   + + F 97.

138. 28 February 1235. Buonadito del fu Guglielmo of Ottavo sold to the episcopate five pieces of land and one fourth "illarum terrarum . . . [document is torn] et rerum massaritiarum in loco et finibus Octavi ubi dicitur ad Colle," for £7.   + + D 13.

139. 28 March 1235. Piero del fu Buondoro of Corciano, a colono of the episcopate, promised that he and his descendants would pay annually 8 stai of must wine in addition to the 4 stai of must wine he previously paid. For this he received 50 soldi from the episcopate.   * H 53.

140. 31 March 1235. Junte del fu Picione and his wife returned one piece of land in the area of Marlia to the episcopate and were absolved from all rent payments they owed to the episcopate. After this they received 40 soldi from the episcopate "pro melioramento." + + O 25.

141. 20 October 1236. Buonaiuto del fu Viviano Rustichello returned to the episcopate those lands at Marlia which he held from the episcopate for an annual rent of 9 stai of wheat, 20.5 stai of barley, 3 stai of must wine, 6 denari, one rooster every three years, one "curro" of wood, one curro of hay, and a second rooster every six years. Buonaiuto said he did this "of his spontaneous will" because he was unable to pay his rents. His debts to the episcopate were then forgiven. * A 28.

142. 1236. Land near the pieve of San Terenzio of Marlia was sold to the episcopate for a price of 40 soldi; on it the episcopate and the pievano of San Terenzio planned to build a mill. * E 24.

143. 23 January 1240. Conrado del fu Benetto and the brothers Benetto and Aldegorio del fu Berghintoro sold to the episcopate a prato (1.5 stiori) at Santa Maria a Monte for £40 10s. + + E 91.

144. 2 March 1240. The pievano of the pieve of Santa Maria a Monte sold a piece of land to the episcopate "pro exsolvendo debito" which the pievano owed for rent of the episcopate's mill at Santa Maria a Monte, for a price of £7 10s. + + E 91.

145. 21 May 1240. Aquilante del fu Buonadeo sold to the episcopate a piece of land (measuring 2 stiori, 3 pannori) at Montignano near the "prato del Vescovo" at Santa Maria a Monte for £9 4s. 3d. + + E 91.

146. 25 August 1240. Uberto del fu Buonacurso of Sorbano del Vescovo traded to the episcopate "omnia jus et meliorandum" of a piece of land at Sorbano in "Friulo," which then was held by one Turco, for an annual payment to the episcopate of 20.5 stai of wheat. Uberto confessed to having received £17 10s. from the episcopate and then the "jus et meliorandum" were returned to Uberto for an annual payment of 7.5 stai of wheat (as well as the original payment of 20.5 stai of wheat). + + A 72.

147. 1242. Fourteen men of San Gervasio returned to Tinioso del fu Rustico of San Gervasio, the episcopate's proctor, the "frantorium et edificium frantorii quod ipsi construerunt . . . et quod . . . edificaverunt illicite. . . ." For this restitution they accepted £3 10s. from the episcopate's proctor. * P 11.

148. 16 October 1242. Gerardo del fu Vitale of the cappella of San Terenzio of Marlia sold to the episcopate's camerario, Baleante, one piece of land "qui fuit de podere predicti qd. sui patris et quod tenebat ab episcopatu." Baleante then reinvested Gerardo with the land, obliging him not to sell it. "Pro qua vendictione et pro augmento redditus ordei quem faciebat episcopatui de stariis septem et medio ordei ad starium affictale et augmentatur in stariis octo ordei . . . recipere debet libras quattuor et dimidiam denariorum quos denarios debet idem camerarius solvere in debitis ipsius Gerarduccii illis creditoribus quibus obligaverat terram suam." (This would seem to give the episcopate a return of about 30 percent on the £4 10s.) + + S 93.

149. 1242. Buonaguida, the widow of the late Buoneconte of Diecimo, ended all claim she had on a podere in Legnana. For this she received 40 soldi from the episcopate.   * D 100.

150. 13 February 1245. Bianco del fu Guiduccio of Marlia traded to the episcopate one piece of land at Marlia for a price of £8.   + + A 88.

151. 9 May 1246. Barbiero and his brother Bonaventura of the cappella of San Martino of Ducentula in Marlia received £10 from the episcopate's camerario "pro melioramento" of the lands they held from the episcopate, and they therefore agreed that their annual rent should be raised by 4 stai of wheat. (The episcopate seems to have received a return of about 12 percent on its money.)   * A 91.

152. 29 January 1251. Borocco and his son Buonaiuto of Marlia sold to the episcopate one piece of land in Marlia (measured one quarra) on which they collected an annual rent of 4 stai of wheat, for £11.   + + T 4.

153. 3 February 1254. Benetto del fu Gerardino of Savignano in the pieve of San Pancrazio gave to the episcopate one piece of land at Marlia (where the episcopate expected to build a mill pond for its mill) for "anulum unum auri in perfinito."   * S 43.

154. 1255. The episcopate bought one piece of land at Diecimo "in loco atrata" for £7.   + + Q 11.

155. 6 May 1262. Spetta del fu Armanno of Moriano and her brothers sold to the episcopate three pieces of land at Sesto Moriano "que terre fuerint de podere Johannis qd. Thutti," on which Giovanni owed 3 libre of oil. They received £8 of "monete minoris de Lucca."   + + S 48.

156. 23 September 1289. Jacopo del fu Vitale of the pieve of San Pancrazio sold to the episcopate the melioramentum of the lands he held from the episcopate for an annual rent of 20 stai of must wine, for a price of £10 7d. Jacopo then promised to pay annually 1 staio of wheat, 1 libra of oil, and 1 staio 1 quarra of must wine for possession of the melioramentum.   *LA,* IX, fol. 296^{r-v}.

157. 8 October 1299. Piero Ciacchori and his brothers Niero and Martino sold to the episcopate one piece of land at Marlia which they held from the episcopate for an annual rent of 4 stai of wheat and 4 stai of millet. They received £30 for the sale.
     LA, IX, fols. 325^v–26^v.

158. 29 January 1310. Diamante, widow of the late Duodo Frammi, sold in pawn to the episcopate her lands and their rents at Puliciano (?) for £40. The rents totalled 72 stai of wheat, millet, and beans.   *LA,* IX, fol. 337^v.

Total Number of Agrarian Contracts by Area and Year

The following list is a breakdown of the total number of agrarian contracts which I have found for lands belonging to the bishopric between 1100 and 1370. I have divided the areas of the diocese (and Sala di Garfagnana, which actually was in the diocese of Luni) into seven geographical regions. Because of the problems of locating lands precisely (see Elio Conti, *La formazione della struttura agraria moderna,* I, Studi Storici, 51-55 [Rome, 1965], 81-96), I have chosen a geographical organization rather than dividing lands according to the type of land let (e.g., mountain, plain, or hills).

The following chart indicates those districts in which episcopal officials were occupied in any given year. It does not, except in a most general way, give an indication of whether the lands were in mountains, hills, or plain. In most areas (except Garfagnana and the Luccan plain), the lands were a mixture of hill and plain.

I have considered the lands north of the confluence of the Serchio and Lima rivers to be in Garfagnana. According to Repetti, *Dizionario,* II, 400-404, and Pacchi, *Garfagnana,* p. 24, medieval Garfagnana extended as far south as Diecimo. I have left Diecimo in the middle Serchio because administratively the fourteenth-century episcopate and commune tended to treat the communes of Diecimo and Moriano as a unit. Vallebuia is considered part of the middle Serchio only because it is located on the right bank of the Serchio across the river from the Luccan plain. The Luccan plain includes episcopal lands at Marlia, Lunata, Sorbano del Vescovo, and the contrata of San Columbano. (The geography of the Luccan plain is described by Luigi Pedreschi, "Contributo alla conoscenza delle 'corti' della piana di Lucca," *Rivista Geografica Italiana,* 57 [1950], 145-57). The Valdarno includes Santa Maria a Monte, Montopoli, and Lavaiano. The Valdera comprises the lands of San Pietro di Valdera, Padule, Sovigliana, Capannoli, and Forcoli. The other areas of the diocese have been included under "other" along with those contracts in which I was unable to ascertain where the lands were located.

The contracts are taken from the Fondo diplomatico and the Archivio della Cancelleria, *Libri antichi,* of the Archivio arcivescovile of Lucca.

Year	Garfagnana	Middle Serchio	Luccan Plain	Valdarno	Valdera	Other	TOTAL
1100–09			1	1			2
1110–19		4	2	1			7
1120–29			2				2
1130–39		1					1
1140–49		2	3				5
1150–59							
1160–69		1		1			2
1170–79			1				1
1180–89		2	1	1			4
1190–99			3			1	4
1200			1				1
1201				1			1
1202			1				1
1203			1				1
1204				3	2		5
1205		1					1
1206			1				1
1207							
1208				1		1	2
1209							
1210							
1211				4			4
1212				1			1
1213							
1214			1	8			9
1215			2				2
1216			5				5
1217			4				4
1218			1				1
1219			1				1
1220			4				4
1221						1	1
1222							
1223		2		3	1		6
1224		1	1	1	3		6
1225		2	1	1		1	5
1226				2			2
1227	1	1		4			6
1228		1	2				3

Year	Garfagnana	Middle Serchio	Luccan Plain	Valdarno	Valdera	Other	TOTAL
1229			1	3	3		7
1230		1		2			3
1231			3	1			4
1232		5	5	10	1	1	22
1233		2	1		1		4
1234		1	3	12	1		17
1235		3	4				7
1236		2	5	2	1		10
1237							
1238	1	1	2	2	1	1	8
1239		1	3	8	3	1	16
1240		1	3	1	4		9
1241		2	1	3	1	1	8
1242	4	2	3	1	1		11
1243		2	4		3		9
1244			1	1	1		3
1245			1		2		3
1246		1	6	2			9
1247			1		1		2
1248		2					2
1249		3		1			4
1250		6					6
1251		4	1			2	7
1252		3		3			6
1253		3		1			4
1254		11	1		1	1	14
1255		7	1				8
1256		2	4	1			7
1257		2	7	1	3		13
1258		4	3	9	23		39
1259	3		2	19	16	2	42
1260		2		3	1		6
1261		9		2			11
1262	1		2	1		1	5
1263	1		1	2			4
1264		2	2				4
1265				1			1
1266		3	1	17			21
1267				20			20

Year	Garfagnana	Middle Serchio	Luccan Plain	Valdarno	Valdera	Other	TOTAL
1268	1	1		2			4
1269				2			2
1270				1			1
1271				1			1
1272							
1273							
1274		2					2
1275		1					1
1276		1		1			2
1277				1			1
1278				2			2
1279		.			1		1
1280							
1281				2			2
1282			1		1		2
1283							
1284					1		1
1285			1				1
1286							
1287							
1288							
1289			1				1
1290		1	1				2
1291		2					2
1292					1		1
1293							
1294				1			1
1295		1					1
1296							
1297							
1298			3				3
1299			2				2
1300							
1301		1	1				2
1302	1	2		1			4
1303							
1304					1		1
1305		2					2
1306			1				1

Year	Garfagnana	Middle Serchio	Luccan Plain	Valdarno	Valdera	Other	TOTAL
1307							
1308	1	2	4				7
1309		1	1			1	3
1310		1	2		2		5
1311		1	2				3
1312		1	1			1	3
1313							
1314							
1315		8					8
1316		3	2				5
1317		4	4				8
1318	3	2	1				6
1319			1		1		2
1320		1	3		7		11
1321		5	1	1	10		17
1322		5	2		4	1	12
1323		2	1		5		8
1324			1				1
1325							
1326–30			1				1
1331–35		1	2		1	1	5
1336–40			1			1	2
1341–45		2	2				4
1346–50		1	2				3
1351–55		2	3				5
1356–60		4	2				6
1361–65	1		2				3
1366–70	1	2	1				4
Total	19	167	164	177	109	19	655

APPENDIX 4

Types of Rent Payments

Measuring the absolute value or relative importance of rents by assigning a monetary value to each type of rent is of dubious value when we have only fragmentary information on commodity prices, relationships of various types of dry measures, or the devaluation of Luccan money. A simple count of the number of times grain, wine, oil, etc., are mentioned is not optimal because it values each part of a mixed rent payment as highly as a payment in a single commodity. (L. A. Kotelnikova, "L'evoluzione dei canoni fondiari dall' XI al XIV sec. in territorio lucchese," *Studi medievali,* ser. 3, 9 [1968], 609ff., and Rosario Romeo, "La signoria dell' abate di Sant' Ambrosio di Milano sul comune rurale di Origgio nel secolo XIII," *RSI,* 69 [1957], 474ff., used these two systems to analyze rents.)

Table 6 first records an inventory of payments made in a single year (see p. 102 above and Chapter 6, note 90), and then measures the change in frequency of various types of rent payments. I divided the contracts chronologically into seven 25-year periods and assigned a value of 60 points to the total rent payment specified in each contract or listed under an individual in the inventories of rents. I chose 60 points since it is divisible by 5, 4, 3, 2, or 1. If, for example, the whole payment was a single payment in money, then the whole 60 points was added to the column under "Money." If the total payment was divided among grain, wine, and money, 20 points were assigned to each of those three columns. By tabulating the rents in this way we can measure the frequency of each type of payment and its relative importance. The rent contracts analyzed are from Fondo diplomatico and the *Libri antichi* of the Archivio arcivescovile.

Under "Other" I have included payments in pepper, wax, labor services, and the like. Broad beans are included with grains because they were used as a grain substitute.

152

TABLE 6

Rent Payments in the Valdarno (1186–1187) and Moriano (1200–1375)

	Number of Payments	Grain		Oil		Money		Wine		Other	
		Total Points	%	Total Points	%	Total Points	%	Total Points	%	Total Points	%
*Valdarno (*N 92)*											
1186–1187	296	4,800	27.02	60	.33	10,980	61.82	60	.33	1,860	10.5
Moriano											
1201–1225	5	120	40.0	20	6.6	80	26.7	80	26.7	—	—
1226–1250	25	700	46.7	260	17.3	390	26.0	100	6.7	50	3.3
1251–1275	80	2,097	43.4	647	13.4	912	19.0	807	16.6	367	7.6
1276–1300	13	495	63.5	240	30.8	15	1.9	15	1.9	15	1.9
1301–1325	2	120	100.0	—	—	—	—	—	—	—	—
1326–1350	1	—	—	60	100.0	—	—	—	—	—	—
1351–1375	275	6,470	39.2	2,730	16.5	2,030	12.4	2,810	17.0	2,460	14.9

Commodity Prices, Twelfth to Fourteenth Centuries

The following can be taken only as indications of commodity prices. Those taken from chronicles (Tolomeo's *Annales*, and *Le croniche di Giovanni Sercambi, Lucchese*, ed. Salvatore Bongi, Fonti per la storia d'Italia, 19-21 [3 vols., Rome, 1892], I, 8-9) are usually prices during famines or at other times were prices were exceptionally high or low. The other prices are found in varied documents. Some prices, cited in litigations usually before communal courts, may be official communal prices (possibly pegged artificially high or low) representing the price which the episcopate could expect to receive for the product in communal markets (or possibly the wholesale price which the peasant would receive when selling the grain in the countryside). The prices are all for immediate delivery—not grain speculations. We are also without information about possible devaluations of the Luccan lira. The final variation of which we must be aware is the normal seasonal variation in prices, which we can still find in the modern agrarian market. Grain prices might vary 25 to 50 percent during the year. Lacking a single type of source, we may not claim any exceptional accuracy for our list of commodity prices.

"Grain"	Price per Staio	Reference
1128	26d.	chronicle, Tolomeo, p. 46 (unexplained)
1294	1s. 3d.	litigation, * D 30
Wheat		
1177	5s. 6d.	chronicle, Sercambi, p. 8 (famine)
1181	7s.	chronicle, Sercambi, p. 9 (famine)
5 March 1182	7s.	litigation, *Regesto del Capitolo*, II, No. 1460
5 June 1182	8s.	litigation, + + R 72
22 June 1192	4s. 5d.	litigation, * Q 44
22 March 1193	3s. 4d.	litigation, + + S 65
6 March 1196	5s.	litigation, + + F 89
5 March 1230	4s. 8d.	admin. record, * K 45

154

15 December 1243	6s.	litigation, ++ G 7, ++ S 49
1246	1s. 7d.	chronicle, Tolomeo, p. 310
21 May 1255	4s. 9d.	litigation, ++ G 8
28 August 1257	7s. 6d.	admin. record, *LA*, I, fol. 24^v
25 February 1275	6s. 4d.	admin. record, ++ B 66
8 November 1324	5s. 10d.	admin. record, * O 20
3 August 1325	8s. 4d.	admin. record, * O 8
1364	15s.	admin. record, *Martilogio,* line 796
1364	16s.	admin. record, *Martilogio,* line 875

Millet

1177	4s. 6d.	chronicle, Sercambi, p. 8
1181	6s.	chronicle, Sercambi, p. 9
1181	5s. (panico)	chronicle, Sercambi, p. 9
1181	4s. 6d. (saggina)	chronicle, Sercambi, p. 9
1182	7s.	chronicle, Sercambi, p. 9
1182	6s. (panico)	chronicle, Sercambi, p. 9
1182	5s. 6d. (saggina)	chronicle, Sercambi, p. 9
25 January 1218	3s.	litigation, ++ H 91
5 March 1230	2s. 8d.	admin. record, * K 45
8 November 1324	6s.	admin. record, * O 20

Broad Beans

1178	5s.	chronicle, Sercambi, p. 8
1181	6s. 6d.	chronicle, Sercambi, p. 9
1182	7s. 6d.	chronicle, Sercambi, p. 9
3 August 1325	5s.	admin. records, * O 8

Must Wine

14 March 1231	5d.	litigation, ++ D 59
1256	1s.	admin. records, *Inventari,* No. XII, line 135

Aged Wine

1254	1s. 6d.	admin. records, *Inventari,* No. XII, lines 120–21
1256	2s.	admin. records, *Inventari,* No. XII, line 81

Barley

15 December 1243	3s. 4d.	litigation, ++ G 7
3 August 1325	5s.	admin. records, * O 8

Chestnuts

1364	3s. 6d. (unprocessed)	admin. records, *Martilogio,* line 880
1364	8s. (husked)	admin. records, *Martilogio,* line 882

APPENDIX 6

Rent Payments Increased by the Bishopric

The following list contains all the examples I have found of rents raised by the bishopric. In many cases we only have a notice that the rent had been changed, with no reason given. In other cases, the document will state that the bishopric purchased improvements made by the tenant. At other times, the transaction was in the form of a sale of land (possibly a freehold) which the buyer then returned to the vendor for a perpetual rent. This last kind of transaction is commonly referred to as a perpetual loan. Occasionally, the episcopate accomplished a rent change by evicting the former tenant for non-payment of rent and then letting the land to another for a higher rent. All these transactions have been included in the list because they all represent various ways that the episcopate could increase the rents on agricultural lands.

1. 1137. Viviano del fu Moretto sold "nomine pignoris" to the episcopate one piece of land that was vineyard and meadow in Vallebuia, which he held from the episcopate for an annual rent of 2 soldi. The land was returned to him at an annual rent of 9 soldi and 8 stai of must wine. The sale price was 55 soldi. (This seems to indicate an interest rate of about 31 percent). ++ O 21.

2. 1147. The episcopate bought "jus, actionem et melioramentum" for 60 soldi. See App. 2, No. 67.

3. 18 March 1164. The episcopate bought a rent of 4 libre of oil for 50 soldi. See App. 2, No. 95.

4. 9 June 1179. The episcopate bought a "melioramentum" for 40 soldi. See App. 2, No. 98.

5. 31 May 1191. The episcopate bought a rent of 1 libra of oil for 20 soldi. See App. 2, No. 110.

6. 25 October 1203. Orlando di Parzino Buzicari promised an annual payment of 4 stai of wheat in place of his former payment of a rooster, a "focaccia," a quarra of "grain" and 14 denari. The 4 stai of wheat were to be paid to the castaldo of Palaia. ++ L 16.

156

7. 28 March 1223. The episcopate bought a rent of 3 libre of oil for £6.   See App. 2, No. 123.

8. 28 June 1229. Bishop Opizone let "per tenementum perpetuum" to Benvenuto del fu Catenace of Lavaiano the podere formerly held by Catenace (for an annual rent of 2 quarre of wheat, 2 quarre of millet, and 2 quarre of barley). Benvenuto promised an annual rent of 3 quarre of wheat, 2 quarre of millet, and 2 quarre of barley. In addition Benvenuto paid a servitium of 2 soldi so that his rent might not be further increased.   + + E 64.

9. 27 November 1231. The episcopate bought a rent of 1 libra of oil for 25 soldi. See App. 2, No. 128.

10. 27 February 1232. The episcopate bought a rent of 1 libra of oil for 28 soldi. See App. 2, No. 129.

11. 1 April 1232. The episcopate bought a rent of 2 stai of wheat for £4 10s. See App. 2, No. 132.

12. 22 June 1232. The episcopate bought a rent of 12 stai of must wine for £4 5s. See App. 2, No. 134.

13. 2 September 1232. The episcopate gave to Vitale Ricci "unam petiam terre que est campus sine arboribus . . . cuius melioramentum . . . dictus primicerius [pro episcopatu]" had bought from Viviano Buonmassari at Marlia. The land formerly paid 20 stai of must wine to the episcopate, and now it was to give an annual rent of 3.5 stai of wheat and 3.5 stai of millet.   * B 75.

14. 27 February 1235. The episcopate bought a rent of 1.5 libre of oil for £3. See App. 2, No. 137.

15. 28 March 1235. The episcopate bought a rent of 8 stai of must wine for 50 soldi. See App. 2, No. 139.

16. 31 March 1235. The episcopate bought a melioramentum for 40 soldi.   See App. 2, No. 140.

17. 29 October 1239. The episcopate changed the rent payments of six tenants from San Terenzio of Marlia by allowing them to return their lands which owed "certas redditas et certa servitia." The lands then were returned to the men as perpetual possessions for rents in wheat: six pieces of land for 16 stai; eight pieces of land for 24 stai; ten pieces for 24 stai; seven pieces for 16 stai; three pieces for 11 stai; and four pieces of land for 13 stai. All other rights to the lands remained with the episcopate, and the six men swore fidelitas to the bishop, ". . . et pro predicta fidelitate nullo modo censeantur manentes vel ascripti aliqui viri manentie seu obnexe conditionis, set censeantur fideles ut alii liberi homines."   * F 87.

18. 25 August 1240. The episcopate bought a rent of 7.5 stai of wheat for £17 10s. See App. 2, No. 146.

19. 16 October 1242. The episcopate bought a rent of 8 stai of barley for £4 10s. (a return of about 30 percent). See App. 2, No. 148.

20. 31 October 1242. The following is contained in the body of a lease contract: ". . . unam petiam terre predicto episcopatui pertinentem que est campus et est ubi

dicitur ad silvam in confinibus Sancti Terentii [de Marlia] . . . et quam terram fuit de podere Vitalis Cigorine quod tenuit ab episcopatu et quam terram Gerarduccius qd suprascripti Vitalis vendidit suprascripto camerario pro episcopatu. . . ." No price was given.   + O 98.

21. 9 May 1246. The episcopate bought a rent of 4 stai of wheat for £10 (a return of about 12 percent).   See App. 2, No. 151.

22. 25 September 1248. Vita del fu Domenico received the "maseo" or "podere" formerly held by the late Bardilius at Aquilea. Vita promised to pay "omnes redditus qui de ipso podere et terris omnibus fieri et reddi consueverunt in blava, vino, oleo, carnibus, pullis et castaneis tam episcopatui quam aliis personis et locis et etiam eidem episcopatui annuatam loco servitiorum que episcopatus recipere consuevatur de ipso podere et terris et personis in eodem residentibus libras sex olei. . . ." Vita and his descendants "debeant censeri manentes vel coloni vel astricti alicui condi- tionis manentie vel servitutis," and he promised further that they would reside on the podere and not alienate the land nor sell the melioramentum without episcopal per- mission.   + + C 32.

23. 23 September 1254. Vitale del fu Ghiandolfo for himself and his brother received a perpetual lease of five pieces of land at Sesto di Moriano for an annual payment of one staio of wheat. "Et de quibus terris annuatam ut usque suprascripti germanii et eorum majores consueti sunt lucano episcopatui redere starios iiii vini . . . et medium starium castaneis gusciutis. . . ." No reason is given for the change.   AE 18.

24. 1256. Bonizio del fu Gherardino of Castro di Moriano and his wife, Bonaventura del fu Jacopo Roberti, returned to the episcopate two pieces of land in Moriano for which they paid an annual rent of 7 stai of must and 2 denari each year. The lands were returned to the couple for an annual rent of 4 stai of wheat.   + R 100.

25. 11 April 1258. One Bartolomeo and his brother (the parchment is severely damaged by mice) returned to the episcopate two pieces of land at Vallebuia that they held by a perpetual lease for an annual rent of 33 denari. The lands were then returned to the brothers on a 29-year lease for an annual rent of 13 soldi. The reason for the change was not given.   + + D 34.

26. 11 February 1259. Buongiatto, brother of the late Gallo del fu Bernardo and guardian for the sons of Gallo, returned to the episcopate two pieces of land (on the Luccan plain) that Gallo had held from the episcopate for an annual rent of 2 stai of wheat. The lands were then let to Buonacurso del fu Beucrato (who already held the piece of land lying between the two pieces) for an annual rent of 3 stai of wheat and 3 stai of millet.   * B 21.

27. 23 September 1289. The episcopate bought a rent of 20 stai of must wine for £10 7d.   See App. 2, No. 156.

28. 8 October 1299. The episcopate bought the melioramentum of a piece of land which owed an annual rent of 4 stai of wheat and 4 stai of millet for £30.   See App. 2, No. 157.

29. 1299. The episcopate let a piece of land at Marlia for an annual rent of 3 stai of wheat. The land had just been returned to the episcopate by the former tenant (who

had paid 18 denari annually) by the action of the Consuls of the Treguana. + + R 67.

30. 1352. In the *Martilogio* under Mammoli: "Star. XIII Grani. Paganellus Gotti-fredi. Cellinus Pagani tenetur in star. VIII grani. Carta Ser Iacobi." After 1357 Cellino's rent was raised to 14 stai of wheat. *Martilogio,* lines 735ff.

31. 1361. In the *Martilogio* under San Michele di Villorbana: "Star. VIIII Grani. Corsinus Guiduccii de S. Quirico ad Liccianum. Guiduccinus Corsini pro eo. Modo tenet Cellus Puccini, ad reddendum star. X grani, ut aparet per cartam manu Ser Iacobi Nicholai, facta sub anno N. D. MCCCLXI." *Martilogio,* lines 713–16.

32. 1364. In the *Martilogio* under Sorbano: "Star. XII Grani. Nucchorus, dictus Sigardus. Modo debetur redere star. XIIII; incepit in MCCCLIIII." *Martilogio,* lines 168–69.

33. ca. 1364. Chigiano del fu Venturella received a 29-year lease of the ten pieces of land in Diecimo formerly held by Setto di Lupardo Ricci for an annual rent of 3 stai of ground chestnuts and 2 libre of pork (*LA,* IX, fols. 69^r-70^v, 21 September 1316). The *Martilogio* of 1364 (lines 1298–99) lists the "Heredes Chigiani Venturelle, pro Lupardo Riccii," as paying 6 stai of ground chestnuts and "Libr. III Carnium."

34. ca. 1364. Donato del fu Guglielmo and his brother Finuccio received a perpetual lease of 16 pieces of land at Diecimo for an annual rent of 9 stai of wheat, 2.5 stai of ground chestnuts, one chicken every five years, and "servitia" when the bishop was at Diecimo (*LA,* IX, fols. 53^v-56^v, 22 October 1315). According to the *Martilogio* of 1364 (lines 1292–93), Donato paid 13 stai of wheat instead of the 9 stai of wheat listed in the earlier lease. However, this may represent more lands than those included in the lease of 1316 since the phrase "cum terra de Regnana" was included after Donato's name in the *Martilogio.*

35. ca. 1364. In 1318 (*LA,* IX, fols. 88^r-90^v), Luporo del fu Paganuccio received a perpetual lease of the lands of Saracino del fu Bonfiglio at San Terenzio of Marlia. In the *Martilogio* of 1364 (lines 358–64), the payments of "Saracinus Bonfilii" total 42.5 stai of wheat, 10.5 stai of barley and 6 stai of millet.

36. ca. 1364. In the *Martilogio* of 1364 under Carignano, Montuolo, Busdagno, and Ponte Sancti Petri (lines 540–42): "Star. III Grani; III Milii. Lemmus Bonansegne Pavesarii de Luca. Contrate S. Petri Somaldi. Modo tenet Merchatus Lemucchi de Montuolo, ad reddendum star. X, videlicet star. III ½ grani et star. III ½ fabarum et star. III milii."

37. ca. 1364. *Martilogio* of 1364 (lines 1195–2000): "Star. III Grani. Idem [Rofus Iohannis Antonii], pro Urso Bonifatii. Guiduccino Ciuglii, pro eo. Modo Cettinus Cetti, qui fuit de comune Tercilliani, ad reddendum star. XII grani. . . . ."

38. ca. 1364. In the *Martilogio* of 1364 under Fondagno (lines 1209–10): "Star. XI Grani. Guido Bonansegne. Modo Nicholao et heredes condam Iovannelli, ad redden-dum star. X grani et star. VI vini."

APPENDIX 7

Servitia Payments to the Bishopric

1. 18 June 1111. Rodolfo del fu Teuto received one piece of land in Prato di San Columbano (orto measured 5 stiori) from the episcopate for an annual rent of 6 stai of wheat and a servitium of 60 soldi.   * K 65.

2. 17 February 1115. Bishop Rodolfo invested Gottifredo di Rodolfo, Sigismondo del fu Rustico, and Baroncione del fu Ursico with the monopoly on milling grain along the Serchio River from Sesto to Ponte di Moriano for an annual censo of 6 stai (the staio of Moriano). "Unde . . . fecerunt meritum argentum eidem episcopi Rodolfus . . . propter ipsa investio confirmandum."   + + A 20.

3. 2 July 1134. Pathano del fu Simonetto and Dinchelo and Guidetto del fu Gerardo paid "anulum aureum" for the right to lease three houses at San Terenzio di Marlia for a rent of 20 stai of wheat and 20 stai of barley as well as providing a cart each year to carry grain and another to carry wood.   AE 17.

4. 14 November 1140. Gatto del fu Donato paid 80 soldi as a servitium for the right to lease one piece of "terra vineata" at Vallebuia which owed an annual rent of 56 stai of must wine.   + M 12.

5. 17 December 1144. Robertino del fu Martino paid 40 soldi for a lease of one half of the maseo (at Marlia?) formerly held by his father "for the usual rents." AE 80.

6. 13 March 1147. Bernardo del fu Bondo received all the lands in the curia of Santa Maria a Monte which the late Sartino had held, at the same rent Sartino had paid. "Et pro suprascripta investione confirmanda curia [referring to the episcopate's castaldo] recepit servitium a suprascripto bernardo xx solidos bonos et exspendibiliter lucensis monete."   + + G 3.

7. 2 May 1188. Tancredo, advocate of the episcopate, with the bishop's castaldi of Santa Maria a Monte invested Ubertellino del fu Manfredo with the right to measure wine barrels in the district of Santa Maria a Monte. "Et pro investione urceorum mensuratorum vini . . . predicti investitores sub nomine servitiis viginti solidorum . . . reciperunt ut deinceps omni tempore firmun et stabile permaneat atque persistat."

160

GRAPH 3

Servitia Payments by Five-Year Periods, 1201–1305

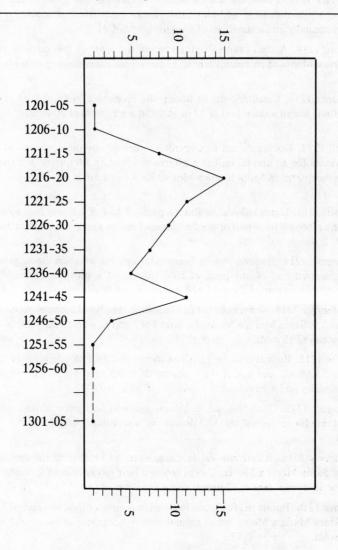

Ubertello was to pay a censo of 1 libra of pepper each Christmas. He would receive 2 denari for each measure he made.   + + C 78.

8. 31 October 1205. Benvenuto del fu Romagnolo of Legnano received a lease of one piece of land at Diecimo at an annual rent of 4 stai of wheat and for which he paid a servitium of £3.   * E 64.

9. 10 January 1211. Priore the son of Bellagorto received one piece of land "cum arboribus et vinea et ficibus" at Montecalvoli (near Santa Maria a Monte) at a rent of 4 denari annually and a servitium of 9 soldi.   * K 41.

10. 30 April 1214. A man (name illegible) received a lease of one piece of land at Santa Maria a Monte at an annual rent of 12 denari for a servitium of 40 soldi.
+ + E 31.

11. 31 March 1214. Canallerio del fu Malagollia received a piece of land at Santa Maria a Monte for an annual rent of 12 denari and a servitium of 20 soldi.
+ + E 32.

12. 7 April 1214. Benvenuto del fu Gerardino received one piece of land at Santa Maria a Monte for an annual rent of 6 quarre of wheat and 6 quarre of barley (according to the quarra of Santa Maria a Monte) for a servitium of 50 soldi.
+ + E 33.

13. 26 April 1214. Uguccione del fu Baroto received half of a house in the castle of Santa Maria a Monte for a rent of one half staio of barley and a servitium of 20 soldi.
    + + E 36.

14. 13 August 1214. Buonito del fu Sesmondo and his brothers Buonigatto and Paragone received half of one piece of land (measured 4 stiori) at Santa Maria a Monte for an annual rent of 2 denari and a servitium of 18 denari.   + + E 30.

15. 7 September 1214. Benvenuto del fu Gerardino (see No. 12 above) received one piece of land at Santa Maria a Monte for a rent of 6 stai of wheat and 6 stai of barley and a servitium of 45 soldi.   + + E 31.

16. 30 June 1215. Buonacurso del fu Abarello received half of one piece of land at Santa Maria a Monte and half of the house on the same property for an annual rent of 2 stai of barley and a servitium of 5 soldi.   + + E 38.

17. 15 August 1215. Corradino del fu Villano received one piece of land at Santa Maria a Monte for an annual rent of 2 denari and a servitium of 8 soldi.
+ + E 40.

18. 25 January 1216. Rubaconte del fu Carnelevare (a brother of the episcopate's castaldo at Santa Maria a Monte, Giova) received four pieces of land at Santa Maria a Monte for an annual rent of 12 denari and a servitium of £6.   + + E 41.

19. 11 April 1216. Buono del fu Buono received one piece of land (measured 15 pannore) at Santa Maria a Monte for an annual rent of 1.5 quarre of barley and a servitium of 2 soldi.   + + E 42.

20. 15 May 1216. Pietro del fu Bellacosa and Gerardo del fu Gervasio received half of a house in Santa Maria a Monte for an annual rent of 2 denari and 3 soldi "nomine servitii ut . . . per hemptionem locatio sit perpetua."   + + E 43.

21. 2 October 1216. Berlinguarda del fu Villano, widow of the late Ventura, received one third of one piece of land at Santa Maria a Monte for an annual rent of 1 denaro and a servitium of 16 soldi.   + + E 44.

22. 16 October 1216. Buonattiario del fu Cerbio received one piece of land at Monte-calvoli (near Santa Maria a Monte) for an annual rent of 3 stai of wheat and 3 stai of millet and a servitium of 2 soldi.   * K 41.

23. 17 April 1217. Buono del fu Buono (see No. 19 above) received a one-eighth portion of a mill at Santa Maria a Monte for an annual rent of 6 quarre of wheat and 28 eels and a servitium of 7 soldi.   + + E 47.

24. 17 April 1217. The same Buono received two pieces of land within the castle of Santa Maria a Monte for a rent of 1 quarra of barley and a servitium of 6 soldi.
+ + E 48.

25. 18 June 1217. Sigerio del fu Guidiccione and his brothers Corbaccione and Rainero received the lands formerly held by Serotino del fu Ughuccione at Santa Maria a Monte for an annual rent of 5 stai of wheat and 5 stai of millet or barley and a servitium of 13 soldi.   + + E 31.

26. 1217. Campulo del fu Faville received one piece of land at Santa Maria a Monte for an annual rent of one half quarra of barley and a servitium of 20 soldi.
+ + E 31.

27. 23 February 1218. Buonacurso del fu Abarello (see No. 16 above) and Ugolino del fu Guittone received one piece of land at Santa Maria a Monte for an annual rent of 4 quarre of wheat and a servitium of 16 soldi.   + + E 51.

28. 22 March 1219. Grandone del fu Moretto received two pieces of land at Santa Maria a Monte for an annual rent of 2 denari and a servitium of 20 soldi.
+ + E 54.

29. 5 January 1220. The widow of the late Mainetto received the late Mainetto's podere for the usual rents and a servitium (the rents and servitium payment are not found in the extant portion of the lease).   + + E 57.

30. 7 February 1220. Buonasera del fu Guido received 14 pieces of land at Santa Maria a Monte for an annual rent of 5 stai of wheat and 5 stai of millet and a servitium of 5 soldi.   + + E 58.

31. 19 December 1220. Rubaconte del fu Carnelevare (see No. 18 above) received four pieces of land at Santa Maria a Monte formerly held by Ventura del fu Salcerio for an annual rent of 12 denari and a servitium of £25.   + + E 63.

32. 1220. Ventura del fu Pitto received two pieces of land at Santa Maria a Monte for an annual rent of 2 quarre of wheat and a servitium of 22 soldi.   + + E 56.

33. 14 May 1222. Amato del fu Tasca of Gello (south of the Arno) received "totum illud podere qui regitur per domenicum masareum eiusdem episcopi et Episcopatus" for the usual rent and £3 "pro qua investione."   + K 42.

34. 3 June 1222. Martino del fu Bernarduccio received one piece of land at Santa Maria a Monte for an annual rent of 4 coppe of must wine and a servitium of 8 soldi.
+ + E 68.

35. 31 March 1223. Buonafronte del fu Pasquale received one piece of land (measured 2 stiori) at Santa Maria a Monte for an annual rent of 2 quarre of barley and a servitium of 10 soldi.   + + E 71.

36. 27 May 1223. Sirenna del fu Upezino of Montecastello received the podere at Lavaiano (in the Valdarno) formerly held by one Carenaccio for an annual rent of 2 denari and a servitium of 40 denari.   * R 58.

37. 13 October 1223. Grandone (see No. 28 above) received one piece of land at Santa Maria a Monte for an annual rent of 2 denari and a servitium of 5 soldi.
+ + E 72.

38. 30 January 1224. Venethiano del fu Michele received one piece of land at Montecastello for an annual rent of 1 quarra of wheat and a servitium of 15 soldi.
* R 79.

39. 16 August 1224. Sirenna (see No. 36 above) received the lands at Montecastello formerly held by the late Greca for an annual rent of 2.5 libre of oil and a servitium of 20 soldi.   * V 69.

40. 18 August 1224. Alliano del fu Mezovillano received one piece of land at Santa Maria a Monte for an annual rent of 2 denari and a servitium of 7 soldi.
+ + E 73.

41. 15 February 1225. Buonaiuto and Benedetto del fu Giorgio of Pescia received the rents paid by four men at Monte Barellis [Monte Bicchieri? south of the Arno near Montopoli] for an annual payment of 2 soldi and a "meritum seu servitium" of 5 soldi.   * C 69.

42. 9 April 1225. Buonacurso of Tramonte received all the lands that the late Romeo of Tramonte had held from the episcopate for an annual rent of 1 staio of wheat and 1 staio of dried, husked chestnuts and a servitium of 100 soldi.   + G 98.

43. 19 September 1225. Frongino del fu Guidone received one piece of land at Santa Maria a Monte for an annual rent of 5 stai of wheat and millet and a servitium of 10 soldi.   + + E 75.

44. 16 March 1226. Jacopo del fu Buongesello received one piece of land at Santa Maria a Monte for an annual rent of 2 denari and a servitium of 10 soldi.
+ + E 77.

45. 2 January 1227. Ventura del fu Tancredo and Alperto del fu Aldrigolo received one piece of land at Montopoli for a pensione of 10 denari annually and a servitium of 5 soldi.   * S 100.

46. 4 February 1227. Angerello del fu Baldro received one piece of land (measured 18-20 pannore) at Santa Maria a Monte for an annual rent of 1 quarra of wheat and 1 quarra of barley and a servitium of 8 soldi.   + + E 79.

47. 1227. Ventura del fu Rilevato received two pieces of land at Santa Maria a Monte for an annual rent of 2 quarre of barley and a servitium of 15 soldi.
+ + E 82.

48. 6 August 1228. Lanfranco son of Data "manens et colonus ipsii episcopatus" received the podere of the late notary Arrigo of Pastina for an annual rent of 7 stai of wheat, 1 somma of wine, and 12 denari, as well as 100 soldi "pro intratura." * D 33.

49. 28 June 1229. Benvenuto del fu Catenace of Lavaiano received the lands or podere formerly held by his father at Santa Maria a Monte (and for which his father had paid 2 quarre of wheat, 2 quarre of millet, and 2 quarre of barley) for an annual rent of 3 quarre of wheat, 2 quarre of millet, and 2 quarre of barley and a servitium of 2 soldi.   + + M 15-19; + + E 64.

50. 28 June 1229. Aldino del fu Martino of Montecastello received the podere (seven pieces of land at Montecastello) formerly held by Buonadonna, widow of the late Dato, for annual rents of 4 quarre of wheat, 4 libre of oil, and 6 denari and a servitium of 20 soldi.   + + E 64.

51. 2 December 1229. Bonifacio of Pariano received two pieces of land at Montopoli for an annual rent of 2 stai of wheat and a servitium of 4 soldi.   * S 100.

52. 18 August 1231. Bernardo del fu Bernardo of Montopoli received the podere of the late Pegalotto del fu Cacciaguerra, promising to make all the payments formerly made by Pegalotto and a servitium of 100 soldi.   * T 3.

53. 21 November 1231. Bartolomeo del fu Martinello received a podere (in Moriano?) which was part of his wife's dowry and for which he promised to pay all rents owed and a servitium of 50 soldi.   + + P 45.

54. 19 January 1232. Buondino del fu Ghiscardo received one piece of land (with figs, vines, and olive trees) at Montopoli for an annual rent of 8 stai of millet and a servitium of 3s. 10d.   * T 36.

55. 7 March 1232. Martino del fu Orlandino received four pieces of land at Montopoli for an annual rent of 18 denari and a servitium of 23 soldi.   * T 36.

56. 8 September 1232. Ugucione del fu Tolomeo received the one half of a podere at San Gervasio formerly held by his father, promising to pay 12 denari annually, 6 hens three years out of four, 6 "socacias" (six days' ploughing service?), and 3 "amulas" (amphoras?) of wine each year and "nomine servitii" 13 soldi.   * P 2.

57. 17 September 1232. Ferramonte del fu Giunte received one piece of land at Montopoli for an annual rent of 3 denari and a servitium of 23 soldi.   * T 36.

58. 22 December 1234. Martino del fu Tederigo received one piece of land at Montopoli for an annual rent of 2 stai of wheat and a servitium of 10 soldi.   * T 36.

59. 13 May 1238. Guidone del fu Galgano received one piece of land ("campus et vinea insimul") at Montecatini for an annual rent of 4 denari and £12 10s. "pro suprascripta locatione."   + + S 77.

60. 13 July 1239. Ughiccione del fu Tolomeo received one piece of land in San Gervasio for rents (unspecified) and a servitium of 2 soldi.   * P 9.

61. 12 December 1239. Varo del fu Uomodideo received one piece of land (measured 3 stiori) at Santa Maria a Monte for an annual rent of 1 quarra of wheat and 1 quarra of barley and a servitium of 12 denari.   + + E —.

62. 19 February 1240. Ricardo del fu Tesalduccio and Franco son of Bernardo received one piece of land at San Gervasio for an annual rent of 1 moggio of wheat ("id est xxiv quarras ad rectam quarram pisani.") and a servitium of £4. ++ K 41.

63. 17 July 1241. Bianco del fu Sannaco received one piece of land at Santa Maria a Monte for an annual rent of 9 quarre of wheat and barley and a servitium of 3s. 6d. ++ E.

64. 6 February 1242. Albertino del fu Francardello of Tempiano received one piece of land at Tempiano (near Santa Maria a Monte) for an annual rent of 28 denari and a servitium of 2 soldi.   ++ K 41; * C 74.

65. 17 February 1242. Lotteringo del fu Lambertuccio received a piece of land at Montecastello for a rent (unspecified) and a servitium of 3 soldi.   ++ K 41.

66. 26 September 1242. Buonacurso del fu Corso of Forcoli received one piece of land at Forcoli for an annual rent of 1 quarra of wheat and a servitium of 5 soldi. * R 89.

67. 7 September 1243. Bellomo del fu Manno and his son Marcovallo confessed to owe the episcopate 100 soldi for unpaid rent on their two pieces of land in Corciano (near Marlia). When this had been paid, the camerario of the episcopate returned the lands to them for a servitium of 2.5 libre of oil and the annual rent of 36 stai of must wine, 1 staio of wheat, 1 staio of barley, 2 libre of oil, 16 denari, one cock every four years, one hen every two years, one-quarter curra of wood, and "una opera ad claudendum pratum Marlie" every two years.   ++ K 62. (See above, App. 2, Nos. 107, 128, and 134).

68. 31 October 1243. Ricardo del fu Tebalduccio, Pandicampo del fu Guarthone, and Vitale del fu Buonfiglio for one half, and Franco son of Bernardo and his brother Pietro for the other half, of one piece of land at San Gervasio (owing an annual rent of 36 quarre of wheat) paid a servitium of £4.   * P 15.

69. 4 November 1243. Riccobene del fu Giunta and Giovanni of San Gervasio received two pieces of land (one described as a maseo) for an annual rent of 3 quarre of wheat and a servitium of £2 6s.   * P 14.

70. 29 September 1244. Ingheramo del fu Magalotto received two pieces of land at Santa Maria a Monte for an annual rent (document is torn) and a servitium of 12 denari.   ++ E.

71. 6 April 1245. Buonamico del fu Trafullo of Forcoli received one piece of land at Forcoli for an annual rent of 2 quarre of wheat and a servitium of 5 soldi.   * Q 57.

72. 6 August 1245. Pietro del fu Pietro of San Gervasio received one piece of land at San Gervasio for an annual rent of 2 denari and a servitium of 7 soldi.   * P 16.

73. November 1246. Benvenuto del fu Giovanni of Montecastello received the "feudum" formerly held by Sirenna del fu Upezino at Montecastello for a promise of the use of one horse for the bishop and £4 "pro servitio et intratura huius feudi. . . ."
          * V 35. (See Nos. 36 and 39 above.)

74. 22 September 1248. Vita del fu Donuccio promised to pay all the rents customarily owed as well as 6 libre of oil "annuatim loco servitiorum" for the maseo or podere in Aquilea (Moriano) of the late Bardelio. Further he promised to remain a colono of the episcopate, to remain on the land, and not to sell the melioramentum of the land without the bishop's permission.   + + C 32.

75. 30 December 1248. One Fide received two pieces of land at Santa Maria a Monte for an annual rent of 9 quarre of wheat and barley and a servitium of 4 soldi.
+ + E.

76. 27 July 1256. Jacopo Ciacche del fu Lucchese received one piece of land at Santa Maria a Monte in exchange for another piece of land. He agreed to pay an annual rent of 1 quarra of barley and 6 denari for servitium.   AD 86.

77. 7 February 1301. Ciancomo Aldobrandini received a house in the contrada of San Columbano for an annual rent of £30 and 100 soldi "nomine intrate."
LA, IX, fol. 1^{r-v}.

Notes

PREFACE

1. See App. 2, No. 117. The official title is the "episcopate of San Martino of Lucca" and in the eleventh and twelfth centuries it was most often referred to with the full title. Beginning in the thirteenth century, notaries abbreviated the title to "episcopatus Lucanus." I have chosen to follow the thirteenth-century usage and refer to the "Luccan bishopric."

2. Nanni, *La Parrocchia,* p. 199, No. 4.

3. Robert L. Benson, *The Bishop-Elect, a Study in Medieval Ecclesiastical Office* (Princeton, 1968), p. 377; see also pp. 53–54, 278–81.

4. *Inventari,* pp. 36–42.

5. *Martilogio.*

6. E.g., Dominus Baleante, who between 1239 and 1249 was variously described as "Camerarius," "Vicarius," and "Vicarius in temporalibus."　＋＋ H 35 (17 October 1239), ＋＋ O 28 (12 July 1246), and * A 91 (9 May 1246).

7. On the archiepiscopal archive of Lucca see Duane J. Osheim, "The Episcopal Archive of Lucca in the Middle Ages," *Manuscripta,* 17 (1973), 131–46; Martino Giusti, "Lucca archivistica," and Hansmartin Schwarzmaier, "La società lucchese nell'alto medioevo e gli archivi ecclesiastici di Lucca," offprints from *Archivi e Cultura,* 5 (1971). On Italian episcopal archives in general see Robert Brentano, *Two Churches: England and Italy in the Thirteenth Century* (Princeton, 1968), pp. 292–324.

1. THE SETTING

1. On the early history of Lucca see *Paulys Real-Encyclopädie der classischen Altertumswissenschaft,* XIII. 2 (1927), cols. 1537–39; Lucca's early history is conveniently summarized in Augusto Mancini, *Storia di Lucca* (Florence, 1950), pp. 1–11. This earliest reference, from Livy (XXI.59.10), could be read as "Luca" or "Luna"; Luca is preferred since Sempronius probably retreated to the area of Parma and then down the Serchio Valley rather than make a more dangerous retreat to the seacoast at Luna. See, e.g., Arturo Solari, *Topografia storica dell'Etruria,* II (Pisa, 1914), 313. Useful bibliographies of recent studies on Lucca are contained in Mancini, *Storia di Lucca,* pp. 351–54; Piero Pierotti, *Lucca, edilizia urbanistica medioevale* (Milan, 1965), pp. 217–23; and Isa Belli Barsali, *Guida di Lucca* (2nd ed., Lucca, 1970), pp. 241–51.

2. On the foundation of the colonia cf. Adrian Nicholas Sherwin-White, *The Roman Citizenship* (Oxford, 1939), p. 74, who argues that the colony referred to in Livy XLV.13.10 is at Luna and not at Luca. Luca became a colonia under the Empire, Pliny *HN* 3.50, and a municipium under the late Republic, Cic. *Fam.* 13.13.

3. Solari, *Etruria* (n. 1 above), pp. 313, 335, gives both the surface area and population figures. The latter must be taken as very crude estimates at best, for Solari based them on the density of these same areas in the early twentieth century. The population, however, within the present walls of Lucca, for example, was about 23,000 in 1837, and about 35,000 by 1960. Arguments assuming static population densities cannot be accepted.

4. Ibid., pp. 312-13.

5. On the Via Francigena see Fedor Schneider, *Die Reichsverwaltung in Toscana* (Rome, 1914), 29-30; on the importance of the Serchio Valley and Garfagnana, idem, *Die Entstehung von Burg und Landgemeinde in Italien* (Berlin, 1924), pp. 127ff.

6. On the lands south of the Arno, see Enrico Fiumi, "I confini della diocesi ecclesiastica del municipio romano e dello stato etrusco di Volterra," *ASI*, 126 (1968), 40ff.

7. Cited in Repetti, *Dizionario*, II, 882.

8. On the foundation of churches before 1000 see Nanni, *La Parrocchia*, pp. 14ff; see also Schwarzmaier, *Lucca*, pp. 27-36.

9. See also the economic and social reasons for the change discussed below, pp. 12-15.

10. The modern archdiocese of Lucca is considerably smaller than the medieval diocese. Pope Leo X removed the ancient pieve of Pescia and the churches of the Valdinievole and Valleriana from Luccan episcopal jurisdiction in 1519. These churches comprise the diocese of Pescia which Benedict XIII created in the eighteenth century. In the seventeenth century, the diocese of San Miniato was formed out of the southern part of the medieval diocese of Lucca. In the eighteenth century, Pietrasanta, Ripafratta, and Barga were added to the archdiocese of Pisa. And finally, in the nineteenth century, the northern part of Garfagnana was joined to the diocese of Massa-Carrara. On the dismemberment of the medieval diocese of Lucca see Guerra, Guidi, *Storia ecclesiastica lucchese*, pp. 15-16; and Bongi, *Inventario*, I, 114-15.

11. David Herlihy, *Medieval and Renaissance Pistoia* (New Haven, 1967), p. 18, found a greater continuity between Roman and medieval Pistoia than I have found at Lucca.

12. Herlihy, "Agrarian Revolution," has investigated population growth for the whole of Italy and southern France. Since a large portion of the contracts used by Herlihy are from Luccan sources, his conclusions seem especially applicable to Lucca.

13. Giuseppe Bindoli, "Le prime e le seconde Mura di Lucca," *Atti*, n.s., 1 (1931), 3-51. Lucca had three walls: the Roman wall, the thirteenth-century medieval wall, and the sixteenth-century wall which is still intact.

14. David Herlihy, *Pisa in the Early Renaissance* (New Haven, 1958), p. 42. Pisa built walls in the twelfth century enclosing ca. 114 hectares and these walls were extended south of the Arno to encircle the quarter of Kinsica at the end of the thirteenth century. Cf. Emilio Cristiani, *Nobiltà e popolo nel comune di Pisa* (Naples, 1962), p. 164, who argues that the walls south of the Arno were begun in the mid-twelfth century and hence the full 185 hectares were probably enclosed much earlier than Herlihy supposed.

15. Among recent scholars Herlihy, *Pisa*, p. 35 n. 1, preferred the more conservative figure, while Mario Lopes Pegna, *Firenze dalle origini al medioevo* (Florence, 1962), p. 335, accepts an estimated area of 97 hectares.

16. Lopes Pegna, *Firenze*, p. 339.

17. Herlihy, *Pistoia*, p. 74.

18. On the various densities see, e.g., Josiah C. Russell, "Thirteenth Century Tuscany as a Region," *TAIUS: Texas A & I University Studies*, 1 (1968), 46ff. The article has now been reprinted in substantially the same form in the same author's *Medieval Regions and Their Cities* (Bloomington, Ind., 1972), pp. 40-51.

19. Bindoli, "Mura," 42-43 (n. 13 above); Elena Paderi, "Variazioni fisiografiche del bacino di Bientina e della pianura lucchese durante i periodi storici," *Memorie della Società Geografica Italiana*, 17 (1932), 104.

20. *Bevölkerungsgeschichte Italiens,* II (2nd ed., Berlin, 1965), 165–66.

21. Herlihy, *Pisa,* p. 43; this figure depends on an arbitrary estimated per capita wine consumption of five to six barrels a year. Herlihy also does not take into account the wine consumed by travelers stopping at Lucca, and the wine consumed by families, on which no tax was owed (that is, wine brought into the city for personal consumption).

22. Fiumi, *San Gimignano,* p. 153, used a similar multiplier for an oath of 1227 taken by the men of San Gimignano.

23. Tuscan demographic figures have been summarized conveniently in Russell, "Thirteenth Century Tuscany" (n. 18 above), pp. 45, 46 and Tables 1 and 2. Russell's figures must be used with caution. His estimate for Pisa is from Herlihy, *Pisa,* pp. 36ff., but the figures given by Cristiani, *Nobiltà e popolo,* pp. 166–68, are to be preferred. See also Enrico Fiumi, *Demografia, movimento urbanistico e classi sociali in Prato dall'età comunale ai tempi moderni* (Florence, 1968), p. 83, who has revised upward the population estimates for medieval Prato.

24. There is no recent study of general Luccan commercial history. On the woolen industry see Thomas Blomquist, "The Drapers of Lucca and the Marketing of Cloth in the Mid-Thirteenth Century," in *Economy, Society, and Government in Medieval Italy,* eds. David Herlihy, Robert S. Lopez, and Vsevolod Slessarev (Kent, Ohio, 1969), especially pp. 68, 73 notes 23–24. (The volume was simultaneously published as nos. 1 and 2 of vol. 7 [1969] of *Explorations in Economic History.)*

25. Florence M. Edler, "The Silk Trade of Lucca during the Thirteenth and Fourteenth Centuries" (Ph.D. dissertation, The University of Chicago, 1930). See also Raymond de Roover, *Money, Banking and Credit in Mediaeval Bruges* (Cambridge, Mass., 1948), p. 20.

26. *Statuti urbanistici medievali di Lucca,* ed. Domenico Corsi (Venice, 1960), pp. 56, 58, 59. The statutes transcribed there cannot be dated exactly, though it is likely that some were first redacted in the early thirteenth century (see pp. 36–37 on the dating).

27. See Thomas W. Blomquist, "The Castracani Family of Thirteenth-Century Lucca," *Speculum,* 46 (1971), 462–63; see also Eugenio Lazzareschi and Franceso Pardi, *Lucca nella storia, nell'arte e nell'industria* (Pescia, 1941), pp. 213ff. Even in the nineteenth and twentieth centuries explorations have failed to discover significant mineral deposits in the province of Lucca.

28. On Luccan agriculture, see below, pp. 96–113.

29. *The Italian City-Republics* (London and New York, 1969), p. 60.

30. See below, p. 17.

31. Tommasi, *Storia di Lucca,* pp. 18, 24.

32. *Annales,* p. 93 (year 1203). The role of these two groups is surveyed in Waley, *City-Republics* (n. 29 above), pp. 165–97.

33. Bongi, *Inventario,* II, 335ff.

34. Ibid., I, 37–49, lists and describes the extant statutes of the rural communes subject to Lucca; *Statuto del comune di Montecarlo,* ed. Domenico Corsi, Fonti sui comuni rurali toscani, 4 (Florence, 1964), p. 49, lists those statutes that have been published.

35. The arguments and the acrimony continued, and even in the nineteenth century antiquarians argued over the extent of medieval jurisdictions as matters of civic pride. See, for example, Domenico Bertini, *Mem e doc,* IV, i (1818), 49ff.

36. Herlihy, *Pistoia,* pp. 225ff., describes Florentine influence at Pistoia after 1250; on Luccan participation see Tommasi, *Storia di Lucca,* pp. 121–22.

37. Theodor Mommsen, "Castruccio Castracani and the Empire," *Medieval and Renaissance Studies,* ed. Eugene F. Rice, Jr. (Ithaca, N.Y., 1959), pp. 19–32, especially 31f. The article is translated and reprinted from *Atti,* n.s., 3 (1934), 33–45.

38. *Tuscia,* I, xl and II, ix, list the comparative figures. About 1275: Lucca 32, Arezzo 14, Pisa 11, Florence 13, Siena 3; ca. 1300: Lucca 43, Arezzo 26, Pisa 27, Florence 15, Siena 6.

39. Herlihy, *Pisa*, pp. 99–100.

40. The hospitals are named in a "catalog of churches" of the mid-fourteenth century transcribed in Bongi, *Inventario*, IV, 116–36. Bongi dated the list ca. 1387, but cf. *Tuscia*, I, 244 n. 3, where Pietro Guidi argues that the document should be dated ca. 1350.

41. Volpe, "Sarzana," *Toscana medievale*, p. 503, quoting a document of 13 September 1232.

42. Cesare Sardi, "Le vie romane e medievali nel territorio lucchese," *Atti*, 34 (1910-14), 198.

43. Ibid., p. 177; according to Giuliano Pisani, *La beneficenza in Lucca prima del Mille* (Lucca, 1907), pp. 100-109, the Spedale di Santa Maria was first mentioned in 1291 and the Spedale del Borgo in 1301.

44. According to the "Estimo of 1260" transcribed in *Tuscia*, I, 246–73, the hospitals of Santa Maria Forisportam, of the monastery of San Bartolomeo in Silice, of the monastery of San Giorgio, of Lunata, of Rughi, of Strada (near San Pietro in Campo), of Pescia, of San Filippo, of San Alluccio, of Bruscieto, and of San Giovanni in Montecatini were along the Via Cassia.

45. Herlihy, *Pisa*, p. 102.

46. On roads between Lucca and Pisa, ibid., pp. 99–100.

47. Gioacchino Volpe, *Pisa*, pp. 8ff.

48. The lands of the jura were sometimes enumerated in imperial privileges. The earliest enumeration by a bishop was that of Pope Alexander II (Anselmo I) in the 1060s: *Mem e doc*, V, iii, No. 1795. See also the "constitutions" of Bishop Enrico of about 1300, rub. xlvii, edited in Raoul Manselli, "La sinodo lucchese di Enrico del Carretto," in *Miscellanea Gilles Gerard Meersseman*, I, Italia Sacra 15 (Padua, 1970), 228-29. On the jura see below, pp. 51–69.

49. On agriculture see below, pp. 96–113.

2. FORMATION OF THE MEDIEVAL LUCCAN BISHOPRIC

1. On the life of San Frediano see Guerra, Guidi, *Storia ecclesiastica lucchese*, App. III, pp. 35-63; on the significance of San Frediano's work, Cesare Sardi, *Le contrattazioni agrarie del medio evo studiate nei documenti lucchesi* (Lucca, 1914), pp. 22-23.

2. These donations have been studied by Nanni, *La Parrocchia*, pp. 5ff., and Robert Endres, "Das Kirchengut," pp. 245-49; on proprietary churches and monasteries and the role of the Lombard nobility see Schwarzmaier, *Lucca*, pp. 27-36, 44-45.

3. The inventory was published in *Mem e doc*, V, iii, no. 1758, and in *Inventari*, No. II, pp. 13-22. Gino Luzzatto analyzed the document in *I Servi nelle grandi proprietà ecclesiastiche italiane dei secoli IX e X* (Senigallia, 1909). This study was republished in his *Dai Servi della gleba agli albori del capitalismo* (Bari, 1966); see especially pp. 22-27 (in the reprint).

4. Endres, "Das Kirchengut," pp. 267-68.

5. Ibid., pp. 260-73.

6. Catherine E. Boyd, *Tithes and Parishes in Medieval Italy* (Ithaca, N.Y., 1952), pp. 70ff.

7. Harry Bresslau, *Handbuch der Urkundenlehre für Deutschland und Italien* (2nd ed., 2 vols., Leipzig, 1912-31; rpt. Berlin, 1958), II, 248-49.

8. Nanni, *La Parrocchia*, pp. 91ff.

9. *Mem e doc*, V, ii, No. 904 (880); similarly, e.g., Nos. 945 (886), 935 (885), 1026 (898); *Mem e doc*, V, iii, Nos. 1501 (979), 1513 (980), 1646 (989).

10. *Mem e doc*, V, iii, Nos. 1448 (974), 1525 (983), 1532 (983).

11. "An Italian Estate," p. 19.

12. *La Parrocchia*, pp. 97ff.

13. See, e.g., *Mem e doc,* V, ii, Nos. 1099 (907), 1105 (907), 1174 (917).

14. On rural counts see Volpe, *Toscana medievale,* pp. 327ff.; idem, *Medio evo italiano,* pp. 58-59.

15. On the family see Schwarzmaier, *Lucca,* pp. 96ff.; see also Repetti, *Dizionario,* VI, 58-63. On the early struggles between the Aldobrandeschi and the communes of Siena and Orvieto see Daniel Waley, *Mediaeval Orvieto* (Cambridge, 1952), pp. 17-19. On the expansion of their power base in southern Tuscany, Volpe, *Toscana medievale,* pp. 11ff.

16. *Mem e doc,* V, iii, No. 1466 (975).

17. Ibid., No. 1471 (976).

18. Ibid., III, i, 101ff.

19. On the rural counts at Lucca see Antonio N. Cianelli, "De' conti rurali nello stato lucchese," *Mem e doc,* III, i, 85-245.

20. See App. 1; see also Schwarzmaier, *Lucca,* pp. 85-133.

21. On castle building, see below, pp. 55-57.

22. On the changes that occurred in the eleventh century see Cinzio Violante, *La società milanese nell' età precomunale* (Bari, 1953) and *La pataria milanese e la riforma ecclesiastica,* Studi Storici, 11-13 (Rome, 1955).

23. On the reform see Gerd Tellenbach, *Church, State and Christian Society at the Time of the Investiture Contest,* trans. R. F. Bennett (Oxford, 1940; rpt. 1959); cf. the study by H. E. J. Cowdrey, *The Cluniacs and the Gregorian Reform* (Oxford, 1970), pp. xix ff., 135-56; Ovidio Capitani, "Esiste un' 'Età Gregoriana'? Considerazioni sulle tendenze di una storiografia medievistica," *Rivista di storia e letteratura religiosa,* 1 (1965), 454-81; on the Synod of Sutri, idem, "Immunità vescovili ed ecclesiologia in età pregregoriana e gregoriana," *Studi medievali,* ser. 3, 3 (1962), 525-75, especially 541ff., and 6 (1965), 196-290.

24. The reform of the chapter has been studied by Erich Kittel, "Der Kampf um die Reform des Domkapitels in Lucca im 11. Jahrhundert," in *Festschrift Albert Brackmann,* ed. Leo Santifaller (Weimar, 1931), pp. 207-47.

25. On the various titles used to designate the canons see Nanni, *La Parrocchia,* p. 14; Kittel, "Der Kampf," (n. 24 above), p. 208.

26. Schwarzmaier, *Lucca,* pp. 52-53, 58-61; the quotation is from p. 61; see also Giovanni Dinelli, "La origine della 'Jura' del Capitolo di S. Martino in Lucca," *Bollettino Storico Lucchese,* 12 (1940), 149-57.

27. Kittel, "Der Kampf" (n. 24 above), pp. 211-12.

28. The documentation is sparse. We have only secondary indications of alienations of lands and of married clergy. See, e.g., the bulls of Leo IX and Alexander II, *Mem e doc,* V, iii, Nos. 1789, 1790, 1795.

29. See the judgement of Augustin Fliche, *La réforme grégorienne* (3 vols., Paris and Louvain, 1924-37), I, 342ff.

30. *Mem e doc,* V, iii, No. 1794; cf. Martino Giusti, "Le canoniche della città e diocesi di Lucca al tempo della Riforma Gregoriana," *Studi Gregoriani,* 3 (1948), 321-67, esp. p. 331, who finds Anselmo's silence on the subject of common life difficult to explain.

31. On Anselmo II see the short biographical essay by Cinzio Violante in *Dizionario biografico degli italiani,* I (1960), 398-407, and the works cited therein.

32. *Vita Anselmi episcopi Lucensis auctore Bardone presbytero,* ed. Roger Wilmans, *MGH,* Scriptores, 12 (Hanover, 1856; rpt. Stuttgart and New York, 1963), p. 15; on the *Vita Anselmi,* see Edith Pásztor, "Una fonte per la storia dell' età gregoriana: la 'Vita Anselmi episcopi lucensis'," *Bullettino dell' Istituto storico italiano per il Medio Evo e Archivio Muratoriano,* 72 (1961), 1-33; the letter of Gregory VII is in *Das Register Gregors VII,* ed. Erich Caspar, *MGH,* Epistolae Selectae, 2 (Berlin, 1920), V, 1 (11 August 1077).

33. *Register,* VI, 11 (28 November 1078).

34. Ibid., VII, 2.

35. On the importance of the familial connections of the canons see Schwarzmaier, *Lucca*, pp. 58-61 and 153-54.

36. Tommasi, *Storia di Lucca*, Doc. I, pp. 2-3.

37. Kittel, "Der Kampf" (n. 24 above), p. 245; Giusti, "Le canoniche" (n. 30 above), p. 324. The donation is found in *Regesto del Capitolo*, I, No. 525.

38. Cowdrey, *The Cluniacs* (n. 23 above), pp. 121-35; Tellenbach, *Church, State and Christian Society* (n. 23 above), pp. 77-85; Giovanni Miccoli, *Pietro Igneo: studi sull età gregoriana*, Studi Storici, Nos. 40-41 (Rome, 1960), pp. 10ff.; on common life in the European church see *La vita comune del clero nei secoli XI e XII*, Atti della Settimana Internazionale di Studio: Mendola, settembre 1959 (2 vols., Milan, 1962).

39. Nanni, *La Parrocchia*, pp. 103, 120-21.

40. Giusti, "Le canoniche" (n. 30 above); on the significance of collegial organization in Italy see Robert Brentano, *Two Churches: England and Italy in the Thirteenth Century* (Princeton, 1968), pp. 97ff.

41. *Regesto del Capitolo*, III, No. 1669.

42. Ibid., I, No. 677.

43. Martino Giusti, "Le elezioni dei vescovi di Lucca specialmente nel secolo XIII," *Rivista di Storia della Chiesa in Italia*, 6 (1952), 205-30.

44. Nanni, *La Parrocchia*, pp. 31ff., 38ff.

45. *Le Liber censuum de l'église romaine*, eds. Paul Fabre and L. Duchesne, Bibliothèque des Écoles Françaises d'Athènes et de Rome, 2nd ser., 6 (3 vols., Paris, 1889-1952), I.1, 67-70.

46. *Tuscia*, I, Nos. 4191-4234.

47. Kehr, *Italia Pontificia*, pp. 414-37, registers S. Frediano's privileges; Migne, *PL*, 163, cols. 131-32.

48. For tithes let by Giovanni see ++ O 42, ++ G 48, ++ O 78; for Anselmo I see Kehr, *Italia Pontificia*, p. 491.

49. ++ G 63 (28 July 1159).

50. ++ I 13 (March 1180).

51. On the advantages of tax farming see William M. Bowsky, *The Finance of the Commune of Siena, 1287-1355* (Oxford, 1970), pp. 120ff.; Herlihy, *Pisa*, pp. 86ff.

52. The figures are given in the *Martilogio* of 1364, pp. 103, 104, 109. We do not know at what point the tithes (except those given to the Hospital of San Jacopo) were alienated by the episcopate. We may assume that the payments began at least ca. 1300, possibly earlier. In 1364 they certainly represented little more than recognition rents.

53. *Mem e doc*, IV, i, No. 143.

54. For donations to churches at Lucca see Nanni, *La Parrocchia*, pp. 38-48; in general see Boyd, *Tithes and Parishes* (n. 6 above), pp. 126-27.

55. The figures are taken from a chronological catalog of beneficenze in Giuliano Pisani, *La Beneficenza in Lucca prima del Mille* (Lucca, 1907), pp. 100-107. Pisani's figures for the period before 1000 are quite accurate, but for the period after 1000 his results must be taken as only tentative: Endres, "Das Kirchengut," p. 245, records 22 donations for the ninth and tenth centuries, but Pisani's figures include only those donations specifically made for charitable works or for the foundation of hospitals.

56. *Lucca*, pp. 65-66.

57. On the rebuilding and construction of Lucca's churches see Isa Belli Barsali, *Guida di Lucca* (2nd ed., Lucca, 1970), passim.

58. There is no study of the early Christian archeology in the diocese of Lucca. For information on the pievi I must thank Sac. Giuseppe Ghilarducci, director of the Archivio arcivescovile

of Lucca and a student of the early Christian archeology of northern Tuscany. For the privilege of Calixtus, see Kehr, *Italia Pontificia*, p. 392.

59. See, e.g., ++ G 15 (1080), ++ H 84 (1099), ++ K 63 (1109), ++ H 76 (1101).

60. *Mem e doc*, IV, ii, No. 112; the opera sometimes was called the Opera di San Martino. There were occasionally other opere for special projects. On the Opera of San Martino, see Bongi, *Inventario*, IV, 136.

61. This diffusion of religious life is but another aspect of what David Herlihy, *Pistoia*, pp. 241-58, has called "Civic Christianity." Though the new piety is more evident in the later Middle Ages and Renaissance (see, e.g., Gene Brucker, *Renaissance Florence* [New York, 1969], pp. 172-212), it really began in the Gregorian and post-Gregorian periods. See, e.g., Gioacchino Volpe, *Movimenti religiosi e sette ereticali nella società medievale italiana (secoli XI-XIV)* (2nd. ed., Florence, 1961).

62. David Herlihy, "Treasure Hoards in the Italian Economy, 960-1139," *Economic History Review*, ser. 2, 10 (1957), 1-14.

63. Cinzio Violante, "I vescovi," pp. 205-06.

64. Francesco Maria Fiorentini, *Memorie della Gran Contessa Matilda*, with notes and documents edited by Gian-Domenico Mansi (Lucca, 1756), pp. 90, 124-25; Matilda's donations to the episcopate are listed in Alfred Overmann, *Gräfin Mathilde von Tuscien* (Innsbruck, 1895), pp. 135, No. 21 (7 May 1075), and 143, No. 34 (26 September 1079).

65. ++ K 5; Nanni, *La Parrocchia*, p. 37.

66. Nanni, *La Parrocchia*, pp. 22-30; Schwarzmaier, *Lucca*, pp. 27-35.

67. Endres, "Das Kirchengut," pp. 245-46; it is not clear whether most of these donations were made out of piety or necessity.

68. On the donation of lands of the Cadolinghi see Robert Davidsohn, *Forschungen zur älteren Geschichte von Florenz* (4 vols., Berlin, 1896-1908; rpt. Turin, 1954), I, 83-91.

69. See, e.g., the series of documents recording a single transaction on 16 October 1043: AB 37 is called an "offersionis cartula" offering the lands to the episcopate "pro anime sue remedio"; AB 39 (same day), a "Repromisionis pagina," where the owner, having received a "meritum de anulo de auro" (no value is listed), promised not to molest the episcopate's possession of the lands; AB 40 (same day) is a "Breve" recording the donation, promise, and meritum.

70. The transactions between 1100 and 1153 are found in App. 2, Nos. 1 to 76. The resumption of 1120 is No. 21.

71. *Mem e doc*, V, i, 325-26 (28 April).

72. For transactions between the Gherardesca and the episcopate see App. 2, Nos. 2, 13, 16, 25, 43, 46, 47, 53, 56, 64, 65, 76.

73. On the Gherardesca and the archbishop of Pisa see *Regestum Pisanum*, ed. Natale Caturegli, Regesta Chartarum Italiae, 24 (Rome, 1938), Nos. 296, 303, 363, 377, 378, 379, 380, 399, 440, 558. On Forcoli, see Repetti, *Dizionario*, II, 324-25; Volpe, *Pisa*, pp. 28-29. On the Gherardesca see Repetti, *Dizionario*, VI, 46-54; Volpe, *Pisa*, pp. 390ff.

74. App. 2, No. 40.

75. Ibid., Nos. 12, 14, 26, 45.

76. Guerra, Guidi, *Storia ecclesiastica lucchese*, pp. 108-09.

77. Herlihy, *Pistoia*, pp. 25-26.

78. *Mem e doc*, IV, ii, No. 105; Tolomeo, *Annales*, p. 77.

79. Guidi and Pellegrinetti, *Inventari*, Nos. VI, X, XIV (*Martilogio*). These conclusions are valid only for the Valdera and the eastern part of the diocese. In other areas in the middle Serchio, at Santa Maria a Monte and elsewhere, the episcopate continued to possess jurisdiction and to receive profits of justice throughout the medieval period. See below, pp. 83-85.

80. Cf. Brentano, *Two Churches* (n. 40 above), who emphasizes the urban nature of the Italian church, as opposed to the more rural English church.

81. The problem has recently been studied by David Herlihy, "The History of the Rural Seigneury in Italy, 751-1200," *Agricultural History,* 33 (1959), 58-71.

82. Tolomeo, *Annales,* p. 20; the conquest of the Luccan contado is recounted in Tommasi, *Storia di Lucca,* pp. 26-51.

83. Volpe, *Pisa,* pp. 9-10.

84. Giovanni Dinelli, "La fortezza medievale di Ripafratta," *Atti,* n.s., 10 (1959), 192.

85. *Mem e doc,* IV, ii, No. 96.

86. Cf. Giovanni De Vergottini, "Origine e sviluppo storico della comitatinanza," *Studi Senesi,* 43 (1929), 385ff., who argues that through the first half of the twelfth century, especially at Pisa and Siena, the bishop or cathedral chapters acted on behalf of the commune in its relations with feudal lords. He further contends (455) that *districtus, episcopatus, comitatus,* and *diocese* became equivalent terms for the territory under the civil jurisdiction of the commune. While this might have been the case generally, "districtus" was used in the Luccan documents to indicate that area placed under the jurisdiction of the Luccan commune by the concession of Henry IV ("Districtus sex miliarum"). "Episcopatus" was used almost exclusively to mean that which belonged to the bishop, and almost never as an equivalent of "diocese." On the lords of Versilia and Garfagnana see Giovanni Dinelli, "I confini geografici della Versilia," *Bollettino Storico Lucchese,* 11 (1939), 69-70; and Pacchi, *Garfagnana,* pp. 85-93.

87. See above, pp. 16-18; see also the remarks of Violante, "I vescovi," pp. 215-17.

88. See the complete statement of Pietro Vaccari, *La territorialità come base dell'ordinamento giuridico del contado nell'Italia medioevale* (2nd ed., Milan, 1963); cf. the remarks of Violante, "I vescovi," p. 195 n. 1.

89. See Violante, *La società milanese* (n. 22 above), Chapter I, on the development of the markets of the Po Valley.

90. On the functions of the castles, see Fabio Cusin, "Per la storia del castello medievale," *RSI,* ser. 5, 4 (1939), 491-542; and Vaccari, *La territorialità* (n. 88 above), pp. 159-72; for Lucca see below, pp. 54-58.

91. See, e.g., Georges Duby, *Rural Economy and Country Life in the Medieval West,* trans. Cynthia Postan (French ed. Paris, 1962; London and Columbia, S.C., 1968), p. 45.

92. E.g., ++ M 15-19 (28 June 1229), a podere or farm located at Lavaiano (south of the Arno) was let and the rent was to be carried to Santa Maria a Monte.

93. + P 16 (1059); ++ F 19 (1211); ++ Q 97 (1235).

94. * N 92. Six men acknowledged having to "reducere unam salmam vini a colcarelli usque ad huc [curiam Sancte Marie Montis]." Doubtless some of the others who owed service "cum asino" carted produce to the regional centers.

95. In *Moneta e scambi nell'alto medioevo,* Settimane di Studio del Centro Italiano di Studi sull'Alto Medioevo, 8 (Spoleto, 1961), pp. 159-60.

96. On the similar actions of a cathedral chapter see Giorgio Chittolini, *I beni terrieri del capitolo della cattedrale di Cremona fra il XIII e il XIV secolo,* Biblioteca della *Nuova Rivista Storica,* 30 (Milan, Rome, Naples, 1965).

97. Nanni, *La Parrocchia,* pp. 145ff.

3. ADMINISTRATION OF EPISCOPAL TEMPORALITIES

1. On the earliest officials see Schwarzmaier, *Lucca,* pp. 305-07; Maria Nesti, "I documenti degli archivi di Lucca durante gli anni 1041-44 del Vescovato di Giovanni II," Tesi di Laurea presented to the Facoltà di Lettere at the Università di Pisa (Pisa, 1967-68), No. 43.

2. Laura Gemignani, "Le carte private degli archivi di Lucca durante il Vescovato di Anselmo di Baggio," Tesi di Laurea presented to the Facoltà di Lettere at the Università di Pisa (Pisa, 1956-57), No. 70.

3. *Mem e doc,* IV, ii, No. 108.

4. App. 2, No. 33; similarly see Nos. 15, 46, 66, 95, 113.

5. *Mem e doc,* V, iii, No. 1799; similarly Nos. 1801, 1809.

6. On the two offices and the debates over their significance see Volpe, *Medio evo italiano,* pp. 55-76 and especially 67-68. This is a review article, first published in 1908 and 1911, of Silvio Pivano, *Stato e chiesa da Berengario I ad Arduino, 888-1015* (Turin, 1908) and Silvio Alvisi, *Il comune d'Imola nel secolo XII* (Bologna, 1909).

7. *Mem e doc,* V, iii, No. 1768; on the advocates at Lucca see also Schwarzmaier, *Lucca,* pp. 273-85, 309-22.

8. *Mem e doc,* V, iii, Nos. 1166, 1200.

9. Ibid., Nos. 1279, 1281; at least we might assume that the "Johannes notarius et judex" found among the witnesses without any patronym was the same Giovanni.

10. Ibid., IV, ii, No. 100.

11. Ibid., V, iii, No. 1796.

12. ++ M 53 (1135), ++ A 18 (1205), ++ B 31 (1218), * F 1 (1218).

13. Bongi, *Inventario,* II, 300ff. Unfortunately, records of this court for the period before 1328 have been lost.

14. + B 64 (1191), ++ S 91 (1178), ++ R 72 (1182), ++ A 97 (1189), * Q 53 (1191), ++ D 34 (1196), * Q 44 (1192), ++ S 65 (1193), ++ O 32 (1194), AC 35 (1194), ++ D 34 (1195), * K 85 (1196), + B 66 (1196).

15. Bongi, *Inventario,* II, 301-02. Bongi first found records of the court in the years 1235 and 1236, but cf. * R 90, the record of a case heard by the court in 1223.

16. On the castaldo see below, pp. 39-41.

17. ++ I 96.

18. * S 4.

19. Endres, "Das Kirchengut," p. 359.

20. See, e.g., *Mem e doc,* V, iii, Nos. 1048 (901), 1102 (907), 1191 (921), 1298 (943).

21. Ibid., Nos. 1515, 1516, 1518, 1526, 1532, 1533, 1542, 1559, 1588, 1591, 1610, 1628, 1631, and 1641; also Schwarzmaier, *Lucca,* pp. 42-43.

22. *Toscana medievale,* p. 23.

23. Ibid., pp. 25ff.

24. On the Avvocati, see Schwarzmaier, *Lucca,* pp. 310-17; Antonio N. Cianelli, "De' conti rurali nello stato lucchese," *Mem e doc,* III, i, 140-47. (N.b., for the sake of clarity, Avvocato or Avvocati (Ital.) refers to the family, while advocate or advocates (English) refers to the office of advocate which may or may not be held by a member of the Avvocati family.) Frederick II's concession is quoted, ibid., p. 143.

25. *Inventari,* No. VI, p. 26.

26. Tommasi, *Storia di Lucca,* pp. 157-58. They were Lamberto degli Avvocati in 1184 and Rainerio degli Avvocati in 1234.

27. Cianelli, "Conti rurali" (n. 24 above), p. 147.

28. For Duodo see ++ M 46 (17 January 1196); for Normanno, ++ B 50 (9 February 1189) and *Inventari,* No. VI, p. 26 (10 February 1192).

29. AE 17 (1135), + M 12 (1141), AE 80 (1145), + Q 51 (1176), ++ R 15 (1181), ++ R 67 (1181), and ++ B 50 (1189).

30. For Riccardo see ++ R 26 (18 October 1181) and ++ T 99 (18 October 1187); for Guido see ++ I 50 (4 August 1187), ++ B 50 (17 February 1190), ++ E 2 (25 May 1201), ++ I 96 (12 June 1203).

31. Paganellus advocatus Lucani Episcopatus, A 90 (16 December 1182) and * Q 76 (2 May 1209); Paganello may be two different advocates. Benedetto del fu Pietro Rofredi Advocato, App. 2, No. 104 (9 February 1189) and ++ A 97 (14 October 1189); the notary Guglielmo, ++ O 32 (22 August 1194) and ++ D 34 (20 April 1195).

32. For a twelfth-century family tree see Schwarzmaier, *Lucca*, p. 315; + L 91 (1120), + + C 75 (1159), + P 28 (1165).

33. Volpe, *Toscana medievale*, p. 23.

34. + F 4 (13 September 1240). The episcopal advocate, Manso di Saraceno, appealed to the bishop of Florence, judge delegate in this case, that Rainerio degli Avvocati "non litigare vel molestare eundem pro dicto episcopo vel episcopatu et ipsum Episcopum et episcopatum super locationibus domarum et terrarum eiusdem episcopatus et super conventionibus et creationibus castaldionum eiusdem episcopatus et confirmationibus eorumdem neque super aliquo extimatione vel cognitione aliquarum causarum, litium vel contraversarum quarum iurisdictio spectat ad lucanum episcopatum . . . item ut non petat vel exigat aliquam conmestionem pro se vel suis equis in palatio lucani Episcopi."

35. Members of the Avvocati family taking an active role in episcopal administration are mentioned in the following documents: Duodo, + M 46 (17 January 1195); Normanno del fu Sesmondino, + + B 50 (9 February 1189), *Inventari,* No. VI, p. 26; Rainerio del fu Tancredo, + G 98 (29 April 1224), * K 54 (29 April 1232), * R 84 (1236); Riccomanno del fu Vicedomino, + G 98 (25 January 1227), + F 77 (23 October 1227), + + N 79 (26 March 1232), * Q 46 (11 July 1232); Tancredo, * K 45 (3 May 1230), * G 36 (9 May 1230); Cecio del fu Avvocato, + + S 77 (31 March 1232), + + K 23 (11 October 1232), * A 28 (20 October 1236); Lamberto, + + T 9 (21 November 1234); Buono del fu Buonacurso, * A 28 (20 October 1236), + + O 29 (1236), + + G 7 (20 May 1243), + + S 49 (20 May 1243); Enrico, + + O 10 (8 September 1237); Guido son of Cecio, + + A 5 (11 December 1237).

36. * G 99 (4 April 1222), + + C 31 (4 March 1224), + F 24 (4 March 1229), + + C 67 (5 March 1230), + + D 34 (14 March 1232), + + A 7 (15 June 1233), * T 36 (22 December 1233), + + O 25 (31 March 1235), + + A 28 (13 June 1237), and + + M 93 (8 January 1245; this document only identifies the principal as "Orlanduccio advocato seu sindico"). (It is noteworthy that only two of the ten documents recording actions by Orlanduccione occurred after 1235, while the Avvocati continued to exercise their office.)

37. * H 90 (17 April 1241), "Rainerius petebat . . . [from the communal court] ut inducere eum in possessionem vicedominatus et advocatie episcopatus lucani secundum tenutam sibi datam per dominum Pandolfum Capitaneum Sacri Imperii in Tuscia generalem. . . . Et super eo videlicet quod dictus Mansus pro lucano Episcopatu dicebat dictam tenutam esse cassam. . . ."

38. For Saraceno del fu Buonaconte see + + E 26 (5 October 1212), * Q 75 (19 March 1214), + G 98 (11 May 1214).

39. Giova, + + E 37 (13 May 1215), "sindicus seu advocatus vel procurator vel vicecomite domini Roberti." Giova was a principal in 14 other documents, but only rarely was he called a viscount. Riccomanno, see above, n. 35. Frate Ricovero, + + C 53 (3 March 1243), + + D 55 (15 December 1255), + K 42 (20 March 1242), + G 45 (13 August 1242), + + O 28 (23 January 1247), * A 90 (25 March 1250), + H 26 (23 July 1251), + + P 71 (23 July 1251), + + S 86 (22 June 1253), + + B 40 (29 July 1255). In 23 other documents Ricovero was called variously proctor, familiaris, or castaldo. Arrigo, son of Morello of Coreglia, * K 54 (5 May 1257) "vicecomiti et procuratori et sindico speciale venerabilis patris domini Henrigi." Ser Ricco del fu Jacopo of Coreglia, * D 62 (1257), "Ricco notarius de Corelia vicedominus venerabilis patris domini Henrigi." In ten other documents he was described as proctor or syndic. Riccomanno, + + C 44 (9 December 1261), "rector hospitalis Sancti Ansani de Ponte Moriani et vicecomes domini Henrigi." Orlando del fu Cipriano, * S 5 (6 September 1274).

40. * G 99 (4 April 1222), Bishop Roberto selected Orlanduccione del fu Tedesco Bonzomori as a familiare of the episcopate "promictendo et convenendo ei per sollempnem stipulationem dare et dari facere eidem Orlanduccio donec vixerit victum et vestimentum et calciamentum

bene et decenter et predictus Orlanduccius promisit servire dicto Episcopo et suis subcessoribus in mensa et in omnibus aliis locis et eundo cum eo equos cum uno ex equis Episcopi. . . ."

41. * H 90.

42. *LA,* IX, fol. 116ʳ (1320); + + C 37 (1327).

43. *San Gimignano,* p. 45.

44. + + O 10 (8 September 1257). I am unable to identify the Berlinghi family and the document does not explain the basis of the argument.

45. *LA,* I, fol. 8ʳ⁻ᵛ (24 March 1257).

46. On the podestàs of the rural communes see below, pp. 63, 68, 75–76.

47. On the notaries see Herlihy, *Pisa,* Chapter I, "The Notarial Chartulary"; on the familial origins and political role of the notaries at Padua, J. K. Hyde, *Padua in the Age of Dante* (Manchester and New York, 1966), pp. 154–75.

48. + + O 32 (22 August 1194); similarly, + + D 34 (20 April 1196; 9 May 1196), + + B 66, * K 85.

49. + + A 51 (4 December 1231), the vicars Ubaldo and Opizone and "Romeus tinctor qd. Reguli . . . compromiserunt in Jacobum notarium filium Luchesi almosneri advocatum lucani Episcopatus inter se arbitratorem . . ."; * R 61 (3 February 1231), "Coram domino Ubaldo primicerio et Magistro Robertino canonicis dicti Episcopatus et Guidone notario et converso dicti Episcopatus et aliis personibus."

50. + + D 34 (20 April 1254); the only other documents in which he appears as a participant are litigations before communal courts, + + G 21 (21 December 1254) and + + T 7 (1255).

51. Ricco appears as an episcopal official in 23 documents. See, e.g., + + O 33 (16 March 1258), * P 79 (12 February 1259), + G 86 (5 May 1261).

52. For Alberto see, e.g., * P 96 (27 July 1259) and * R 76 (13 December 1262).

53. + + Q 9 (21 April 1280).

54. For other documents referring to notaries acting as episcopal officials see AB 94 (1258), + + Q 89 (1264), + + R 71 (1265), + + S 86 (1267), + + A 68 (1270), AB 89 (1302), + + F 28 (1304), + + T 8 (1311), + + M 47 (1308), + D 10 (1308), + H 21 (1309), * F 60 (1311), + + Q 85 (1322), + + D 55 (1324), + + C 37 (1327).

55. On this change see Daniel Waley, *The Italian City-Republics* (London and New York, 1969), pp. 182–97; for what is known of the Luccan experience see above, p. 5.

56. Tommasi, *Storia di Lucca,* App., p. 27.

57. + + N 3.

58. + + D 31.

59. + + D 50 (1146), + + R 26 (1181), + + I 50 (1187).

60. + + N 18 (16 October 1193).

61. + + L 55.

62. E.g., * N 17, * N 26, * N 40, AB 54.

63. *LA,* I, fol. 2ᵛ (24 March 1257), records the appointment of Tantobuono di Albare as the castaldo of San Gervasio.

64. * S 4 (1 November 1269), "Dominus Nantelmus primicerius, dominus Paganellus de Porcari et dominus Philippus lucani canonici, vicarii lucani Episcopatus pro dicto eorum officio vicariatus pro lucano Episcopatu et vice et nomine lucani Episcopatus fecerunt, costituerunt, et ordinaverunt Junctam dictum de Subgromineo qui moratur in Sancta Maria de Monte absentem tanquam presentem dicti lucani Episcopatus sindicum, procuratorem, certum nuntium et actorem et castaldionem in Santa Maria de Monte tantum ad exigendum et recolligendum et sibi dari et solvi faciendum, redditos, affictos, pentiones, et libella et jura lucani Episcopatus petendum et proseguendum et defendendum et prout olim consuetus erat recolligere et recipere terre domini henrici olim lucani Episcopi. Et generaliter ad omnia et singulam

faciendum qua ad predictam spectant et que verus et legiptimus sindicus, procurator et castaldio facere potest."

65. * M 31 (12 August 1261), "Raynerio de Secgio castaldus Episcopi in curia Moriani"; + + Q 2 (8 May 1261), "carfagnane castaldus et procurator domini Henrigi."

66. *LA,* IX, fols. 313^r-314^r (there are two folios marked 313), "dominus Paganellus d.g. lucanus episcopus . . . fecit, constituit et ordinavit Solominum notarium de montetopari qd. Martini . . . ipsius episcopatus vicecomitem, castaldionem, sindicum et procuratorem . . . in infrascriptis terris de ultra Arnum videlicet in septiro, leccia, perignano, sancto Piero, monteculaccio, solaria, padule, capannole, forcole, alica, montefoscoli, tavelle, montecastello, tregiaria, Sancto Gervasio, palaria, ripezano, colleoli, montecchio, pratielione, et toiano ad petendum, recipiendum, exigendum et confitendum pro ipso domino episcopo et episcopatu . . . qui seu que ipsi domino episcopo et episcopatui debentur et debebuntur hinc ad tres proximos futuros annos ab omnibus et singulis personis, locis, collegiis et universitatibus. . . . Et ad agendum et defendendum contra omnem personam et locum in curia et extra in omnibus et singulis causis, litibus, et questionibus que propterea inoverentur coram quocumque et quolibet judice ecclesiastico et civili. . . ." Herlihy, *Pisa,* p. 199, lists grain prices at Pisa. Another castaldo paying a fixed annual fee is recorded at San Lorenzo di Moriano in 1347, *LA,* X, fol. 205^{r-v}.

67. E.g., + + Q 91 (20 April 1281), "Gualandus notarius de Pisis qd. Guidonis Gualandi castaldio et sindicus et procurator venerabilis Patris"; + + F 28 (3 January 1304), "Turchinus qd. Beni notarius civis lucanus vicecomes et castaldio. . . ."

68. I found only one reference to "Rusticus castaldus Episcopi de Sancto Gervasio," * P 1 (23 October 1204). There are ten references to Ventura and Nenita: for Ventura, e.g., + + E 9 (23 February 1232), "nuntio et procurator lucani Episcopatus," and + + D 91 (20 February 1238), "castaldus seu villicus lucani Episcopatus in Santa Maria in Montem"; for Nenita, + + D 91 (18 September 1232).

69. For Giova see, e.g., + + E 30 (13 August 1214), + + E 73 (19 August 1224); for Gualfreduccio, * R 72 (11 April 1259), and * R 72 (10 January 1262).

70. On Giova and his brothers see + + E 25 (12 December 1211), + + E 20 (13 August 1214), + + E 39 (26 July 1215), + + E 41 (25 January 1216), + + E 63 (19 December 1220), + + E 74 (13 January 1225), + + E 12 (5 February 1238), + + O 14 (1233), and + + E 69 (1232), where both Giova and Rubaconte were named as members of the major and minor councils.

71. * S 5 (6 September 1274).

72. * S 19 (9 March 1257).

73. *Regesto del Capitolo,* I, Nos. 721, 939, 999.

74. *Inventari,* No. V, pp. 23-25.

75. In 1183, the chapter's treasurer was one Guido del fu Bernarduccio "cammarlingo eccl. et canonice S. Martini," *Regesto del Capitolo,* II, No. 1496.

76. *Inventari,* No. XI, pp. 43ff.; for Baleante see, e.g., + + L 27 (23 March 1241) and + + L 44 (30 November 1241).

77. On Baleante see, e.g., + + A 78 (19 December 1240), "camerarius domini Episcopi et Episcopatus"; * A 9 (9 May 1246), "canonicus lucanus vicarius in temporalibus domini Guertii"; + + C 32 (22 September 1248), "vicarius episcopatus et domini Guertii."

78. The only exception I have found is * K 45 (1230), "Tancredus camerarius," who may be the layman described in the same year as "advocatus et vicarius domini Opizi lucani Episcopi" and possibly a member of the Avvocati family. * G 36.

79. For Jacopo see + + D 34 (3 August 1256), + + A 90 (14 December 1265); for Agolante, + + D 55 (29 December 1257); for Presbyter Guido di Gragno, + B 14 (29 September 1258).

80. *Inventari,* No. XIII, pp. 53-58.

81. Martino Giusti, "Le elezioni dei vescovi di Lucca specialmente nel secolo XIII," *Rivista di Storia della Chiesa in Italia,* 6 (1952), 219-20.

82. Tommasi, *Storia di Lucca,* pp. 72-73; also Carlo De Stefani, "La signoria di Gregorio IX in Garfagnana," *ASI,* ser. 5, 28 (1901), 1-14.

83. Frate Ricovero, "familiaris et vicecomes domini Guercii," e.g., + G 45 (13 August 1242), + G 34 (9 May 1258).

84. * E 66.

85. + + S 77 (26 November 1262), "Dominus Soffredus plebanus Masse vicarius provincie vallis neule pro venerabile patre domino Henrico lucano Episcopo"; Nanni, *La Parrocchia,* p. 173.

86. *LA,* I (1256-57), e.g., fols. 4^{r-v}, 7^r, 9^r, 10^r, 11^r, 11^v-13^r, 14^{r-v}, 17^r.

87. Ibid., e.g., fols. 3^{r-v}, 5^v-6^v.

88. Tommasi, *Storia di Lucca,* pp. 141, 149, 151. The other communal vicariates were Valdilima, Valleriana, Barga, Coreglia, Camporgiana, Castiglione di Garfagnana, Camaiore, Pietrasanta, Massa del Marchese and Lunigiana (including Sarzana and Carrara). The functions of the communal vicars are studied by Domenico Corsi, "Le 'Constitutiones Maleficiorum' della Provincia di Garfagnana del 1287," *ASI,* 115 (1957), 347-59.

89. Giusti, "Le elezioni" (n. 81 above), pp. 210-11.

90. For Opizone, e.g., + + A 51, + + D 34, + + K 36; for Ubaldo, + + B 87, + + P 53, A 20.

91. + + S 72 (1236), "Dominus Buondimandus camerarius"; + + K 41 (1249), "Dominus Conradus vicarius et primicerius"; + + C 99 (1236), "Dominus Ugolino primicerius et proctor"; * R 11 (1239), "Presbyter Baleante canonicus lucanus et camerarius"; + + D 55 (1250), "Dominus Gualteroctus canonicus et camerarius"; + + G 24 (1251), "Presbyter Accursus canonicus Sancte Marie Forisportam et camerarius domini Guercii"; * P 21 (1254), "Dominus Petrus cammerarius ac vicarius domini Guercii"; + + B 86 (1254), "Frate Ricovero vicecompte, et procurator domini lucani Episcopi"; * M 37 (1239), "Frater Ricuperus procurator et sindicus et familiaris domini Guercii"; + + K 41 (1249), "Dominus Ronaccius canonicus lucanus vicarius venerabile patris patris domini Gercii"; + + D — (1256), "Presbyter Jacobus canonicus ecclesie Sancte Marie Forisportam lucani camerarius."

92. See above, pp. 42-43.

93. On Guercio's spiritual activities see Paolo Dinelli, *Mem e doc,* VII, 53-58; on his relations with the commune see below, p. 75.

94. Giusti, "Le elezioni" (n. 81 above), pp. 218ff.

95. Ibid., p. 219.

96. + + K 42 (1261); cf., e.g., + + I 22 (1218), a document making a castaldo for Moriano "cum consilio familiarum eius omnium vel maioris partis. . . ."

97. Nanni, *La Parrocchia,* p. 201, quoting from a document of 1286 in the Archivio Capitolare di Lucca, Libro LL, 41, fol. 27^r.

98. Jacopo appears as treasurer first in 1256 under Bishop Guercio. The other documents refer to his actions as Enrico's treasurer. See, e.g., + + A 90 (14 December 1266).

99. + + C 44 (9 December 1261).

100. Seventeen leases made by Orione are extant; see, e.g., + + S 44 (2 December 1260) and AB 92 (11 February 1268).

101. + + L 36 (18 January 1270): "domini antelminus primicerius et filippus canonici lucani canonache Sancti Martini et vicarii lucani Episcopatus pro se ipsis et pro domino Paganello item canonico et conlega eorum ex auctoritate eorum offitii vicariatus et nomine lucani Episcopatus consensu dominorum Guidi archipresbyteri et Gerardini et Gualtrocti et Guidi de

Anania et Guilielmi de Gragna et Petri et Soffredis et Orlandi canonicorum suprascripte canonache et ipsi idem canonici fecerunt et constituerunt et ordinaverunt et creaverunt dominos Angelium et Franciscum monacos Monasterii Sancti Michelis de Guamo presentes et recipientes . . . sindicos, proctores, actores, responsales, advocatos, defensores, custodes, administratores, et negotiatores, gestores in omnibus et singulis eorum et lucani Episcopatus causis, litibus, questionibus, negotiis et factis ecclesiasticis et secularibus . . . ad agendum, petendum, causandum, defendum, excipiendum, replicandum, libellos dandum et recipiendum et lites contestandum et de calumpnia et veritate dicendum . . . et soluctiones et pagamenta recipiendum et nuntios et castaldiones faciendum et factos removendum . . . dantes eis plenum et liberum et generalem mandatum promictentes firmum tenere totum et ea omnia que per eos vel alique eorum actum seu procuratum fiant."

102. + + D 55 (12 January 1324), + + C 37 (1327).

103. See App. 1.

104. *LA,* IX, fols. 292^v-293^v; 310^v-311^r.

105. Ibid., X, fol. 10^{r-v}; the document of institution is quoted in the body of a lease of 1332.

106. This must remain hypothetical until the chapter and its rich archives have been thoroughly and systematically studied. For another aspect of the economic crisis see below, pp. 113-16.

107. *Pistoia,* pp. 241-58; the quotation is from p. 246.

108. *Tuscia,* I, No. 4252.

109. Nanni, *La Parrocchia,* p. 172; on the patronatus see ibid., pp. 171-81.

110. On Florence, see Gene Brucker, *Renaissance Florence* (New York, 1969), Chapter V, "The Church and the Faith."

4. THE EPISCOPAL JURA

1. On the bishop's jura see Nanni, *La Parrocchia,* pp. 117ff. Two other Luccan religious bodies also possessed jura during the Middle Ages. The cathedral chapter of San Martino retained its jura in Versilia until the French suppressed it in 1799; See Giovanni Dinelli, "La origine della 'Jura' del Capitolo di S. Martino in Lucca," *Bollettino Storico Lucchese,* 12 (1940), 149-57. The abbot of the monastery of San Salvatore of Sesto possessed a jura in an area near the lake of Bientina which passed to the Luccan commune in the mid-thirteenth century; see Tommasi, *Storia di Lucca,* p. 156.

2. *LA,* IX, fol. 123^r; the document only notes approval and states that one half of all profits of justice shall be the bishop's. The extant statutes of Montopoli and Santa Maria a Monte date from the period of Florentine jurisdiction when the episcopate's rights in the Valdarno no longer were recognized. The statutes of both communes have been edited by Bruno Casini, *Statuto del comune di Montopoli (1360),* Fonti sui comuni rurali toscani, 5 (Florence, 1968), and *Statuto del comune di Santa Maria a Monte (1391),* Fonti sui comuni rurali toscani, 2 (Florence, 1963).

3. The exemplum was edited by Domenico Corsi, "Il 'Breve' dei consuli e dei podestà del comune di Santa Maria a Monte (secoli XII-XIII)," *Atti,* n.s., 10 (1959), 151-72.

4. *Medio evo italiano,* p. 68; Volpe is speaking of the "nobiliores" or "nobilissimi" in the early eleventh-century episcopal towns, but his observation is valid for the rural communes.

5. On the *Libri antichi,* see Duane J. Osheim, "The Episcopal Archive of Lucca in the Middle Ages," *Manuscripta,* 17 (1973), 142-45.

6. *LA,* IX, fols. 6^r-8^r (1302).

7. The communal register probably was similar to the *Liber censuum* of Pistoia. On the Archivio di Stato of Lucca, see Bongi, *Inventario,* I and II.

8. Bongi, *Inventario,* I, xi ff.; the quotation is from p. xi.

9. *Mem e doc,* V, iii, No. 1795; see also the imperial concessions of Otto IV (1209) and Charles IV (1355) which include other areas added after 1063, ibid., IV, i, No. 30 (Charles's contains the text of Otto's).

10. C. Manaresi, "Alle origini del potere dei vescovi sul territorio esterno della città," *Bullettino dell' Istituto storico italiano per il Medio Evo e Archivio Muratoriano,* 58 (1944), 221-334.

11. *Mem e doc,* V, i, p. 115; ibid., IV, ii, No. 59; Schwarzmaier, *Lucca,* pp. 50-58.

12. The role of the rural counts and the juridic history of castles are discussed above, pp. 13-15, 23-25.

13. *Mem e doc,* IV, i, No. 46.

14. Ibid., V, ii, No. 306. It is impossible to know just where this "Villa" was located. It may designate Villa Basilica as Repetti, *Dizionario,* V, 774, assumed. But it could also refer to the "Villa" located near Bientina, Moriano, Fosciana, or in the Valleriana. On these possibilities see Nanni, *La Parrocchia,* "indice dei nomi e delle cose," p. 231.

15. *Mem e doc,* V, iii, No. 1287 (8 December 941) and No. 1571 (19 September 983).

16. *Mem e doc,* V, ii, No. 330 (802) and No. 679 (850).

17. *Dizionario,* V, 6; Walprando's will is *Mem e doc,* IV, i, No. 46; the trade of land at Tocciano is ibid., V, ii, No. 44; the "Tucciano near Luciano" is No. 46. For the location of Luciano and Tucciano see Nanni, *La Parrocchia,* p. 66.

18. *Ricerche storiche sulla Provincia della Garfagnana* (Modena, 1785; rpt. Bologna, 1967), p. 86.

19. Nanni, *La Parrocchia,* p. 16; he cautions, however, that the church referred to may be San Casciano a Vico instead of the church at Moriano.

20. Ibid., p. 72 n. 81; Nanni cites all references to the pieve in the period before 1000.

21. *Mem e doc,* V, ii, No. 607 (844) and No. 648 (847). The key phrase is "pertinens Eccl. vestre S. Maria plebe baptismale sita loco Sexto."

22. Ibid., V, iii, No. 1161.

23. Ibid., V, i, 115.

24. See, e.g., Santa Maria a Monte, 1066-73, ibid., V, iii, No. 1795; Mammoli, 1080, ibid., IV, ii, App., No. 84; Montecatini, 1075, Alfred Overmann, *Gräfin Mathilde von Tuscien* (Innsbruck, 1895), No. 21.

25. *Mem e doc,* IV, ii, App., No. 59; on Anchiano and its lords see Antonio N. Cianelli, "De' conti rurali nello stato lucchese," *Mem e doc,* III, i, 152-60; see also Schwarzmaier, *Lucca,* pp. 52-53, 103. On castles in the Florentine contado see Riccardo Francovich, *I Castelli del contado fiorentino nei secoli XII e XIII,* Atti dell' Istituto di Geografia della Università di Firenze, 3 (Florence, 1973), pp. 15-24.

26. See above, pp. 10-15.

27. See above, p. 13; Nanni, *La Parrocchia,* pp. 97ff.

28. *Mem e doc,* V, iii, No. 1795.

29. Pacchi, *Garfagnana* (n. 18 above), No. 11.

30. Ibid., No. 33.

31. *LA,* IX, fols. 4^{r-v} (1 November 1301), 57^{r}-58^{r} (undated but 1301-23).

32. See above, pp. 22-25.

33. *Mem e doc,* IV, ii, App., No. 84 (1074-80).

34. *Mem e doc,* V, iii, No. 1279 (941).

35. Overmann, *Gräfin Mathilde* (n. 24 above), No. 34.

36. Maria Nesti, "I documenti degli archivi di Lucca durante gli anni 1041-44 del Vescovato di Giovanni II," Tesi di Laurea presented to the Facoltà di Lettere at the Università di Pisa (Pisa, 1967-68), Nos. 68 and 69.

37. *Mem e doc,* V, iii, No. 1788; the document is badly lacerated and if information on rights and duties was included, it is no longer legible.

38. Nanni, *La Parrocchia,* p. 37.

39. In general see above, pp. 22-25; on the sales and gifts of castles or parts of castles to the episcopate see Nanni, *La Parrocchia,* p. 37; Nesti, "I documenti" (n. 36 above), No. 68; Maria Pianezzi, "I documenti degli archivi di Lucca durante gli anni 1045-50 del Vescovato di Giovanni II," Tesi di Laurea presented to the Facoltà di Lettere at the Università di Pisa (Pisa, 1967-68), No. 62; *Mem e doc,* IV, ii, No. 108; ibid., V, i, 325-26; ibid., No. 1800; Overmann, *Gräfin Mathilde* (n. 24 above), Nos. 34, 37, 54; App. 2, Nos. 2, 12, 13, 14, 16, 20, 22, 25, 26, 30, 31, 32, 33, 36, 41, 43, 45, 46, 47, 49, 50, 53, 60, 61, 62, 63, 64, 76, 77, 78, 85, 86, 92, 102.

40. On the Luccan conquest of its contado see Tommasi, *Storia di Lucca,* pp. 26, 63, 65; on the Pisan commune and the Valdera, Volpe, *Pisa,* pp. 178-90.

41. *Mem e doc,* V, i, 325-26.

42. *Mem e doc,* IV, ii, App., No. 99 (Moriano, 1121); ++ G 92, ++ D 40 (Valivo di Sopra, 1122); ++ B 36 (Castro di Moriano, 1159); * E 22, ++ G 2, + L 26 (Colcarelli, 1169); similarly, ++ Q 21 (Castelvecchio di Garfagnana, 1179) and * A 22 (Aquilea in Moriano, 1191). The oath of the "men of Moriano" probably included the men of Castro di Moriano and Aquilea: the men of Moriano differentiated among themselves to a greater and greater extent during the late twelfth and thirteenth centuries, and by the mid-thirteenth century there were seven rural communes in the district of Moriano. According to litigation over the district of Moriano in 1277 (* G 31), "jurisdictio comunium plebis sexti moriani, castri moriani, sancti cassiani, sancti laurentii, sancti michaelis de vilorbana, sancti quirici de licciano et aquilee pleno jure pertinet ad lucanum Episcopatum...."

43. See above, p. 19.

44. See, e.g., *LA,* IX, fols. 22ᵛ-23ʳ (10 September 1303), "Molaçano"; 24ᵛ-25ᵛ (5 November 1305), Cerreto; 27ʳ⁻ᵛ (20 January 1306), Vergemmole; 72ᵛ-73ʳ (20 April 1317), Castagnore; 297ᵛ-298ᵛ (21 March 1284), Vico Pelago; 348ᵛ (16 May 1308), Cassio; 352ʳ⁻ᵛ (11 December 1308), Verio.

45. *Tithes and Parishes in Medieval Italy* (Ithaca, N.Y., 1952) pp. 178-95; Boyd did not establish the exact period in which the alienation of the rural tithes occurred, nor the extent to which these rural communes may have ended the collection of tithes altogether.

46. Nanni, *La Parrocchia,* pp. 160ff.; Nanni cites similar cases in 1186 and 1206. See also the litigations over rights of patronage, above, pp. 19-20.

47. Montopoli, ++ D 36, and Nanni, *La Parrocchia,* p. 167; Santa Maria a Monte, * G 85; Aquilea, ++ H 71. On popular selection of rectors in general see Nanni, *La Parrocchia,* pp. 159-81. Nanni argues that the litigations over patronage are an indication that the church was attempting to reclaim its rights. It is more likely that these litigations indicate that the de jure rights of the church were compromised with the interests of the laity in the selection of spiritual leaders.

48. * F 46.

49. Fedor Schneider, "Nachlese in Toscana," *Quellen und Forschungen aus Italienischen Archiven und Bibliotheken,* 22 (1930-31), No. III.

50. ++ P 40; according to the tithe lists in *Tuscia,* I and II, the churches of Montecalvoli were subject to the pieve of Santa Maria a Monte; the mill in question probably was the bishop's mill at "piediripa" which the episcopate continued to control well into the fourteenth century.

51. Salvatore Bongi, "Quattro documenti de' tempi consolari (1170-1184) tratti dal R. Archivio di Stato in Milano," *Atti.* 21 (1882), 288-89; the convention between Santa Maria a Monte and Montecalvoli is no longer extant.

52. Domenico Corsi, "Santa Maria a Monte nelle guerre tra il comune di Pisa e quello di Lucca attraverso le cronache e alcuni documenti inediti," *Bollettino Storico Pisano,* 36-38 (1967-69), 68 n. 52.

53. *Mem e doc,* IV, ii, No. 111.

54. On the definitions of the words see Charles Du Cange, *Glossarium Mediae et Infimae Latinitatis,* 10 vols. (1883-87; rpt. Graz, 1954), s.v.

55. AC 7 (8 May 1207).

56. AE 20 (30 September 1210).

57. + + K 48; similarly + + A 97 (1189), further litigation over Diecimo and Fondagno.

58. On transhumance, see, e.g., Philip Jones, "Italy," *Cambridge Economic History,* I (2nd ed., Cambridge, 1966), 380.

59. * M 29; + + P 78.

60. Corsi, "Il 'Breve' " (n. 3 above), pp. 151ff.; see also Corsi's transcription in "Le 'Constitutiones Maleficiorum' della Provincia di Garfagnana del 1287," *ASI,* 115 (1957), 347-70.

61. AB 50 (15 June 1223); there was already one commune in Moriano, at Castro di Moriano, which was distinct from the commune of Sesto di Moriano.

62. See, e.g., David Herlihy, "Direct and Indirect Taxation in Tuscan Urban Finance, ca. 1200-1400," *Finances et comptabilité urbaines du XIIIe au XVIe siècle,* Colloque international—Blankenberge, 6-9-IX-1962. Actes (Brussels, 1964), pp. 389-90. Herlihy cannot pinpoint exactly when profits from justice slipped in importance, saying only that after the middle of the thirteenth century, "direct taxes in the form of the *estimo . . . ,* as far as we can judge, [were the] most remunerative in supporting the city budget, at least in the inland communes" (p. 401). The chronology is vague, but we may assume that profits of justice remained of major importance in the first part of the thirteenth century.

63. *Pisa,* pp. 46ff.

64. See, e.g., litigations + + A 7 (15 July 1236) and + + A 28 (13 June 1237). The inquests into legal status usually followed the form used in + + A 8 (28 November 1228).

65. *Pisa,* p. 26, citing the agreement of 1180 in *Mem e doc,* IV, ii, No. 111.

66. I have found only six cases where communal consuls had private dealings with the episcopate: Bernardo del fu Bernardo of Montopoli, * T 3 (18 August 1231), received a podere from the episcopate; Bonensegna del fu Barone of Montopoli, * T 89 (1236), returned his portion of the hospital at Ripalta to the episcopate, and * S 84 (3 May 1258), received a 12-year lease of three pieces of land at Montopoli for an annual rent of four stai of wheat; Buono notario, AB 90 (1276), received a ten-year lease of a "casamentum seu sedium in burgo montopoli" for an annual rent of eight soldi. Ventura di Tancredo of Montopoli, * S 100 (2 January 1227), received a perpetual lease of one piece of land at Montopoli for a rent of ten denari annually and an entry-fine of five soldi; Ugolino del fu Buonamico of Sesto di Moriano, + + C 53 (3 March 1243), received a perpetual lease of 22 pieces of land at Sesto, + + Q 97 (23 October 1254); Ugolino's sons Diociguardo and Bello received a perpetual lease of nine pieces of land at Sesto; see also *Martilogio,* lines 916-919; Rubaconte del fu Carnelevare (+ + O 14), see above, p. 41.

67. *San Gimignano,* p. 45.

68. Herlihy, "Santa Maria Impruneta: A Rural Commune in the Late Middle Ages," in *Florentine Studies: Politics and Society in Renaissance Florence,* ed. Nicolai Rubinstein (London, 1968), pp. 251-52; idem, *Pistoia,* pp. 122ff., for the extremely high price of wheat in the thirteenth century—the reason it had replaced wine as the most valuable cash crop.

69. *Statuto del comune di Montopoli* (n. 2 above), p. 41.

70. Ibid.

71. Blomquist, "Drapers of Lucca" (see Ch. 1 n. 24 above), p. 68; Florence M. Edler, "The Silk Trade of Lucca during the Thirteenth and Fourteenth Centuries" (Ph.D. dissertation, The University of Chicago, 1930), pp. 58-93.

72. Fiumi, *San Gimignano*, pp. 51-52.

73. Ibid., p. 174.

74. Volpe, *Toscana medievale*, pp. 163ff.

75. App. 7, No. 7; * D 15 (1210).

76. * D 27 (13 December 1226).

77. + + E 87 (21 September).

78. The term *Lambardi* or *Lombardi* often was used to name families of rural counts or in some cases a consortium of families. These men may represent collateral lines of a single family, although I have found no indication of a familial relationship.

79. + + E 91 (16-19 January 1239); + + D 16 is a second copy of the litigation. The case had begun at least four years earlier: see the procurations in the unnumbered rolls under the sign + + D; there are five dated between 6 and 9 November 1235.

80. + + E 69 (1232); + + O 14 (1233).

81. + + E 99.

82. + + O 23 (1237).

5. THE EPISCOPAL JURA AND THE LUCCAN COMMUNE

1. Tommasi, *Storia di Lucca*, App., No. 1; Robert Davidsohn, *Storia di Firenze* (8 vols., Florence, 1956-68), I, 394-95.

2. Tolomeo, *Annales*, pp. 20, 27, 29, 30, 44, 46.

3. Bernardi Maragonis, *Annales Pisani a. 1004-1175*, ed. Karl Pertz, *MGH*, Scriptores, 19 (Hanover, 1866), a. 1144 (Pisan style).

4. Frederick's privilege to the men of Garfagnana is in Domenico Pacchi, *Ricerche storiche sulla Provincia della Garfagnana* (Modena, 1785; rpt. Bologna, 1967), No. XII. In general see Daniel Waley, *The Italian City-Republics* (London and New York, 1969), pp. 110ff.

5. Volpe, *Toscana medievale*, p. 362; Tolomeo, *Annales*, pp. 94-97.

6. Volpe, *Toscana medievale*, p. 503.

7. See, in general, Davidsohn, *Storia di Firenze* (n. 1 above), I, 851-54; II, 21-22, 224ff.; Pacchi, *Garfagnana* (n. 4 above), pp. 64-70.

8. See below, App. 2, Nos. 9 (1108), 10 (1108), 11 (1109), 14 (1114), 24 (1121), 40 (1129), and 45 (1130). Tommasi, *Storia di Lucca*, App., Doc. No. 2 (1107); Tolomeo, *Annales*, pp. 46, 50; Robert Davidsohn, *Forschungen zur älteren Geschichte von Florenz* (4 vols., Berlin, 1896-1908; rpt. Turin, 1964), I, 83-91.

9. See above, pp. 25-26.

10. *Annales Pisani* (n. 3 above); see also Volpe, *Pisa*, pp. 65-66, 178ff.

11. See below, p. 76.

12. Waley, *City-Republics* (n. 4 above), p. 111; similarly, Volpe, *Pisa*, pp. 178-79.

13. Davidsohn, *Storia di Firenze* (n. 1 above), I, 497-99; V, 351-54.

14. Ibid., II, 20-21.

15. Ibid., Eduard Winkelmann, *Acta imperii inedita seculi XIII et XIV* (2 vols., Innsbruck, 1880-85; rpt. 1964), I, Nos. 30, 32, 34.

16. Volpe, *Toscana medievale*, p. 426.

17. Tolomeo, *Annales*, p. 104.

18. Ibid., App. II, p. 302.

19. Pietro Pressutti, ed., *Regesta Honorii Papae III* (2 vols., Rome, 1888-95), I, Nos. 3503, 3669, 4143. Davidsohn, *Storia di Firenze* (n. 1 above), II, 46-47, 122-23; Bongi, *Inventario*, II, 308. The papal letters might actually indicate that the whole affair was part of the strife that had been a feature of Luccan political life since the 1190s. Solution of the problem must await a study of the "nobiltà e popolo" of Lucca in the thirteenth century.

20. For this and the following sections on Santa Maria a Monte see Tommasi, *Storia di Lucca*, pp. 84-85, and Domenico Corsi, "Santa Maria a Monte nelle guerre tra il comune di Pisa e quello di Lucca attraverso le cronache e alcuni documenti inediti," *Bollettino Storico Pisano*, 36-38 (1967-69), 51-70. Both Tommasi and Corsi argue that the events of 1252 at Santa Maria a Monte were prompted by fears of treason, although they cite no evidence of treason at the time.

21. Volpe, *Toscana medievale*, pp. 502-03.

22. ++ L 23 is the agreement of 1229 which mentions an earlier agreement with Bishop Roberto (1202-25); the constitutions of 1308 are in *Mem e doc*, III, iii, Book I, rub. xxxvi.

23. AD 38. It seems unlikely that Bartolomeo handled the matter in such a formal manner, but we have no record of any protests by the bishopric's vicars. Bartolomeo did eventually serve as podestà for that year, which may indicate that his declaration was pro forma. Corsi, "Santa Maria a Monte" (n. 20 above), p. 60.

24. Corsi, "Santa Maria a Monte," p. 63.

25. Ibid., p. 67.

26. * L 42.

27. ASL, *Capitoli*, XXXIII, pp. 4-13 (24 May 1379).

28. Corsi, "Santa Maria a Monte" (n. 20 above), p. 59. The bishopric itself, however, could be called upon for aid. A rather cryptic document of 1248 (* O 10) was a "Memoria de eo quod lucanum comune habuit et precipit de proventibus lucani episcopatus . . . anno MCCXLVIII." It recorded without further comment that the commune had received £576 11s. 3d. If we assume that the bishopric's income in 1248 was nearly equivalent to its estimated income of £3,500 in 1260 (*Tuscia*, I, 246), then the commune levied a tax of about 16 percent on the bishopric.

29. The bishop still collected profits from justice at Montopoli and Santa Maria a Monte in the late fourteenth century, long after the two communes had been incorporated into the Florentine state; see AB 99 (11 June 1353), the city council of Montopoli ordering that the Luccan bishopric should receive half the profits from justice. Bruno Casini, *Statuto del comune di Santa Maria a Monte (1391)*, Fonti sui comuni rurali toscani, 2 (Florence, 1963), rub. xiii, p. 50.

30. ++ O 23 (29 September); the reason the two knights were being sent is not included in the document; they probably served in the imperial army in Lombardy.

31. A 92 (12 October 1267); * B 88 is a second copy of the appeal.

32. * G 31; Tommasi, *Storia di Lucca*, pp. 104, 126.

33. * O 21 (1229).

34. *LA*, IX, fols. 294^r-295^r (15 February 1287). Apostil, "Commissio factum per Episcopum lucanum in dominum Andriolum Judicem super grassa victualium in civitate lucana ut Judex commissum sibi officium posset constringere fideles lucani Episcopatus."

35. Salvatore Andreucci, "Papa Clemente V° in una controversia fra il Vescovo e il comune di Lucca," *Giornale storico della Lunigiana e del territorio lucense*, n.s., 16 (1965), 65-73.

36. *Statuto del Comune di Lucca dell' anno MCCCVIII* (=*Mem e doc* III, iii), p. 340.

37. ASL, *Capitoli*, XXXIII, pp. 72ff. (July 1330).

38. ASL, *Capitoli*, I (this volume is also cited as *Libro Grande di Privilegi*), fols. 25^r-36^r. Ser Federigo argued that the men of Sorbano del Vescovo "substinuerunt et substinent onera

realia et personalia pro lucano comuni salvendo impositas et collectas et alia onera lucano communi et faciendo exercitus et cavalcatas et alia servitia pro lucano communi et habendo extimum factum per lucanum communem. . . ."

39. The transcription is found in *Le croniche di Giovanni Sercambi, lucchese,* ed. Salvatore Bongi, Fonti per la storia d'Italia, 19-21 (3 vols., Rome, 1892), I, 72.

40. Bongi, *Inventario,* II, 24.

41. ASL, *Anziani avanti la libertà,* X, fol. 24ᵣ⁻ᵛ.

42. * I 58 (26 June 1346), Ser Spinello complained to the Gabella maggiore that "Ciomeus de Podio et ser Bartholomeus Bonotelli de villa baçilica proventuales seu officiales proventus venditionum, alienationum et dotium anni domini MCCCXLIII seu ante vel postea gravant et molestant indebite et iniuste plures et plures homines et personas de dictis communibus . . . pro comperis et alienationibus per eos factis inter se . . . et pro dotibus per eos receptis. . . ." This is unjust, "cum ipsa comunia et homines ipsorum communium non veniant in carta compere per eos facte de dicto proventu sed expresse sunt exclusi a vendictione et gabella predicta maxime cum non sint sub jurisdictione lucani communis sed sunt sub jurisdictione et dominio tam in temporali quam spirituali domini lucani episcopi et episcopatus lucani. . . ." * S 38 (1 September 1347) is a similar complaint directed at the farmers of the gabelles on wine and comestibles. Spinello added that they were also being forced to mark their wine and oil containers with the Luccan communal mark. Again the judge of the Gabella maggiore supported the communes of the jura with a general affirmation that "communia et homines eorumdem non teneri nec cogi debent vel posse ad aliquas gabellas solvendas vel ad aliqua alia honeria realia vel personalia subeunda lucano communi."

43. *Regesti del R. Archivio di Stato in Lucca,* ed. Luigi Fumi, II (Lucca, 1903), Nos. 481-85.

44. ASL, *Capitoli,* I, fols. 41ᵣ⁻44ᵛ (15-27 July); the documents refer to a "lis et discordia" between the communes of Moriano and the commune of Lucca, but the agreement seems to be a pro forma recognition of rights as well as a negotiation of tax payments. The agreement was probably substantially the same as that made in the early 1350s. *LA,* LXVI, fol. 28ᵣ⁻ᵛ (19 April 1354), records a payment to the Luccan commune of 10 fl. of the 70 fl. the communes at Moriano owed for the gabelles on wine, bread, and pork.

45. ASL, *Capitoli,* XXII, p. 389 (24 February 1371).

46. * I 58 (26 June).

47. A 63 (16 March 1347), on the back "Sententia lata per Iudicem Gabelle 1347 pro Episcopatui et Jura Moriani."

48. A 67 (3 January 1348).

49. ASL, *Capitoli,* XXXIII, p. 5 (May 24).

50. Marvin B. Becker, *Florence in Transition* (2 vols., Baltimore, 1967-68), I, 233. Cf. the review by Lauro Martines, *Speculum,* 43 (1968), 689-92.

6. SOURCES OF WEALTH

1. On episcopal treasures see above, pp. 42-43; for the records of the medieval bishopric, Duane J. Osheim, "The Episcopal Archive of Lucca in the Middle Ages," *Manuscripta,* 17 (1973), 131-46; the best description of a commune's financial administration is William M. Bowsky, *The Finance of the Commune of Siena, 1287-1355* (Oxford, 1970), pp. 1-15. On the possibilities of a study of expenditures see Ann Katherine Chiancone Isaacs, "Fisco e politica a Siena nel Trecento," *RSI,* 85 (1973), 26-27. For an episcopal inventory composed during a vacant see, *Inventari,* No. XIII, pp. 53-58.

2. Augusto Mancini, *Storia di Lucca* (Florence, 1950), p. 26; Guerra, Guidi, *Storia ecclesiastica lucchese,* p. 202.

3. See above pp. 19-20; *Martilogio,* lines 28, 210, 969, 1410, 1469, 1514, 1518, 1524, 1537, 1561, 1571, 1646, 1671, 1672, 1678, 1681, 1695, 1698, 1706, 1709, 1718, 1719, 1721, 1723, 1740, 1744, 1759, 1763, 1766, 1783. Only five of the entries explain the reasons for the payments: three paid for lands and houses (two soldi for land at Ripa and two stai of wheat at Palaia, and one staio of wheat and 18 soldi for land in the Luccan suburbs); San Jacopo paid for tithes; and one hospital paid 10 soldi for a mass.

4. See above, p. 19.

5. On proctors' expenses see Robert Brentano, *Two Churches: England and Italy in the Thirteenth Century* (Princeton, 1968), pp. 20-28.

6. *Tuscia,* I and II.

7. Ibid., I. 243-75.

8. Kehr, *Italia Pontificia,* p. 387, quoting *Le Liber censuum de l'église romaine,* eds. Paul Fabre and L. Duchesne, Bibliothèque des Écoles Françaises d'Athènes et de Rome, 2nd ser., 6 (3 vols., Paris, 1889-1952), I.1, 67; see also *LA,* IX, fols. 309^v-310^r (30 January 1291), where the bishopric asked for an extension on the due date of the payment it still owed.

9. See above, pp. 75-76.

10. Tommasi, *Storia di Lucca,* p. 106.

11. On loans to the Luccan bishopric see Violante, "I vescovi," p. 205; *Mem e doc,* IV, ii, No. 118 (1119), * Q 45 (1187), + + P 47 (1139), * L 25 (1210), * A 64 (1118), * S 82 (1157), * O 9 (1194), * K 28 (1224), * H 13 (1239), + + R 22 (1254), * F 74 (1301), + L 27 (1306), + + D 10 (1308). In most cases we have no more than the slightest idea of the interest paid, since the loan documents usually only noted the properties given in pawn and not what they were worth in annual interest. On voluntary loans to communes, see Bowsky, *Finance* (n. 1 above), pp. 189-224, especially 223, who noted that interest rates on communal loans varied from 10 to 60 percent.

12. *Martilogio,* line 1458, "Ecclesia S. Petri Siricaioli porte S. Donati" paid one libra of wax; line 1794, "Ecclesia S. Martini de Fagognano" paid two libre of wax. Doubtless other of the unspecified payments in the *Martilogio* were for similar confirmations.

13. Violante, "I vescovi," pp. 216-17, posed the problem in his survey of the economic role of the bishop in the eleventh and twelfth centuries. He emphasized the political reasons for the change: "E mentre in effetti il potere cittadino passava alle nuove forze produttive che costituivano il 'Comune di Popolo,' la potenza economica—spesso decadente—del vescovo sembrava fondarsi sempre più unicamente sul patrimonio fondiario. . . ."

14. See App. 3, a geographical and chronological breakdown of the extant leases.

15. Typical examples of Italian agricultural leases have been translated in Georges Duby, *Rural Economy and Country Life in the Medieval West,* trans. Cynthia Postan (French ed. Paris, 1962; London and Columbia, S.C., 1968), pp. 439-40, Nos. 87, 88; we need not wonder at the vagueness of references to the location of, e.g., "the lands formerly held by the late Guido." Even in mid-twentieth century rural America, farmers may continue to refer to a farm as "the old Nelson place" 20 years after the last Nelson died.

16. "I vescovi," p. 210.

17. Transcribed by Eugenio Lazzareschi, "Fonti d'archivio per lo studio delle corporazioni artigiane di Lucca," *Bollettino Storico Lucchese,* 9 (1937), 78; I am using the translation of the oath found in Robert S. Lopez and Irving W. Raymond, eds., *Medieval Trade in the Mediterranean World* (New York and London, 1961), pp. 418-19.

18. See, e.g., the diplomas of Otto IV of 1209 and of Charles IV of 1355, *Mem e doc,* IV, i, No. 30.

19. * R 88 (1227).

20. See, e.g., *Martilogio; LA*, VIII, fol. 11^v (12 August 1343), the commune of Molegano admitted owing 12 soldi annually for tithes; fol. 24^r (11 August 1344), the commune of Lerciano confessed to owe two libre of wax for tithes; fol. 45^r (11 February 1343), the commune of Terillio paid four libre of wax for its tithe. *LA*, IX, fols. 22^v-23^r (10 September 1303), the commune of Molazzano promised 12 soldi annually for tithes; similarly, fols. 24^r-25^r, 27^{r-v}, 72^v-73^r, 297^v-298^r, 299^v-300^v, 347^r, 348^v, 352^v-356^v.

21. *Mem e doc*, V, ii, No. 855 (874); iii, No. 1293 (942), 1530 (983); cf. Lynn White, *Medieval Technology and Social Change* (Oxford, 1962), p. 83, who, following Arturo Uccelli, ed., *Storia della Tecnica dal medio evo ai nostri giorni* (Milan, 1944), p. 132, argues that there may have been a fulling mill on the Serchio in 983. I have found no mention of any kind of mill on the Serchio in the tenth century.

22. *Regesto del Capitolo*, I, Nos. 239, 608n, 639, 754, 805; II, Nos. 1215, 1230, 1238, 1296; III, 1562, 1649, 1771.

23. "The Advent and Triumph of the Watermill," in *Land and Work in Mediaeval Europe*, trans. J. E. Anderson (Berkeley and Los Angeles, 1967), pp. 136-68. The essay was originally published in *Annales d'histoire économique et sociale*, 7 (1935), 538-63.

24. Enrico Fiumi, "Sui rapporti economici tra città e contado nell' età comunale," *ASI*, 114 (1956), 41.

25. + + A 20, the bishop promised "quia deinceps in antea non abeamus potestatem neque licentem . . . molinum abendi neque ponendi neque tenendi" in the district.

26. + + P 40, the abbot "investivit Ottonem d.g. lucanum episcopum eique pactum et conventum fecit quod ipse Manfredus abbas vel eius successores non litigabit neque molestabit . . . prefatum Ottonem . . . videlicet del molino et aldio atque sepe suprascripti episcopatus."

27. + + E 37; the original lease given to the pieve is + + B 50 (1192); "large fish" is a rather vague term. In 1294, however, large fish were defined as those worth more than 12 denari (* L 22). The pieve of Santa Maria a Monte still held the mill as late as the 1260s: * S 49 (1261). The bishop used the same type of lease to construct his mill at Marlia, where the rector of the church of San Terenzio of Marlia agreed to construct a mill on episcopal lands: * B 85 (1236).

28. + + E 47.

29. + + E 42 (1216), + + E 48.

30. * S 5 (6 September 1274); although the lease included no explanation of the nonpayment of the revenues, it may be that the problem was in part political. The Pisans held Santa Maria a Monte in the years just prior to 1274 and there was a pro-Pisan party in the town; neither group would have been willing to help the Luccan episcopate collect its rents. On Giunta as castaldo, see, e.g., * R 83, + S 52, * T 24.

31. * L 22 (1294).

32. *LA*, IX, fols. 73^v-75^r (28 May 1317).

33. * B 86 (10 December 1354); + + G 33 is a second copy of the same document.

34. *Regesti del R. Archivio di Stato in Lucca*, ed. Luigi Fumi, II (Lucca, 1903), No. 154 (1 March 1343) to Pope Clement; No. 167 (April 1343) to Walter, duke of Athens and lord of Florence.

35. *LA*, IX, fol. 38^v (3 January 1346), records the return of the mill to the episcopate because milling was prohibited; fol. 56^r (3 August 1346) is a new lease of the mill at Marlia.

36. The episcopate's estimated wealth in 1260 is listed in *Tuscia*, I, 246. I used £60 as the worth of the rent because that is the figure given in the rent contract of 1317. The value of the rents may have been much greater in 1260 when the episcopate controlled the district of Santa Maria a Monte. If it were as high as £100, then the mill represented about 3 percent of the episcopate's estimated wealth.

37. AC 77, + + C 27, * M 52, * P 11; *LA*, IX, fols. 4^{r-v}, 214^{r-v}.

38. Brentano, *Two Churches* (n. 5 above), pp. 103-05.

39. On the reorganization of episcopal properties see above, pp. 22–29.

40. See, e.g., *Mem e doc,* V, iii, No. 1795; Nanni, *La Parrocchia,* p. 118; San Columbano lay just outside the thirteenth-century walls although it was well developed. San Pietro Somaldi and the adjoining area of Fratta were just outside the mid-thirteenth century city walls.

41. *La società milanese nell' età precomunale* (Bari, 1953), p. 226 n. 33.

42. *Regesto del Capitolo,* I, Nos. 102, 316.

43. Violante, *La società milanese* (n. 41 above), pp. 226–30.

44. *Mem e doc,* V, iii, No. 1789; * H 90 (1241).

45. * D 39 (17 April 1165); the document is actually a "Promissionis pagina": Villano del fu Corso Maltacci, having received a "meritum" in accordance with a decision of the consuls of the Treguana, agreed to the annual 6d. payment "de terreno videlicet suprascripti episcopatus unius case que est sala in civitate luca prope portam Sancti Donati." Giuseppe Matraja, *Lucca nel Milleduecento* (Lucca, 1843; rpt. 1963), No. 261. Since Matraja chose the year 1200, before the completion of the thirteenth-century walls, San Pietro Somaldi and Fratta were outside the area he included in his work.

46. * G 46 (1232), ++ F 100 (1257); ++ R 54 (1259); the urban rents between 1300 and 1319 are found in *LA,* IX, fols. 1^{r-v}, 18^{v}–19^{r}, 19^{v}–20^{r}, 92^{v}–93^{v}, 302^{v}–303^{v}, 331^{v}–332^{r}, 342^{v}–343^{r}, 337^{v}, 341^{r-v}; rents naturally vary according to the type of land, area of the city, and the nature of the house; the documents, however, do not describe the houses completely. On medieval houses at Lucca, see Piero Pierotti, *Lucca, edilizia urbanistica medioevale* (Milan, 1965), pp. 37–46 and Part II, "Catalogo e analisi degli edifici medievali," pp. 59–185.

47. Thomas W. Blomquist, "The Castracani Family of Thirteenth-Century Lucca," *Speculum,* 46 (1971), 461 n. 8.

48. *Inventari,* No. X, pp. 36–42 (12 June 1201).

49. We have no information about the nature of these "feudi" or about the benefits they may have brought the episcopate.

50. I have found 36 rent contracts between 1165 and 1364; AB 95, AB 98, AD 55, ++ B 50 (2 contracts), ++ E 9, ++ E 14, ++ E 23, ++ E 29, ++ E 43, ++ E 53, ++ E 55, ++ E 59, ++ E 86, ++ E 91 (3 contracts), ++ E — (3 contracts), ++ L 28, ++ P 29, ++ R 69, ++ S 77, * C 74, * H 92, * K 20, AB 90, AB 92, ++ S 74, + S 77, * P 13; *LA,* IX, fols. 26^{r}–27^{r}, 354^{r}–355^{r}; *Martilogio,* lines 1791–92.

51. On possible depopulation see below, pp. 113–15.

52. On the geographical distribution of episcopal lands see above, pp. 9, 11, 23–26.

53. The rents in commodities are analyzed in Endres, "Das Kirchengut," pp. 273–79 and 291–92; cf. Cesare Sardi, *Le contrattazioni agrarie del medio evo studiate nei documenti lucchesi* (Lucca, 1914), pp. 139ff., who argues that large scale oil production began only in the fourteenth century, though he himself cites the existence of an olive press complete with aqueducts as early as 1014. The most important later introduction seems to have been the broad bean or fava bean, which is commonly found in the rent contracts after the early thirteenth century.

54. On the lack of demesne farming on the Luccan chapter's lands see Jones, "An Italian Estate," p. 27; on the use of slaves, Luzzatto, *Servi della gleba* (see Ch. 2 n. 3 above), pp. 157ff. Though servile dues seem to have been uncommon, there were exceptions. Some servile dues (*servitia*) were still collected as late as 1364. See ++ S 59 (12 January 1295), a lease which included a promise to pay 1.5 stai of wheat "et omnia alia servitia et angarias faciendum que et quas qd. Beneventus et Malioratus [the former tenants] fecerunt. . . ." *Martilogio,* lines 868–69, 1097, 1103, 1191, 1292–93, 1301, 1304, 1316, 1318, 1320–21, 1346, 1348, 1355, 1551.

55. See, e.g., Elio Conti, *La formazione della struttura agraria moderna nel contado fiorentino,* I, Studi Storici, 51–55 (Rome, 1965), 7ff.

56. "Agrarian Revolution," pp. 23–48; the quotation is from pp. 34–35. Cf. the reservations of Conti, *La struttura agraria* (n. 55 above), pp. 76n, 142n, who considers the sales of complete homesteads to be evidence of continued crisis rather than reconstruction—i.e., that Herlihy's

eleventh-century age of reconstruction is actually a continuation of the crisis. Conti also argues convincingly that the notarial formulae of the eleventh and twelfth centuries are too imprecise to measure the changes in the patterns of landholding accurately.

57. For the eleventh-century donations and purchases see Nanni, *La Parrocchia,* p. 37; Maria Nesti, "I documenti degli archivi di Lucca durante gli anni 1041–44 del Vescovato di Giovanni II," Tesi di Laurea presented to the Facoltà di Lettere at the Università di Pisa (Pisa, 1967–68), Nos. 6, 9, 43, 68, 69, 70, 72; Maria Pianezzi, "I documenti degli archivi di Lucca durante gli anni 1045–50 del Vescovato di Giovanni II," Tesi di Laurea presented to the Facoltà di Lettere at the Università di Pisa (Pisa, 1967–68), Nos. 11, 18, 49–50, 52, 62; Laura Gemignani, "Le carte private degli archivi di Lucca durante il Vescovato di Anselmo da Baggio," Tesi di Laurea presented to the Facoltà di Lettere at the Università di Pisa (Pisa, 1956–57), Nos. 42, 47, 48, 77; *Mem e doc,* IV, ii, App., Nos. 83, 89, 105, 108; V, iii, No. 1800; Alfred Overmann, *Gräfin Mathilde von Tuscien* (Innsbruck, 1895), No. 34; for the twelfth-century sales and donations see App. 2.

58. *La struttura agraria* (n. 55 above), pp. 215–16.

59. *Mem e doc,* V, iii, No. 1795; see also the remarks of Cinzio Violante in *Moneta e scambi nell' alto medioevo,* Settimane di Studio del Centro Italiano di Studi sull' Alto Medioevo, 8 (Spoleto, 1961), pp. 154ff.

60. Nanni, *La Parrocchia,* pp. 95–96; Gemignani, "Le carte" (n. 57 above), Nos. 39, 45, 52, 300.

61. + A 38 (1103), + A 38 (1114), * L 25 (1120), and * H 46 (1131).

62. + + R 15, AD 63 (1158), AC 58, AC 90; App. 2, No. 92.

63. + F 38.

64. See, e.g., the twelfth-century leases, + + R 26, + + R 67. The episcopal leases unfortunately almost never include the size of the pieces of land being let.

65. "An Italian Estate," p. 24.

66. Examples of the ninth-, tenth-, and eleventh-century livelli are found in Endres, "Das Kirchengut," pp. 287ff.; and in *Mem e doc,* IV and V.

67. "Italy," *Cambridge Economic History,* I (2nd ed., Cambridge, 1966), 356; Jones tempered his views in his latest examination of Tuscan agriculture ("From Manor to Mezzadria: A Tuscan Case-Study in the Medieval Origins of Modern Agrarian Society," in *Florentine Studies: Politics and Society in Renaissance Florence,* ed. Nicolai Rubinstein [London, 1968], 193–241), noting that duties to improve the land "by the thirteenth century . . . had dwindled, in most cases, to a purely nominal duty" (p. 215).

68. See, e.g., *Regesto del Capitolo,* III, No. 1727.

69. Sardi, *Le contrattazioni agrarie* (n. 53 above), pp. 146–47.

70. + K 43 (1152), * K 20; other examples are cited in Sardi, *Le contrattazioni agrarie,* pp. 146–47; for a lease which anticipated, if not required, certain improvements, *LA,* VIIIa, fols. 35ᵛ–36ʳ (19 September 1345), "Si aliquo tempore dictus Pasquinus conductor . . . faceret capannam et hedificium capanne seu superficiam, que remaneat et remanere debeat libera et expedicta dicto Episcopo . . . absque aliquibus expensis eidem Pasquino vel suis heredibus restituendis."

71. * A 91; similarly, + + L 10 (1147), + + B 44 (1179), + + I 52 (1191), * B 75 (1232), + + O 25 (1235), + + A 72 (1240); *LA,* IX, fol. 296ʳ⁻ᵛ (1289). These documents do not describe the improvements. In some cases the tenant's sale of the melioramentum may actually be a hidden perpetual loan.

72. + + F 99 (9 February 1240). This lease was to last nine years and specified a rent of two stai of wheat and two stai of millet and continued with the clause ". . . dicti jugales melioramentum dicte terre non debent vendere alicui persone vel loco nec episcopatui nec aliquam inquisitionem facere lucano episcopatui vel episcopo qui pro tempore fuerit de melioramento dicte terre. . . ."

73. *Mem e doc,* V, iii, No. 1795, p. 667.

74. Violante, "I vescovi," pp. 205ff. On bonifica in general see Jones, "Italy," (n. 67 above), pp. 353-67.

75. On terracing and grape arbors in the middle Serchio region see Luigi Pedreschi, *I terrazzamenti agrari in Val di Serchio,* Pubblicazioni dell' Istituto di Geografia dell' Università di Pisa, 10 (Pisa, 1963), pp. 35ff.

76. *Annales,* p. 77.

77. On drainage and flood control see Elena Paderi, "Variazioni fisiografiche del bacino di Bientina e della pianura lucchese durante i periodi storici," *Memorie della Società Geografica Italiana,* 17 (1932), p. 104. The construction of the wall at Saltocchio cannot be accurately dated.

78. + + F 27.

79. "An Italian Estate," p. 24n.

80. * F 1 (21 July), the two litigants selected Arrigo Ciavera del fu Ubertello as arbiter.

81. * G 62.

82. L. A. Kotelnikova, "L'evoluzione dei canoni fondiari dall' XI al XIV sec. in territorio lucchese," *Studi medievali,* ser. 3, 9 (1968), 601-55, p. 618.

83. On the debate over the conversion to commodity rents see ibid., p. 601 and the works cited therein; see especially the discussion of Cinzio Violante in *Moneta e scambi* (n. 59 above), pp. 155ff.

84. Rosario Romeo, "La signoria dell'abate di Sant' Ambrogio di Milano sul comune rurale di Origgio nel secolo XIII," *RSI,* 69 (1957), 474-75.

85. Ibid., pp. 477-78; Violante, *Moneta e scambi.* (n. 59 above), pp. 155-56; Kotelnikova, "Canoni fondiari" (n. 82 above), p. 603.

86. Jones, "An Italian Estate," p. 28.

87. Violante, *La società milanese* (n. 41 above), pp. 99-110, 259-88.

88. *Moneta e scambi.* (n. 59 above), pp. 155-56. The bulk of Violante's studies are concerned with the eleventh and twelfth centuries and the religious reforms. He sees this period as the key turning point in medieval history, and many of his works represent a continuing search for the proper relationships between the great political, economic, and religious changes then occurring.

89. Kehr, *Italia Pontificia,* App., pp. 487-92. These leases represent 12 of the 42 extant leases given in the Luccan diocese during his pontificate.

90. * N 92; before the consuls of Santa Maria a Monte, the bishop's castaldo Fracasso del fu Bernardo made known "omnes rationes qui sunt episcopatus Sancti Martini de Lucca . . . in curia Sancte Marie Montis et in curia Montiscalvoli et in curia de Puteo et curia Ficeclensi. . . ." The 181 payments in money averaged 13.8 denari per payment.

91. See App. 4.

92. Kotelnikova, "Canoni fondiari" (n. 82 above), p. 641, Table 1; pp. 647-48, Table 2.

93. *Le croniche di Giovanni Sercambi, lucchese,* Fonti per la storia d'Italia, 19-21 (3 vols., Rome, 1892), I, 9.

94. App. 5 contains the notations of commodity prices I have found.

95. App. 6, Nos. 1-5.

96. Ibid., No. 7.

97. Ibid., No. 19.

98. See, e.g., Jones, "Italy" (n. 67 above), pp. 419-20; Conti, *La struttura agraria* (n. 55 above), pp. 214-15.

99. L. F. Marks, "The Financial Oligarchy in Florence under Lorenzo," in *Italian Renaissance Studies,* ed. E. F. Jacob (London, 1960), pp. 123-47, especially 124ff.

100. App. 6, No. 17.

101. Ibid., No. 21.

102. Ibid., No. 19.

103. Ibid., Nos. 10, 11, 15, 18, 19, 21; in other cases, e.g., Nos. 7, 9, and 14, we lack indications of commodity prices or else we have only an indication that the rent had been changed.

104. Herlihy, *Pistoia,* p. 140.

105. App. 6, No. 14, at Musciano (1235) in the Valdarno; cf. No. 38 (ca. 1364), the lands are at Fondagno (pieve of Diecimo) although the tenant is from Torcilliano (pieve of Montesigradi).

106. On the significance of the chronological period in which we find the rent increases see below, pp. 113–15.

107. "An Italian Estate," p. 28.

108. On English entry-fines see, e.g., E. A. Kosminskiĭ, *Studies in the Agrarian History of England in the Thirteenth Century,* ed. R. H. Hilton, trans. Ruth Kisch (Oxford, 1956), pp. 249ff.

109. App. 7, Nos. 1–7; for the significance of the chronological restriction see below, pp. 113–15.

110. "An Italian Estate," p. 26.

111. App. 7, Nos. 1–5, 8, 42, 48, 53, 67, 74, 77.

112. App. 7, Nos. 14, 17, 20, 21, 28, 36, 37, 40, 44, and 72 required an annual rent of one or two denari.

113. The typical form of the phrase indicated that the payment was made "nomine servitii ut . . . per hemptionem locatio sit perpetua. . . ." See, e.g., App. 7, No. 20 (15 May 1216).

114. Jones, "An Italian Estate," p. 26.

115. *Regesto del Capitolo,* II, No. 1134.

116. * N 92.

117. + + R 14 (1232), "faciendo inde consuetos redditos et servitia ipsi episcopatui." Similarly, * B 75 (1245) at Marlia, a grain rent and the servitia owed by the former tenant; also + + O 31 (1200), + + S 59 (1295); *Martilogio* (ca. 1364), lines 1092, 1097, 1103, 1174–75, 1177–78, 1180, 1184, 1186, 1189, 1191, 1292–93, 1301, 1304, 1316, 1318, 1320–21, 1346, 1348, 1356.

118. App. 7, No. 74.

119. App. 7, Nos. 3, 13, 20, 24, and 77.

120. Ibid., Nos. 23, 41.

121. Ibid., Nos. 6, 33, 48, and 77.

122. There were almost no successful reclamation projects in the Luccan countryside between the thirteenth and the eighteenth centuries. On bonifica and reclamation see Paderi, "Variazioni fisiografiche" (n. 77 above). The best synthesis of medieval English agriculture is M. M. Postan, *The Medieval Economy and Society* (Berkeley and Los Angeles, 1972); see especially pp. 149ff.

123. See below, pp. 113–15.

124. Jones, "An Italian Estate," p. 26; but cf. his later work, "From Manor to Mezzadria" (n. 67 above), p. 222, in which he seems less impressed by the twelfth-century notices of poderi and simply states that "from the late thirteenth century on, the characteristic leasehold units, on old as well as new estates, were increasingly *poderi*. . . ."

125. "From Manor to Mezzadria," p. 228.

126. *La struttura agraria* (n. 55 above), p. 5.

127. Herlihy, "Agricultural Revolution," statistically analyzed the change in landholding patterns in rural society by studying the ratio of contracts which mention homesteads (lands with buildings) and those simply indicating pieces of land. He argued that the rise in the circulation of pieces of land indicated a rise in population and an attempt to reorganize the small uneconomical agricultural units. See, however, Conti, *La struttura agraria* (n. 55 above), p. 77,

who observed that by the eleventh and twelfth centuries the notarial formula had become too vague to bear the weight of Herlihy's assertions. See also n. 56 above.

128. Luccan episcopal documents only rarely give field sizes of the pieces. Given the wide variations in the sizes of the pieces of land, we have no statistically reliable estimate of field sizes.

129. At best, these figures can only approximate the process of "ingrossamento" since our sample varies in number and in geographical area.

130. ASL, *Estimo*, VII, fols. 1^r-79^v; this volume is a register of all the lands in the Luccan district that owed rents to the Luccan episcopate.

131. Ibid., fols. 28^r-32^v.

132. We must not overemphasize the results of such analyses, since we are assuming that the recording notary only used "podere" when referring to a farm large enough to support a family and in all other cases used the phrase "petie de terra." It is doubtful that any notary cared as much about the distinction as we do.

133. $++$ K 23, $++$ M 15-19, $++$ O 82, $++$ S 14, $++$ S 59, * B 75, * D 33, * I 87, * M 78, * P 1, * P 3, * P 93, * Q 99, * R 14, * R 99, * T 3, * V 10, + F 77, + G 98, + I 25, + K 42, + N 9, AB 35, AC 45, AE 80, $++$ A 29, $++$ A 37, $++$ A 59, $++$ B 91, $++$ C 32, $++$ C 71, $++$ E 57, $++$ E 63, $++$ F 28, $++$ N 87, $++$ O 30, $++$ P 45, $++$ R 14, $++$ S 51, * F 1, * F 87, * G 62; *LA*, IX, fols. 347^v, 350^r.

134. "From Manor to Mezzadria" (n. 67 above), pp. 220-21.

135. * S 100 (1227), * T 36 (1232).

136. + 58 (four leases dated between 24 July and 13 September). These were not perpetual leases: three were for eight years and the other for 20 years.

137. $++$ G 82.

138. $++$ C 100.

139. Similar sales and subleasings are * K 85 (10 June 1232), $++$ N 83 (16 July 1232), $++$ D 34 (7 October 1234), $++$ R 67 (18 February 1240); examples of these kinds of sales and subleases appear only irregularly in the episcopal records.

140. $++$ C 32. The contract only named a rent of six libre of oil; the other rents or services owed were not enumerated.

141. $++$ R 67 (1240), £12 was paid for a perpetual rent of twelve stai of wheat (we have two wheat prices of six soldi per staio listed in 1243, though lower prices are listed late in the 1240s and 1250s). The other perpetual loan contracts I have found are $++$ N 91 (1187), $++$ R 67 (1196), $++$ R 67 (1204), $++$ M 36 (1215), $++$ S 70 (1227), $++$ S 43 (1230), $++$ D 19 (1264), and $++$ C 54 (1273). Close analysis of these contracts must await studies of changes in the value of Luccan money and a conscientious attempt to establish thirteenth- and fourteenth-century commodity prices.

142. $++$ C 100 (1217), $++$ S 6 (1223).

143. $++$ E 54 (1219), $++$ E 62 (1220), $++$ E 72 (1223).

144. On inquests see Osheim, "Episcopal Archive" (n. 1 above), pp. 137-39.

145. *Two Churches* (n. 5 above), p. 349.

146. See, e.g., $++$ A 51 (1231), $++$ A 68 (1270), $++$ A 98 (twelfth century?), $++$ A 99 (1257).

147. See, e.g., Jones, "From Manor to Mezzadria" (n. 67 above), p. 229, who finds that resumption of lands, where it occurred, was for the most part voluntary.

148. *Tuscia*, I, 206-24, 243-75; I have subtracted the 20 entries added after the completion of the *Estimo*.

149. Ibid., pp. 244-45.

150. Ibid., pp. 269-70. The churches included in the *Estimo* of 1260 but not in the tithe lists are marked with an asterisk to the left of the name, e.g., "5369. * Eccl. S. Petri de Pinochio."

151. Ibid., p. 266 notes 3, 4, 6, 7, and 8. The only other cases where similar shifts were noted on the *Estimo* are on p. 265 n. 1 and p. 272 n. 4.

152. *Pistoia,* pp. 70-71, Tables 1 and 2; cf. Emilio Cristiani, "Note sui rapporti tra il comune e il contado di Pistoia nel corso del secolo XIII," in *Il Gotico a Pistoia nei suoi rapporti con l'arte gotica italiana* (Pistoia, 1966).

153. See App. 2. I have found 31 purchases of land between 1201 and 1245 and only five after that period.

154. I have found no indication that the episcopate involved itself in the purchase of new equipment or in the purchase or use of fertilizers.

155. On the role of entry-fines in the debate over the "economic depression of the fourteenth century," see Barbara Harvey, "The Population Trend in England between 1300 and 1348," *Transactions of the Royal Historical Society,* 5th ser., 16 (1966), 23-42.

156. *La struttura agraria* (n. 55 above), p. 216.

7. TUSCAN BISHOPRICS IN THE MIDDLE AGES

1. Sabatino Ferrali, "Le temporalità del Vescovado nei rapporti col Comune a Pistoia nei secoli XII e XIII," in *Vescovi e diocesi in Italia nel medioevo (sec. IX–XIII),* Italia Sacra, 5 (Padua, 1964), pp. 365-408.

2. Jones, "An Italian Estate"; idem, "From Manor to Mezzadria: A Tuscan Case-Study in the Medieval Origins of Modern Agrarian Society," in *Florentine Studies: Politics and Society in Renaissance Florence,* ed. Nicolai Rubinstein (London, 1968), pp. 193-241; David Herlihy, "Church Property on the European Continent, 701-1200," *Speculum,* 36 (1961), 81-105; idem, "Treasure Hoards in the Italian Economy, 960-1139," *Economic History Review,* ser. 2, 10 (1957), 1-14, and "Agrarian Revolution." The exception to this general rule is monastic history; see Philip Jones, "Le finanze della badia cistercense di Settimo nel XIV secolo," *Rivista di Storia della Chiesa in Italia,* 10 (1956), 90-122, and idem, "A Tuscan Monastic Lordship in the Later Middle Ages: Camaldoli," *Journal of Ecclesiastical History,* 5 (1954), 168-83. A lack of interest in the unique problems faced by the churchmen is one of the very few weaknesses in Elio Conti, *La formazione della struttura agraria moderna nel contado fiorentino,* I, Studi Storici, 51-55 (Rome, 1965). An exception to this trend is Cinzio Violante's *Studi sulla Cristianità medioevale* (Milan, 1972), especially pp. 325-79.

3. Fiumi, *San Gimignano,* pp. 15-28; Volpe, *Pisa, Toscana medievale,* and *Medio evo italiano.*

4. On the reform movement in general see the review article (and the works cited therein) by Ovidio Capitani, "Esiste un 'Età Gregoriana'? Considerazioni sulle tendenze di una storiografia medievistica," *Rivista di storia e letteratura religiosa,* 1 (1965), 454-81. The quotation is from Violante, "I vescovi," p. 194.

5. Volpe, *Pisa,* pp. 15ff.; idem, *Toscana medievale,* pp. 152-53; Ferrali, "Le temporalità" (n. 1 above); pp. 365-79; Giovanni Lami, *Lezioni di antichità toscane* (Florence, 1766), pp. cxxi-cxxii; Narciso Mengozzi, *Il feudo del Vescovado di Siena* (Siena, 1911).

6. See Maria Luisa Ceccarelli, *Il monastero di S. Giustiniano di Falesia e il castello di Piombino (secoli XI–XIII).* Presentazione di Cinzio Violante. Biblioteca del *Bollettino Storico Pisano,* Collana storica, 10 (Pisa, 1972), p. 15.

7. *Pisa,* pp. 10-15 (the quotation is from p. 15).

8. Volpe, *Toscana medievale,* pp. 152, 355-57; Ferrali, "Le temporalità" (n. 1 above), p. 382.

9. Violante, "I vescovi," p. 195 n. 1; he is proposing a major revision of Pietro Vaccari's *La territorialità come base dell' ordinamento giuridico del contado nell' Italia medioevale* (2nd ed., Milan, 1963), observing that socio-economic changes are as important as juridical changes.

10. Volpe, *Pisa,* pp. 10, 15; Pietro Santini, "Studi sull'antica costituzione del comune di Firenze," *ASI,* 5th ser., 16 (1895), 24–25; Giovanni De Vergottini, "Origine e sviluppo storico della comitatinanza," *Studi Senesi,* 43 (1929), pp. 385ff.

11. Herlihy, "Church Property" (n. 2 above), p. 96; see also the other articles by the same author, "Agrarian Revolution," "Treasure Hoards" (n. 2 above), and "The History of the Rural Seigneury in Italy, 751–1200," *Agricultural History,* 33 (1959), 58–71.

12. Donations, on the other hand, do continue to be random—but donations to bishoprics in the late eleventh and twelfth centuries were less common than they had been in the mid-eleventh century.

13. See Pietro Santini, "Studi sull' antica costituzione del comune di Firenze" (part 3; see n. 10 above), *ASI,* 5th ser., 26 (1900), 240–45; Volpe, *Toscana medievale,* pp. 107–08, 135, 156ff.; Silvio Adrasto Barbi, "Delle relazioni tra comune e vescovo nei secoli XII e XIII," *Bollettino Storico Pistoiese,* 1 (1899), 82–83.

14. Volpe, *Toscana medievale,* pp. 181, 386ff.

15. "Il capitolo del duomo di Orvieto ed i suoi statuti inediti," *Rivista di Storia della Chiesa in Italia,* 9 (1955), 183–84; Giovanni Antonio Pecci, *Storia del Vescovado della città di Siena* (Lucca, 1748), pp. 103–34.

16. See the remarks of Robert Brentano, *Two Churches: England and Italy in the Thirteenth Century* (Princeton, 1968), pp. 97–105.

17. Natalini, "Il capitolo" (n. 15 above), pp. 188ff.

18. Volpe, *Toscana medievale,* pp. 107–08, 181; idem, *Pisa,* p. 18.

19. Volpe, *Toscana medievale,* p. 481; Brentano, *Two Churches* (n. 16 above), pp. 73–86.

20. See Brentano, *Two Churches,* pp. 80, 82ff., 97ff. I must disagree with Brentano's contention (p. 80) that "the vicar's not being exactly an episcopal administrative substitue was so clearly true in Arezzo until 1256 that the cathedral clergy claimed the right to nominate the vicar general." Since chapters could and often did claim the right to be consulted in various types of episcopal affairs, their nomination of the official did not make the vicar general any less "an episcopal administrative substitute."

21. *Two Churches,* pp. 78–79.

22. Brunetto Quilici, "La chiesa di Firenze dal governo del 'Primo Popolo' alla restaurazione guelfa," *ASI,* 127 (1969), 265–337; Volpe, *Toscana medievale,* pp. 27ff. and 107ff.

23. Volpe, *Toscana medievale,* pp. 425–26; such appointments also occurred at Mantua, Bologna, Imola, and Reggio.

24. Robert Davidsohn, *Storia di Firenze* (8 vols., Florence, 1956–68), I, 619–23, 641–43, 658; Santini, "Studi," *ASI,* 16 (n. 10 above), 23–24.

25. Barbi, "Comune e vescovo" (n. 13 above), pp. 81–83; Ferrali, "Le temporalità" (n. 1 above), pp. 369–70.

26. See Ferdinando Ughelli, *Italia Sacra* (10 vols., Venice, 1717–22; rpt. Nendeln, Lichtenstein, 1970), III, cols. 338–446, 543–56; by the late thirteenth century the Malavolti family did control the Sienese bishopric, but this was long after the commune would have had to fear an attempt to seize power by a bishop or his noble relatives.

27. "I vescovi," especially p. 195 n. 1.

28. See especially *San Gimignano,* pp. 20–21. Fiumi emphasizes the importance of demographic factors in almost all his work.

29. *Pisa,* p. 46. This quotation brings together two of the themes in medieval Italian history that Volpe considered most important—associations of free men and the role of force. Both also appear central to his understanding of nineteenth- and twentieth-century Italian history. On Volpe the historian see the introduction to *Pisa* by Cinzio Violante and the works cited therein.

30. See Volpe, *Toscana medievale,* pp. 74–84, 274–75, 434; Santini, "Studi," *ASI,* 16 (n. 10 above), p. 31; Volpe, *Pisa,* p. 30.

31. See Santini, "Studi," *ASI*, 16 (n. 10 above), p. 31; Volpe, *Toscana medievale*, pp. 274-75; Ferrali, "Le temporalità" (n. 1 above), pp. 404-05.

32. Quoted in Volpe, *Toscana medievale*, p. 274.

33. Salvemini, *Studi storici* (Florence, 1901), p. 90.

34. Davidsohn, *Storia di Firenze* (n. 24 above), V, 353.

35. Domenico Corsi, "Santa Maria a Monte nelle guerre tra il comune di Pisa e quello di Lucca attraverso le cronache e alcuni documenti inediti," *Bollettino Storico Pisano*, 36-38 (1967-69), 54.

36. Joseph R. Strayer and Charles H. Taylor, *Studies in Early French Taxation* (Cambridge, Mass., 1939), pp. 54-55, 88, 93; see also the more recent study by John B. Henneman, *Royal Taxation in Fourteenth Century France* (Princeton, 1971), pp. 6, 14-15.

37. Volpe, *Toscana medievale*, pp. 257-58; Bernardino Barbadoro, *Le finanze della Repubblica fiorentina. Imposta diretta e debito pubblico fino all'istituzione del Monte*, Biblioteca Storica Toscana, 5 (Florence, 1929), pp. 30-31, 59; Davidsohn, *Storia di Firenze* (n. 24 above), I, 354.

38. Quoted in Volpe, *Toscana medievale*, p. 228.

39. Quoted in Lauro Martines, *Lawyers and Statecraft in Renaissance Florence* (Princeton, 1968), p. 249.

40. On Siena's relations with its bishop see Mengozzi, *Il feudo* (n. 5 above). Volpe, too, often saw parallels between internal political relations and the larger papal-imperial struggle. Salvatore Andreucci, "Papa Clemente V° in una controversia fra il Vescovo e il comune di Lucca," *Giornale storico della Lunigiana e del territorio lucense*, n.s., 16 (1965), 65-73, considered the controversy of 1308-09 at Lucca to be a result of a conversion to Ghibellinism.

41. On Massa Marittima see Volpe, *Toscana medievale*, pp. 15-16. On Tuscany see, e.g., Violante, "I vescovi"; Quilici, "La chiesa di Firenze" (n. 22 above), p. 293; Ferrali, "Le temporalità" (n. 1 above), pp. 375ff.

42. Volpe, *Toscana medievale*, pp. 475ff.; Quilici, "La chiesa di Firenze" (n. 22 above), p. 293.

43. "Italy," *Cambridge Economic History*, I (2nd ed., Cambridge, 1966), 409; but cf. more recently in "From Manor to Mezzadria" (n. 2 above), pp. 216-17, where he qualifies the reasons for the debts as "due to destitution or any 'crisis' of manorial revenue, [rather] than to extraordinary causes . . . [including] conspicuous investment in property."

44. See Quilici, "La chiesa di Firenze" (n. 22 above), pp. 293-95; Volpe, *Toscana medievale*, pp. 275-76; and Giovanni Cherubini, "Aspetti della proprietà fondiaria nell'aretino durante il XIII secolo," *ASI*, 121 (1963) 9, 26 n. 67.

Index

Proper names ordinarily are given in Italian even when the text is in Latin. Family names are used only where the names were clearly established in the thirteenth century. Names of individuals are alphabetized by proper name and then by patronym or surname, disregarding titles and nicknames. Individuals for whom I have no patronym or surname are listed first, usually with some indication of occupation or area of origin.

A

Adalascia del fu Gerardo, 133 No. 16
Adalecta, wife of Lamberto di Ugo, 138 No. 78
Advocate, 31-33, 120-21
Agnese di Martino del fu Niero, 143 No. 123
Agolante di Guidone, 43
Albertino del fu Francardello, 166 No. 64
Albertino del fu Rolandino, 63
Alberto del fu Ansaldo, 98
Alberto del fu Bernardo, 137 No. 59
Alberto del fu Gattalioso, 62
Alberto del fu Magistro Ferrante, 37
Alberto del fu Patto, 140 No. 95
Alberto del fu Villano, 132 No. 14
Albone "Carbone" del fu Lamberto, 30
Aldegorio del fu Berghintoro, 145 No. 143
Aldibrando, pievano of S. Maria di Suvilliano, 138 No. 66
Aldino del fu Martino, 165 No. 50
Aldobrandeschi family, 14; Ildebrando, count, 14
Alemagno, archpriest, 46
Alessio del fu Rainero, 138 No. 73
Alexander II, pope: see Anselmo I
Alica, 39, 139 No. 86, 180 n. 66

Altopascio, 8
Amato del fu Tasca, 163 No. 33
Ambrogio, bishop, 55
Amico del fu Bernardo, 64
Amuriccio, 140 No. 90
Anchiano, 53, 55, 56; lords of, 15, 55; *see also* Gherardo II
Anconevollio del fu Palmiero, 133 No. 19
Andrea del fu Pietro, 138 No. 72
Angelo, monk of S. Michele of Guamo, 46-47
Angerello del fu Baldro, 164 No. 46
Anghaia, 143 No. 126
Angiorelli family: *see* Pietro III
Anselmo I, bishop (Pope Alexander II), 16, 17, 18, 19, 22, 23, 27, 31, 32, 53, 56, 57, 97, 98, 99, 129, 172 n. 48
Anselmo II, bishop, 16-17, 18, 22, 23, 27, 31, 57, 118, 129
Antelminelli, Buono, 37
Antelminelli family: *see* Castracani, Castruccio
Antelmino, primicerio, 181 n. 101
Anziani of Lucca, 52, 77-78, 78-79, 82, 93, 100
Aqui, 140 No. 92

199

C